NOVEL AND ROMANCE: THE *ODYSSEY* TO *TOM JONES*

Novel and Romance: The *Odyssey* to *Tom Jones*

Hubert McDermott

Statutory Lecturer in English
University College Galway, Ireland

BARNES & NOBLE BOOKS
Totowa, New Jersey

First published in the United States of America 1989 by
BARNES & NOBLE BOOKS
81 Adams Drive, Totowa, N.J. 07512
ISBN: 0–389–20869–8

Library of Congress Cataloging-in-Publication Data
McDermott, Hubert.
Novel and romance.
Bibliography: p.
Includes index.
1. English fiction—18th century—History and
criticism.   2. Romances—History and criticism.
3. Medievalism in literature.   4. Classicism in
literature.   5. Richardson, Samuel, 1689–1761—Knowledge
—Literature.   6. Fielding, Henry, 1707–1754—Knowledge—
Literature.   7. Influence (Literary, artistic, etc.)
I. Title.
PR858.R7M37   1989   823'.5'09   89–28
ISBN 0–389–20869–8

Printed in Hong Kong

To Anne, Suzanne, John and Barry

Contents

Introduction

The seeds of this book lie in my study, as an undergraduate, of the *Satyricon* of Petronius. The existence of this work seemed to me to cast serious doubts on the common assumption that the novel had suddenly sprung into being in eighteenth-century Western Europe. Later, I turned my attention specifically to the works of Samuel Richardson and Henry Fielding to see why their fiction was regarded as 'new' and 'revolutionary'. In the case of Richardson it became immediately obvious that *Pamela* and *Clarissa* were simply reworkings of models already in existence. The case of Fielding is somewhat more complex, however. For a start, he was an inveterate literary plagiarist, and his novels – even more so than those of Richardson – seemed to bear out my contention that the English novel was not a new invention by any means, but simply a new synthesis of pre-existing narrative modes. Fielding appeared to have borrowed his theory of fiction from the French writers of heroic romance, his technique from Paul Scarron, and his fictional structure from drama. Most important of all, perhaps, he had based his concept of realism on the theory of classical comedy. Fielding had been classically educated and was aware that fiction had been sanctioned in epic, realism in comedy. He therefore set about writing a 'comic epic', with obvious and wide-ranging consequences for fiction. An important effect of Fielding's classical training was the assurance it gave him in acknowledging that he was a composer of fiction. Previous writers, say Defoe – and even Richardson – had denied they were writing fiction at all, and claimed, rather, to be 'editors' of 'authentic papers', which had come into their possession. If Fielding had not rescued it when he did, a rational discussion of fiction might not have taken place until much later.

I commenced this introduction with a reference to Petronius and, ironically, Henry Fielding's reliance on classical theory for his theory of fiction, places him in a special position *vis-à-vis* the Roman author, since both had, in effect, attempted 'comic epics'. Indeed, it is almost certain that the *Satyricon* was a major influence on Fielding: it was one of the very few works of fiction in his personal library. But Henry Fielding was no ordinary literary plagiarist: he

gathered, as we shall see, many diverse traditions of fiction into a
new and exciting synthesis.

A view of Richardson and Fielding which regards them as part
of a continuing tradition rather than as great originals is not the
conventionally accepted one. It is, of course, easy to understand
why students of Richardson and Fielding should be more interested
in what is new in their fiction than in what is traditional. But the
common view of these two authors as great originals helps to
highlight a major problem in the criticism of fiction. The problem
has been created by the twentieth century, which has become so
novel-centred in its approach to fiction that the words 'novel' and
'fiction' have almost become synonymous. Such extensive study
has been devoted to the novel in this century, that its standards
have quietly established themselves as the yardstick for all fiction.
This yardstick is posing problems even for twentieth-century
fiction, but it has posed many more for works of fiction written
prior to 1740. The standards of the novel when applied to seven-
teenth- and early eighteenth-century English fiction, for instance,
can only result in the dismissal of that fiction as 'irrelevant'.

Perhaps Ian Watt's book, *The Rise of the Novel*: *Studies in Defoe,
Richardson and Fielding*,[1] best illustrates the theory that the English
novel sprang into being in 1740. *The Rise of the Novel* has contributed
much to a greater understanding of developments in prose fiction
in the eighteenth century, in England. But Watt discards all vestiges
of a literary context which earlier histories of fiction had at least
sought to provide. And yet, perhaps, it is these early histories –
such as those by Raleigh,[2] Cross,[3] Saintsbury,[4] and Baker[5] – which
are partly to blame for the impatience of the modern critic with
pre-1740 fiction. The authors of these histories seldom suggested
any interrelationship between what we now call the novel, and
prose fiction written prior to 1740. While reading the early volumes
of Baker, for instance, one is continually apt to question their *raison
d'être*. Baker, as John Richetti remarks, 'simply ranged through the
predecessors of the eighteenth-century masters, from Sidney to
Mrs Behn, picking out scenes which struck . . . [him] as vivid,
realistic (full of low-life gusto and/or dialect), and circumstantial,
and then ticketed them with meticulous hindsight as partial
anticipators of the full-blown insight into the depiction of real life
which Defoe and Richardson invented'.[6]

Northrop Frye has adequately summed up the case against the
'invention' of the novel in the eighteenth century. 'The literary

historian who identifies fiction with the novel', he writes, 'is greatly embarrassed by the length of time that the world managed to get along without the novel, and until he reaches his great deliverance in Defoe, his perspective is intolerably cramped'.[7] A correct view of the novel is one which sees it as representing only two centuries in a narrative tradition which can be traced back to Homer, at least. And a major aim of the present study is to demonstrate that fiction has developed from Homer along a continuum on which, undoubtedly, the novels of Fielding and Richardson represent a distinct highlight, but not a separate beginning.

A main concern of mine throughout this study is to avoid being dragged into a controversy over the relative merits of realism and romance in fiction. One could argue that it is the insistence on realism as the *sine qua non* of the novel, i.e. 'fiction', and the concomitant view that romance is, at worst, the polar opposite of realism, at best, 'unrealistic', which has vitiated so much of the criticism of fiction. Almost all the works which I discuss prior to *Pamela*, are what are regarded in modern terminology as romances. But, with certain exceptions, my aim will not be to concentrate on and isolate elements of realism in these works. Even when I come to discuss the works of Richardson and Fielding, I shall be more intent on placing them within a continuing tradition of fiction rather than on emphasising their break with tradition. And if the chapters on Richardson and Fielding seem to concentrate too exclusively on the tradition of romance in their works at the expense of the 'new realism', the reader should understand that I do not necessarily intend to exalt one above the other.

For the purposes of this study, I have chosen as my working definition of fiction, a definition of romance given by Ben Edwin Perry, which reads as follows:

> an extended narrative published apart by itself which relates – primarily or wholly for the sake of entertainment or spiritual edification, and for its own sake as a story, rather than for the purpose of instruction in history, science, or philosophical theory – the adventures or experiences of one or more individuals in their private capacities and from the viewpoint of their private interests and emotions.[8]

This definition has the obvious advantage of being applicable to both novel and romance, since it avoids any reference to the distinguishing characteristics of the novel *vis-à-vis* the romance.

1
Ancient Narrative Modes

Any study of the origins of European fiction must inevitably begin with the ancient Greek epic, the prototype of all narrative forms. Epic has in fact dominated and influenced narrative forms right down to the present day, a fact acknowledged in the expression sometimes used to describe the modern novel, 'latter-day epic'. The modern novel is the true, and possibly the only successor of ancient epic, bearing the same relationship to modern society as the epic did to ancient society.

While it may be a truism to suggest that all works of art depend to a greater or lesser extent on the society for which they are created, the interdependence of epic and society in ancient times is quite remarkable. Ancient epic depended, ironically, on isolation for its development, since it was the seclusion of the society for which it was written that gave it its unique characteristics. Ancient epic reflected all the ideas and ideals of what Ben Edwin Perry calls a 'closed society',[1] i.e. an isolated society. The epic, an oral verse form, was the only narrative form in this society, and was, therefore, all things to all men, being a synthesis of myth, history, and fiction. The ancient epic contained within itself 'all the spiritual, educational, and entertainment values that the age requires'.[2] It would be incorrect to suggest that isolation of a particular community was, *per se*, the most important factor in the development of epic: the quality of life within that community was obviously of greater importance.

In the closed society of which we have been speaking, the relationship between the epic poet and his audience was unique: the poet related a story which the audience knew well, to an audience he knew well. Such rapport was seldom to exist again between artist and audience. And it is important to emphasise the epic poet's allegiance to a traditional story: 'not to fact, not to truth, not to entertainment, but to the *mythos* itself – the story preserved in the tradition which the epic storyteller is re-creating'.[3] Allied to this allegiance on the part of the poet was a demand for such allegiance from his audience. The audience was well aware of its ancestral traditions, and demanded only that the poet rehearse these: this the poet did, with variations only in emphasis, style, and in the minor details of the story.

The closed society for which epic catered was also a homogeneous one, a fact which is obvious from the lack of any rigid gradations of rank: 'there are of course heroes and villains, pious men and criminals', George Lukács writes, 'but even the greatest hero is only a head taller than the mass of his fellows, and the wise man's dignified words are heard even by the most foolish'.[4] Within this closed, homogeneous society, epic further depended for its growth and development on a degree of naïveté and lack of sophistication on the part of both author and audience. One result of this naïveté was a failure to distinguish between fact and fiction, and a total acceptance of everything related in epic as truth. With sophistication came a greater awareness of the distinction between fact and fiction, which had obvious consequences for the genre epic. The fact and fiction previously fused to create an epic poem were inevitably parted, one to become history, the other, fiction. Since romance immediately succeeded epic in ancient times, and was, like epic, a long, fictional narrative, the relationship between the two forms was obviously very close. The extent of this relationship is perhaps best highlighted by emphasising the major distinction between the two forms. 'The epic hero', writes George Lukács, 'is, strictly speaking, never an individual. It is traditionally thought that one of the essential characteristics of the epic is the fact that its theme is not a personal destiny but the destiny of a community.'[5] A. B. Taylor shares this view, and claims that epic is the narrative form which voices 'the feelings and aspirations of a nation animated by some one strong national sentiment against the menace of an external foe'.[6] The theme of romance is *not* the destiny of a community; nor does it voice the feelings and aspirations of a nation. Instead, there is in romance a manifest emphasis on the private rather than the public, reflected in a progression from war to love, from the national hero to the individual significant only for himself and those immediately surrounding him.

Just as epic is the literary form peculiar to the closed society, so romance is the form most representative of what could be called the open society, the society which results when the closed society is opened up to the world and is changed beyond recognition. Epic perfectly reflected the hopes, ideals, and fears of its closed society; romance was to be a fitting reflection of the open society – a society without common hopes, ideals or fears. The so-called inferiority of the romance as compared with the epic, is, in many ways, a reflection of the inferiority of the open as opposed to the closed society. This is how Perry sees the distinction between these two societies:

> In European history the closed societies . . . are . . . periods in which the direction of men's thinking is centripetal, instead of being centrifugal and chaotic, as in an *open* society like that of the present. In the *closed* society custom and fixed beliefs about human values and mankind's relation to the beyond are the guides to life and to men's choice of action, instead of philosophy as with the Socratic dialecticians in an *open* society. Men living in a *closed* society, men of faith and fixed beliefs, like Homer and Sophocles, know the answers to life's problems, however tentative, vague or mystical these answers may be; but they know no 'problems', whereas everything in the advanced, *open* society of today tends to be seen as a problem which only the god Science can be expected to solve.[7]

The progression from a closed to an open society in ancient Greece is relatively easy to describe. At his death in the year 323 BC, Alexander the Great had opened to Greek influence, and vice versa, a world which stretched from the Aegean to the Hindu Kush, from the Jaxartes to the Cataracts. Later, came the conquest of Greece by Rome, which simply continued the process of 'opening' Greece. It was this era – the Hellenistic and Early Roman Empire – which produced the prose romance. It is an era which obviously needs a literary historian and sociologist to do for it – and fiction – what Ian Watt did for the late seventeenth and early eighteenth century in *The Rise of the Novel*. Indeed, similarities between the two eras, ancient and modern, are so striking as to suggest that similar factors in both instances brought about the rise of prose fiction. A cursory glance at the social, economic and literary conditions in the Hellenistic and Early Roman Empire will suggest the extent of the resemblance, while at the same time affording a more concrete description of a so-called open society.

W. W. Tarn and G. T. Griffith, in the course of an excellent work on Hellenistic civilisation, write:

The world of Hellenism was a changed and enlarged world. Though the particularism of the Greek city state was to remain vigorous enough in fact, it had broken down in theory; it was being replaced by universalism and its corollary, individualism. The idea emerges of an *oecumene* or 'inhabited world' as a whole, the common possession of civilised men; and for its use there grows up the form of Greek known as the *koine*, the 'common speech', which was also used by many Asiatics; Greek might take a man from Marseilles to India, from the Caspian to the Cataracts. Nationality falls into the background; common speech and education promote a common culture in every city of the 'inhabited world'; literature, learning, above all philosophy, do to some extent envisage a larger world than Greece, and the upper classes in Rome and parts of Asia came to feel that Greek culture is a thing a man must have, at least in externals.[8]

The authors go on to show how most of the social and economic barriers between countries were down, in this era, and demonstrate, too, how thought was free, as it was not to be again until modern times. It was an age in which the personality of the individual had free scope; an age of specialists, where it took, for instance, four different craftsmen to make a candelabra. Even versions of communism and socialism manifested themselves. There were the age-old problems too – those of prices and wages, with the inevitable strikes. It is interesting to pursue the concept of individualism in the Hellenistic age a little further, particularly since Ian Watt places such emphasis on the development of this concept in modern times as a contributory factor in the rise of the novel. Tarn and Griffith write:

Man as a political animal, a fraction of the *polis* or self-governing city state, had ended with Aristotle, with Alexander begins man as an individual. This individual needed to consider both the regulation of his own life and also his relations with other individuals who with him composed the 'inhabited world'; to meet the former need there arose the philosophies of conduct, to meet the latter certain new ideas of human brotherhood. These originated on the day – one of the critical moments of history – when at a banquet at Opis, Alexander prayed for a union of hearts (*homonoia*) among all peoples and a joint commonwealth of Macedonians and Persians; he was the first to transcend national boundaries, and to envisage, however imperfectly, a brotherhood of man in which there should be neither Greek nor barbarian.[9]

In the Hellenistic and Early Roman Empire, commerce was internationalised. The Hellenistic world became 'one great market controlled by the Greek or Hellenized merchant and the Greek manufacturer'.[10] Business methods were also improved, as was banking. All commercial transactions were based on credit and on coined metal put into circulation by different states. Gold became the standard in monetary exchange, while all the various monetary systems tried to adapt themselves to one another, in order to facilitate business relations. Out of all this activity there arose a new and very wealthy middle class: practical knowledge of business had opened the way for the lowly-born to high positions.

The spread of education in the period under review also contributed to the rise of a new middle class. Schooling was more general, even if confined to teaching the rudiments of the three Rs. Women could, for the first time, get all the education they wanted, and their relative emancipation in this era bears a similarity to that achieved by women generally in Europe, in modern times. Tarn and Griffith[11] see the Macedonian princesses of the two generations after Alexander as exerting the greatest influence on the emancipation of women: these princesses were very much the counterparts of their menfolk, as can be seen from the account of their duties and general activities. Relative freedom broadened down to the ordinary Greek home, and women who wished for emancipation were able to secure it. Tarn and Griffith[12] enumerate also, with evidence from contemporary sources, the wide variety of positions occupied by women in this era. Epicurus had a pupil called Leontion: poetesses began to reappear in the third century BC: an Aristodama of Smyrna toured Greece, with her brother as business manager, giving recitals and receiving many honours: women now received citizenship of other cities, for the same services as men: there were women magistrates in the Roman period: women founded clubs, and took part in club life. There were, as we shall see, writers who wrote with the newly-emancipated female audience in mind.

Developments in the book trade made a significant contribution to the rise of prose fiction in the Hellenistic era. The significance of these developments, in ancient as well as modern times, lies in the removal of literature from the control of a restrictive literary tradition. The beginnings of a book trade in ancient Greece may be placed with some accuracy in the fifth century BC, during the Golden Age of Greek literature. The great masterpieces of the age were widely distributed, which suggests they were manufactured and distributed on a commercial scale. At this time, and until much later, the bookseller was evidently manufacturer, publisher, and retailer all in one. With the enormous increase in the reading public in Hellenistic times, however, and a proportionate increase in the number of writers, the book trade soared, making it quite impractical for a single individual to manage every aspect of the process. The production and publication of works continued to be handled by one individual, but the process of selling the finished article inevitably passed into the hands of another. The trade of bookmaking 'prospered exceedingly', says F. G. Kenyon, 'Commentators, compilers, populizers swarmed as they do today . . . .'[13]

To the modern reader, the process of 'printing' books in ancient times is an absorbing and intriguing subject. The 'printing press' was usually a collection of Greek slaves assembled in a large hall. These slaves were skilled scribes and were paid for their work. The 'printing' was done in either of two ways: the original text was either dictated to the scribes by a reader, or portions of it were shared between individual copyists. A well-organised publisher with the necessary capital was able to put hundreds of copies of an average work on sale within days of receiving the original. Pliny the Younger mentions an edition of one thousand copies[14] of a work published at the author's own expense: one must assume that 'public' editions of ancient 'bestsellers' must have been brought out in much larger quantities. The first edition of any new work was a limited one: demand dictated the number and extent of further editions.

Ludwig Friedlander says we tend, today, to underestimate the productive power of writing as compared with that of the press.[15] He goes on to show how, in relatively recent times, when copy, not print was necessary, the difference between the two is less than is generally imagined. He gives several examples from modern times, one of them the instance of the circulation of two thousand copies of Voltaire's *La Pucelle* in Paris, in a month. How much more easily, then, could the ancients, with their comprehensive organisation and centuries of experience, produce multiple copies in a short time. The actual extent of some ancient editions is suggested by references in various contemporary works. Cicero,[16] for example, said that the depositions of the witnesses in the Catilinarian conspiracy were copied by all the clerks, circulated in Rome, distributed throughout Italy, and sent to all the provinces, so that there was no place in the Roman Empire they had not reached. Varro's great biographical work – which was actually illustrated by some process or other – was, Pliny tells us,[17] circulated to the four corners of the earth. Horace, too, is pleased to think[18] his poems will be read on the banks of the Bosphorus, in Gaul, Spain and Africa, as well as other parts of the Empire. Ovid consoles himself in exile with the thought that his complaint will be heard wherever the world extends,[19] and that he is the most widely-read author in the world.[20]

There is very little evidence available on the actual method of distribution of books in the period under review. What is certain is that it was not a particularly difficult task. The improvement in communications was a great help, as was the spread of a common civilisation. Possibly of greatest importance, however, was the spread of 'common speech' over the greater part of the 'inhabited world'. This meant that a man from even an outlying area of the Empire was sure of an audience if he had something of interest to offer. It is invidious, in the circumstances, to try to draw a comparison between Watt's estimation of 80 000 readers in England at the end of the eighteenth century, and the number of readers in the early Roman Empire. But it does seem that an estimate of 80 000 would be a conservative one, of the number then able to read Greek and Latin.

Friedlander[21] gives a very interesting account of what the retail bookshops in Rome looked like, with their pillars and entrances decorated with notices and copies of books for sale. The shops were also a meeting place for friends of literature who came to inspect the new books, or have a chat. Friedlander also gives examples,[22] of prices, but although these are in sterling it is difficult to say what their equivalent today is. It is best to preface his examples by saying, as he does, that prices were not high. The price of the first book of Martial (118 epigrams, 700 lines), 'elegantly got up', was 5 denarii, or about 20p: cheaper editions were to be had for from about 6 to 10 sesterces, i.e. from about 6p to 10p. Synonymous with the book trade in Ancient Rome is the name Atticus. He was one of the major book-publishers of antiquity, and was also a retailer, supplying both libraries and individuals. Atticus employed large numbers of slave copyists, some of them exceptionally well educated. Books published by Atticus found a ready market because he was known as a publisher of repute. He kept a special team of readers for correcting works, for example. And this leads us to one of the major drawbacks of the ancient 'printing press'. Because of the high capital outlay involved, most publishers insisted on rapid reproduction, with dire consequences for the finished product. Copyists made absurd mistakes and careless errors, and these were not easily corrected.

One must not omit to mention the major role played by the libraries in ancient times, in bringing about a huge increase in the volume of book production. The famous library of Alexandria was founded in 300 BC by Ptolemy I, and Ptolemy II founded a 'daughter' library in his reign, probably for duplicates. Estimates of the number of volumes in the library vary; one estimate puts the number at 200 000 five years after its founding, while an estimate of the number in the time of Caesar is 700 000. In compensation for the destruction of the books in Alexandria, Antony donated the 200 000 volumes in the library at Pergamum to Cleopatra. Besides the libraries at Alexandria and Pergamum, there were state libraries also at Antioch and Rhodes.

There would seem to be no essential difference between the circumstances, briefly outlined above, and those described by Watt[23] as having contributed to the rise of the novel in modern times. And the attitude of the educated literary élite to fiction in both ages seems almost identical, also. This is how John Richetti describes the prose fiction of the early eighteenth century, and the attitude of the literati to this fiction:

> Prose fiction at a popular level essentially requires only a simple exercise of literacy . . . rather than the complicated, enlightened response toward artistic structure and style involving an awareness of allusion and irony which neo-classic literature at its best demands. Put next to these standards, the fiction of the period can best be described as fantasy machines, which must have appeared to the educated literate élite of the eighteenth century precisely what comic books and television seem to the contemporary guardians of cultural standards. Prose fiction forms part of that steady expansion of popular literature in the eighteenth century which traditionalists like Pope and Swift could see only as a pervasive vulgarization of the arts.[24]

The attitude of the educated élite towards fiction in ancient times was equally, if not more prohibitive. This attitude can best be appreciated by examining the demise of epic and the rise of romance. Romance proper began with the breakdown of epic into its constituent parts, each part developing as a separate entity thereafter. The epic was, as we noted earlier, an amalgam of all the ethical, religious, aesthetic and scientific ideas and ideals of the society for which it was written. Gradually, however, with changes in that society, the nature of the epic changed too. Eventually, the constituent parts of the epic amalgam were cultivated, each for its own sake, and became the forms we know as tragedy, comedy, lyric poetry, and so on. One of the most immediate results of the dissolution of epic was the enormous declension in the importance of the story (or fiction), *per se*, as an art form. All its principal values were simply appropriated by forms for which it had previously acted as a kind of crutch. The story, then, became a kind of literary outcast, since its *raison d'être* had – as far as the typical classicist was concerned – disappeared. A story, for the classicist, by definition almost, was something subordinate or incidental, certainly not an end in itself. Then, too, the concept of prose as a means of appealing to the emotional or artistic senses of an audience was utterly alien to the classicist. In this context, it is easy to understand the utter hostility of the educated élite in ancient times towards *fictions* in *prose*. And it is, perhaps, important, also, to appreciate that Europe has never, since classical times, experienced a prohibitive and restrictive literary fashion of such dominance. This fashion rigidly excluded and refused to acknowledge the existence of any so-called literary form unless it was classical in kind. And prose romance, or indeed any kind of prose fiction, was not classical in kind. The idea of a respected author, for instance, expressing himself in prose fiction was quite unthinkable, unless, of course, he had lost his sanity. After reading the *Babyloniaca* of Iamblichus, Photius praises the author's prose style but thinks it a pity that so capable a rhetorician should have demeaned himself by writing childish fiction instead of writing about matters of serious concern.[25] And Philostratus relates how a royal secretary under Hadrian wrote a book about the love of Araspas for Panthia, and ascribed it to a rival rhetorician, Dionysus of Miletus, in order to disgrace him.[26]

Romance, therefore, because it was not classical in kind, was developed originally by authors who were independent of the dominant literary fashion. This independence was made possible, in all probability, by the emergence of the publisher/bookseller who helped to remove literature from the control of a restrictive academic tradition, and bring it, instead, under the laws of the marketplace. In the case of an author of fiction, his new independence meant that he could appropriate artistic aims and methods previously confined to 'legitimate' art forms such as tragedy, comedy, or epic. These appropriations he used as he saw fit, or as best suited his aim of entertaining his readers.

The influence of the new, wealthy and literate middle class on the development of English fiction seems to have its parallel in ancient times also. It would appear that the major developments in ancient fiction were aided by, or coincided with the emergence of a new middle class. The members of this new class, in ancient times also, demanded the 'vulgarization of the arts' to suit their own tastes. Prior to this they had been the forgotten people of literature, aware that their way of life, their outlook on life, was excluded from the literature controlled by an academic tradition. The pressure exerted by this new group brought about the creation of the 'fantasy machine' called Greek romance. And although there are no statistics on this ancient middle class, the Greek romances themselves give a reasonably accurate indication of the type of reader involved, one not significantly different to his – or perhaps more accurately her – counterpart seventeen hundred, or, indeed, two thousand years later.

It is instructive to look at the relationship between the decline of drama and the growth of prose fiction in ancient times. Here, again, the similarities between ancient and modern times should be evident, without elaboration. Robert Liddell talks of the modern novel as 'the rightful heir to the Drama'[27] and explains what he means, thus:

> The history of the Drama is the pre-history of the Novel. It may be said, shortly and dogmatically, but with infinitely more truth than such statements in literary history are commonly made, that the English theatre died in 1700 – a glorious death, after its most brilliant comedy, *The Way of the World* – and that the English novel was born with *Pamela* in 1740. There must be some connection between these two events, and of course there is. Poetry, having separated from Drama, has led an independent life ever since, for the most part little concerned with the representation of character in action. As for the representation

of character in action – here the Novel succeeded to the Play, and minds that in other ages would have been devoted to the Drama have been devoted to fiction.[28]

With very little modification, what Liddell has to say about the modern novel and drama, can be said also of the ancient romance and drama. One would be loath to assign a year to the death of Greek drama, but it can be said that it had gone into a steep decline in the Hellenistic age. Tragedies continued to be written in quantities, for festivals, but they were both artificial and precious. New Comedy was in vogue, with Menander as Congreve's counterpart. In the days of the early Empire, drama had sunk to a very low ebb: neither comedy nor tragedy was written – they were very much out of favour. Instead, mime and pantomime held the stage. Ben Edwin Perry, too, has drawn attention to the similarity between ancient and modern times in this respect:

> Like the modern novel, the ancient, which has the same potentiality of extension upward and outward, succeeded the drama as the dynamic form of fictional entertainment and edification. The literary and social conditions, which brought about this change in the principal medium by which literature as a genuine interpretation of life was henceforth expressed, were very much the same, fundamentally, in both cases. The drama had declined to a low level of effectiveness in two respects: the values that it had to convey, which were normally trivial or narrow as compared with those of Euripidean or Menandrian drama in the ancient period, or with those of the Elizabethan in the modern; and its capacity for communicating even those values to the literary public at large . . . .[29]

Later, Perry remarks that the nature of the innovation in Greek romance

> consists in nothing more or less than the transference to prose narrative, the natural medium for a reading public, of the principal artistic aims and sanctions of serious drama. Chief among these sanctions is the plasmatic license, which allows an author to invent for art's sake, speeches, actions and characters. . . .[30]

This statement of Perry's could be taken simply as a gloss on Robert Liddell's statement about the 'representation of character in action'.

THE *ODYSSEY*

Any discussion of Greek romance must inevitably begin with Homer's *Odyssey*, the archetype, not only of Greek, but of all great romance. The *Odyssey* is archetypal in that it sets the pattern for all subsequent romances, whether in the design of the narrative or the use of specific scenes and incidents to symbolise primary human experiences. That the *Odyssey* is a romance is generally agreed: or to put the matter another way, the term romance seems to express perfectly the essential dissimilarity which exists between *Odyssey* and *Iliad*: E. V. Rieu, in the introduction to his translation of the *Odyssey*, acknowledges the distinction between it and the *Iliad*, describing the *Odyssey* as a novel, the *Iliad* as a tragedy. The *Odyssey*, he writes, 'is the true ancestor of the long line of novels that have followed it'.[31] Ben Edwin Perry has a very plausible theory to explain why the *Odyssey* differs from the *Iliad*:

> The conditions under which the story of the *Odyssey* was told were distinctly different from those which had inspired the story of Achilles in the *Iliad* . . . . Whatever may be the date of the origin of the *Iliad* in the form in which we have it, the story of Achilles pictures the ideals of a comparatively isolated, partriarchal society on the mainland of Greece, while the *Odyssey* reflects the outlook on the world of a later age, in which the interest in sea voyages has been stimulated by the beginnings of colonization and contact with Phoenician traders, and in which the social organization has advanced toward the dissolution of the old kingship and the predominance of the nobility as it appears in Hesiod and Archilochus.[32]

It is one thing to show why the *Odyssey* is, or should be, different to the *Iliad*, another to show just in what this difference consists. Rieu is obviously correct in pointing to the essentially tragic quality of the *Iliad*, a quality which is certainly not present in the *Odyssey*. Other major distinctions between the two works can be isolated by using the headings 'public' and 'private'.

The *Iliad* is a national saga, a patriotic expression of the heart and soul of a nation. There is a hero, Hector, and numerous other characters of almost equal stature, but all are simply the means to the end of reflecting the essence of nationhood. While the problems of Odysseus are symbolic, on one level, of the problems of Everyman, on another level his is essentially a private story of domestic and adventurous life, and one with a happy ending. There are other, perhaps more obvious differences between the two stories. It is not only modern times, for instance, which have recognised the incredible and fantastic nature of Odysseus' adventures. In the preface to his *True History*, Lucian tells us that every episode in his book will be a subtle parody of some fantastic 'historical fact' recorded by any ancient poet, historian, or philosopher, and he continues:

> Of course the real pioneer in this type of tomfoolery was Homer's Odysseus, who told Alcinous and his court an extremely tall story about bags of wind, and one-eyed giants, and cannibals, and other unpleasant characters, not to speak of many-headed monsters and magic potions that turned human beings into animals. He evidently thought the Phaeacians were fools enough to believe anything.[33]

Lucian goes on to say that his chief reaction is 'astonishment – that anyone should tell such lies and expect to get away with it. But if other people can do it why should not I?'[34] This remark may have signalled the launching of innumerable other romancers' careers. Lucian, and, unfortunately, most who followed him, were unaware of the quality of the precedent set by Homer in the *Odyssey*. In an attempt to imitate the *Odyssey*, they simply imitated the externals and failed utterly to capture the soul of that work.

Another obvious distinction between the *Iliad* and the *Odyssey* lies in those very externals of the *Odyssey*. In the *Odyssey* there seems to be an exploitation of adventure for adventure's sake rather than towards an end, as in the case of the *Iliad*. One must admit, however, that very few adventure stories have characters of the quality of Odysseus. Love and sexuality are also introduced as powerful forces into the *Odyssey*: these forces are absent from the *Iliad*. But love in the *Odyssey* deserves to be distinguished from the love portrayed in later romances. In the *Odyssey*, the love presented is a mature love between a couple who have been married for a very long time. In the Greek romances, the love presented has attained the force of a Ben Jonson 'humour', which he describes in *Every Man out of His Humour*, as a 'peculiar quality' which 'Doth so possess a man that it doth draw / All his effects, his spirits, and his powers, / In their confluxions, all to run one way'. In the *Odyssey*, on the contrary, we feel that Homer has devoted as much attention to love as it deserved to have paid to it as a component in the life and personality of man. But Homer does not allow us to forget that Odysseus spends ten years attempting to return to his home *and* to Penelope. Their eventual reunion is one of the supreme moments of literature. Similar reunions were to become a staple ingredient of later romances, but their artificiality and sentimentality simply serve to reveal the extent of Homer's achievement in conveying such piercing joy. It is perfectly fitting, too, that the simile used to depict Penelope's frame of mind at the time should be that of a shipwrecked sailor:

> Penelope's surrender melted Odysseus' heart, and he wept as he held his dear wife in his arms, so loyal and so true. Sweet moment too for her, sweet as the sight of land to sailors struggling in the sea, when the sea-god by dint of wind and wave has wrecked their gallant ship. What happiness for the few swimmers that have fought their way through the white surf to the shore, when, caked with brine but safe and sound, they tread on solid earth. If that is bliss, what bliss it was for her to see her husband once again. She kept her white arms about his neck and never quite let go. (xxiii, 358)

It seems doubtful that E. V. Rieu had the endings, only, of the *Iliad* and the *Odyssey* in mind, when he called one a tragedy, the other a novel. And, yet, the *Iliad* ends 'unhappily', with the death of Hector, while the hero of the *Odyssey*, after many years of wandering and hardship, eventually manages to return to his home and to his wife. And we presume that he and his wife 'lived happily ever after'. This happy ending introduced by Homer into fictional narrative was to become a feature inseparably associated with romance.

It is somewhat ironic that the *Odyssey*, the first great romance, should so brilliantly illustrate Richard Chase's comment on the power of romance to 'express dark and complex truths',[35] truths not readily accessible or available to the novelist. In telling the tale of an exiled king striving to return home, Homer is telling the tale of all of us. All of us know what it is like to be desperately lost and to wonder if we shall ever get 'home' again. And the *Odyssey* gives us hope, because its central message is simply this: that no matter how long, no matter how far from home we are lost, no matter how desperate we become, we shall eventually return home, and to happiness. It is little wonder, then, that the *Odyssey* has become a key word in Western civilisation: all of our individual lives consist of 'odysseys' of one kind or another; each life, short or long becomes *the* 'odyssey'.

The appeal of the *Odyssey* to generation after generation of new readers for almost three thousand years, in spite of its presentation of both an alien culture and civilisation, can be explained only in terms of the projection of timeless psychological experiences. These experiences are most obviously present in Odysseus' fabulous adventures as related by him to the Phaeacians. By standards of 'realism', these adventures must be regarded as utterly naïve and unsophisticated. At least Lucian gave Homer the benefit of the doubt, by presuming that Homer himself *knew* he was telling lies, but expected to get away with it because the Phaeacians were fools enough to believe anything. It can be argued that Homer himself contributed to a misinterpretation of this section of the *Odyssey*. The adventures of Odysseus take place in a very physical world, and the stark realities of this world are too obvious to deny. Such stark realities and such a physical world, coupled with such incredible adventures, tend to confuse the modern reader. In effect, the incredible adventures of the body of Odysseus project adventures of his soul.

Without going into too great detail it is possible to show the general outline of the adventures of Odysseus' body/soul.[36] The predominant feature of the story is the sea, and it controls the destiny of Odysseus from beginning to end: having tossed him from one island to another for two years, it finally maroons him for eight more with Calypso. Even when he does manage to get away from Calypso, the sea breaks up his raft and washes him, naked, to the shores of Scherie. Odysseus' journey by sea is obviously a symbol of a journey into his mind. Homer, like many artists since, instinctively uses the sea as a symbol for the unconscious, and by presenting a real sea journey, projects a spiritual one. The many encounters with strange monsters and the dead, thus become encounters Odysseus has with forces within himself. It is not simply because Homer depicted them so well that the likes of Circe, Polyphemus, Calypso, or any of the other strange beings, are such powerful figures: they are personfications of our own angers, lusts, fears, acting on Odysseus in exactly the same way as they act on us. Odysseus offends Poseidon, god of the sea, in much the same way as we offend our 'Poseidon', our unconscious: and the results are catastrophic, because 'Poseidon' strikes back quickly and viciously. Not until he has submitted himself to the sea, faced its terrors and monsters, and promised to do penance to its god, can Odysseus return home. It is only on such a reading as this that the incredible becomes credible.

Odysseus' first encounter is with the Cicones, and he describes it thus:

The same wind as wafted me from Ilium brought me to Ismarus, the city of the Cicones. I sacked the place and destroyed the men who held it. Their wives and the rich plunder that we took from the town we divided so that no one, as far as I could help it, should go short of his proper share. And then I said we ought to be off and show a clean pair of heels. But my fools of men refused. There was plenty of wine, plenty of livestock; and they kept on drinking and butchering sheep and fatted cattle by the shore. Meanwhile the Cicones went and raised a cry for help among other Cicones, their up-country neighbours, who are both more numerous and better men, trained in fighting from the chariot and on foot as well, as the occasion requires. At dawn they were upon us, thick as the leaves and flowers in their season, and it certainly looked as though Zeus meant the worst for my unhappy following and we were in for a very bad time. Six of my warriors from each ship were killed. The rest of us contrived to dodge our fate and got away alive. (ix, 142)

This is Odysseus' first encounter, and his last with human beings until he is cast ashore on the isle of Scherie. The assault on the Cicones is intriguing: why did Odysseus attack such a town in the first place, never mind sack it? He gives no explanation whatever for his actions, at this, or any other point in his story. The conflict between master and men is shown here for the first time, and will be a significant feature of all future incidents. These conflicts seem to represent conflicts in Odysseus' mind, and suggest that the men are merely projections of the mind of Odysseus, though this does not preclude them from being characters in their own right, much as Iago, say, is very much a flesh and blood character as well as being a projection of forces within Othello's mind.[37] At Ismarus the men rebel against reason and Odysseus, allowing their appetites full sway. Zeus shows them what happens when elements which should be kept in check are unleashed and allowed to run amuck, by unleashing a terrible storm. This storm also marks the shift in the *Odyssey* from the outer world of turmoil to the inner world of even greater turmoil. It is perfectly fitting that at the very beginning of this journey into the interior, Odysseus should meet the Lotus Eaters, who will tempt him not to make the journey, to opt out of life, and never again go home. Odysseus realises that this is not the answer, that one must face and acknowledge one's difficulties before they can be overcome.

The next encounter is with the Cyclops, the 'Calibans' of the *Odyssey*:[38] they represent the most vicious, unrestrained proclivities of human nature. Polyphemus, it should be noted, is the son of the sea, or Poseidon: this is why Odysseus is so brutally punished for maiming Polyphemus. This time, in spite of advice from his men to the contrary, Odysseus forces himself on Polyphemus, eager for a stranger's gift. Odysseus, having released the forces of avarice, lawlessness and savagery in Ismarus, now encounters the very representation of these forces in Polyphemus. It is Odysseus' first encounter with his own unconscious, and it has all the hallmarks of a dreadful nightmare. Odysseus is completely wrong in thinking that he can be victorious, even in a limited sense, in his conflict with Polyphemus, or that he can escape by running away: he must, rather, come to terms with Polyphemus or Polyphemus' father, Poseidon, before he can reach home. It is not without significance that Odysseus is helped, in his bid to outwit Polyphemus, by wine. It is at this point that Odysseus tells us that the wine he is about to give Polyphemus was a present from Maron, son of Euanthes, 'the priest of Apollo' who was patron-deity of Ismarus, 'because he had protected him and his child and his wife out of respect for his office, when we came upon his home in a grove of trees sacred to Phoebus Apollo' (ix,45). This was a saving (in every sense of the word) grace in Odysseus' otherwise abominable behaviour at Ismarus. Apollo, patron of Ismarus, is the god of reason; and when, in Polyphemus, Odysseus meets the image of his own unreasonableness, he manages to outwit him with a gift of Apollo, god of reason. Odysseus beguiles Polyphemus further with word games, another symbol of reason/civilisation, before eventually blinding the Cyclops with his own staff. But Polyphemus calls on his father, Poseidon, to avenge him, and Poseidon's revenge is the story of the remainder of Odysseus' adventures.

The second potentially destructive force which Odysseus has to face is represented by Circe – that of sexuality. Her power is aptly demonstrated when she turns Odysseus' men into swine, while retaining their human minds. The art of Circe is suggestive of the power of lust to turn men into beasts, the mind losing control over the body. Not only does she turn men into swine but also into lions and wolves – the other creatures gambolling around her house: between them they share the excesses of rage, lust and gluttony. Although Circe fails to trap Odysseus in one way, thus failing to transform him into an animal, she does seduce him into complete forgetfulness of his original purpose: she thus succeeds where the Lotus Eaters failed. It is his men, ironically, who finally rouse Odysseus from his lethargy, and remind him of his seemingly forgotten home. Having decided he will set sail, Odysseus is told by Circe that he must first consult Teiresias in Hades. In line with his representation of the unconscious as the sea, Homer depicts the entrance to Hades as lying at the very edge of the sea: Odysseus must journey to the very bottom of his unconscious. In Hades, Teiresias tells him of his future perils and his eventual homecoming. In Hades, too, Odysseus meets his mother, who puts his mind at ease about events in Ithaca: after Anticleia come the wives and daughters of great men; after them the ghosts of famous men. It is highly significant that, after his mother, all the shades of women that Odysseus meets, reflect his deepest fears concerning his own wife. All these women are wives who have, in one way or another, been unfaithful to their marriage vows. And Agamemnon is, appropriately, the first of the men to appear: he tells of his murder by his wife, Clytaemnestra, who had been living in adultery with Aegisthus. It is appropriate, also, that it should be Agamemnon who draws the distinction between Clytaemnestra and Penelope, saying that Penelope is far too sound in heart and mind to dream of murdering Odysseus. So Odysseus is able to leave Hades secure in the knowledge of his wife's fidelity and of a homecoming guaranteed to be happy. Having left Hades and set out once more on his journey home, Odysseus and his men encounter Scylla and

Charybdis. Once again Odysseus is a powerless witness as some of his men are eaten. The remainder then insist on landing on the island of Thrinacia, despite the warnings of both Circe and Teiresias. On this occasion, again, his men override Odysseus' judgement, and while he sleeps (the sleep of reason?) they butcher and eat the sacred cattle of the Sun-God, with disastrous consequences – all but Odysseus are killed. This crime against Helios is reminiscent of Odysseus' earlier crime against Apollo, another sun god. With the death of the last of his men one could argue that Odysseus has had, finally, all the diseased parts of his soul extirpated.

After Thrinacia, a furious storm carries Odysseus to Ogygia, the island of Calypso. Odysseus' meeting with Calypso shows that he has still not been the victor in his conflict with sexuality. But after eight years on the island of Ogygia, Odysseus is described in the following manner:

> His eyes were wet with weeping as they always were. Life with its sweetness was ebbing away in the tears he had shed for his lost home. For the nymph [Calypso] had long since ceased to please. At nights, it is true, he had to sleep with her under the roof of the cavern, cold lover with an ardent dame. But the days found him sitting on the rocks or sands, torturing himself with tears and groans and heartache, and looking out with streaming eyes across the watery wilderness. (v,91)

Odysseus was unable to overcome his crippling inability to act, for eight years: then, within four days, he had built a raft, and arrived home within three weeks. It is obvious that it was Odysseus himself, not Calypso who had imprisoned him on the island. It is a fitting conclusion to this part of his adventures that Odysseus should end up in the sea: he has become part of the destructive element, has come to terms, in so far as one can, with his unconscious. He was now ready to go home. Thus ends the story of Odysseus' fantastic adventures, adventures which become credible only when viewed rather as representations of psychological experiences than as actual events.

The extraordinary narrative structure of the *Odyssey* has been the exemplar not only of subsequent epic poems, but also showed the writers of prose fiction the benefits of such a framework. Homer, in the *Odyssey*, does not really begin his tale *in mediis* but rather *in ultimis rebus* since the tale of *Odysseus*, which is either nineteen or ten years long, depending on the perspective one adopts, begins approximately four weeks prior to his eventual homecoming. The story opens, simply, with a reference to the imprisonment of Odysseus by the Nymph Calypso, who wished to marry him. Indeed, we do not meet Odysseus himself until as late as Book V. Instead, the first four books are devoted to an introduction. This introduction is perfectly ingenious, and takes two forms, direct and retrospective narration. The direct narration serves simply to inform us of the contemporary situation in Ithaca, with the house of Odysseus beseiged by suitors, who for four years have been demanding that Penelope marry one of them: in the meantime, they have contrived to eat her out of house and home. We learn, too, of the concern of the gods for Odysseus' welfare, and witness his son Telemachus visit Sparta and sandy Pylos to see Menelaus and Nestor, to inquire about his father.

The retrospective narration in the *Odyssey* perfectly illustrates Homer's unique artistry. A glance at the diagram of the narrative in Appendix I will make several facts obvious. If Odysseus' own relation of his adventures is excluded, almost all of the retrospective narration occurs in the first four books. In these first four books there are seven narrators, and one of the narrations, that of Menelaus in Book IV, contains within itself another retrospective narration – that of the Old Man of the Sea. The events themselves, as narrated in these first four books of the *Odyssey*, seem to show no regard for either chronological or other progression. But what we *do* have, by the time Book IV has ended, is several unique impressions. Before ever we meet Odysseus, his character and personality have been magnificently sketched by Homer. This sketch ranges from the laudatory comments made about Odysseus by such as Nestor and Menelaus, to the details of incidents in which Odysseus took part. The comments of Menelaus alone are enough to suggest the wonderful qualities of Odysseus, and we consequently look forward expectantly to meeting him. Menelaus talks of all his friends who are dead, and how much he would give to have them back with him; and he continues:

> And yet, though I miss them all and often grieve for them as I sit here in our halls till sorrow finds relief in tears and the tears cease to fall . . . I do not mourn for the whole company, disconsolate as I am, so much as I lament one man among them,

whose loss when I brood over it makes sleep and eating hateful things to me. For of all the Achaeans who toiled at Troy it was Odysseus who toiled the hardest and undertook the most. Yet all that labour was to end in misery for him, and for me in the haunting consciousness that I have lost a friend. (iv,65)

And we know, also, what to expect of the man 'who was never at a loss' when we meet him. We learn that it was Odysseus who conceived the plan of the wooden horse in Troy, and later saved the expedition from disaster.[39] We hear, too, of the time he entered Troy to spy, having first flogged himself to look like a slave, and clad himself with filthy rags. When he did return to his own side, it was with a 'harvest of information" (iv,68).

This random flashback method of Homer performs one other important function, that of fleshing out the background to the story. Very little attention is paid to the nine years spent at the actual siege of Troy, except to mention incidents like the above in which Odysseus featured. More attention, in fact, is paid to the dissension over when, and how the Greeks should sail for home. But the majority of the retrospective narration deals with the fate of the other heroes of Troy, and their attempts to return home – Agamemnon, Menelaus, Ajax and Nestor. These homecomings, or 'nonhomecomings' as the case may be, provide an excellent background for the story of the homecoming of Odysseus, and this background is fully sketched even before Odysseus begins his story. The degree of time and attention given to the story of Agamemnon, is not without significance in all of this retrospective narration. It is the first incident from the past actually referred to in the *Odyssey*, and the extent of the importance of the incident is indicated in that it is Zeus himself who is pondering on the death of Agamemnon. Nestor tells the story of the homecoming and death of Agamemnon in detail,[40] and it is again told by The Old Man of the Sea. Agamemnon himself reiterates the tale when Odysseus meets him in Hades. Homer, by having this story told *four* times, obviously intends some parallel between Agamemnon's story and that of Odysseus. Is Homer trying to create and accentuate suspense around the eventual homecoming of Odysseus by suggesting that it will simply be a variation of that of Agamemnon? And we must take into consideration, also, Odysseus' own misgivings about the fidelity of Penelope, and about circumstances in Ithaca generally. As it transpires, of course, the final condition of Odysseus is quite the reverse of Agamemnon's: but the significance of Agamemnon is thereby altered, not rendered irrelevant.

In these first four books of the *Odyssey*, only two quite short references are made to the adventures of Odysseus. Zeus is the first to refer to the actual adventures, and talks of the reasons for Odysseus' long-delayed homecoming – the blinding of Polyphemus, and the subsequent vengeance of his father, Poseidon.[41] Homer himself makes the second reference, telling how the son of Antiphus was devoured by Polyphemus. These two short, intriguing references serve as a kind of advance publicity for what is to follow, and could be called, in this instance, 'retrospective-prospective' narration. The final piece of retrospective narration in the first four books, brings us up to date on events in Ithaca, and is told by Antinous, who informs us that the suitors have now been kept on tenterhooks for four years by Penelope. He also elaborates on the various devices used by Penelope to fob them off in the course of those four years.

Odysseus' narration of his own experiences imitates the very pattern which Homer himself has used in the structure of the *Odyssey*. Odysseus begins at the end, as it were, by narrating, in Book VIII, the story of his coming to Ogygia and his eight-year exile with Calypso. This narration takes just ten lines, and he devotes the next forty lines to a narration of his sailing to, and arrival in Scherie, the land of the Phaeacians. This latter section of the story we have already witnessed in direct narration, and it serves a useful purpose. We see clearly that Odysseus uses no embroidery whatsoever in his tale; indeed, if anything, he tends to depreciate his experiences. We will keep this in mind, Homer knows, when Odysseus comes to describe his fantastic experiences in the next four books. By the end of Book VIII, we have learned all about the end of the adventures of Odysseus, and of his eight years with Calypso. There are two years of wanderings – or the beginning and middle of the narration – which we have yet to hear, and these are told by Odysseus himself in Books IX to XII, in chronological sequence, with very little interruption.

Homer's narrative in the first twelve books describes a circle, beginning on the island of Ogygia, where Odysseus is a captive, and ending in Book XII with Odysseus describing his landing on that same island. These first twelve books have been used to describe ten years; the twelve remaining books will describe the events of four days. Such is Homer's artistry, however, that we never feel he could have described these four days in less than twelve books.

There are, strangely, two instances of retrospective narration in the final twelve books – strangely, because it seems that we have been given all the information about the past that is needed, and, anyway, the time for retrospection is over, with the urgent and important events to be undertaken. The narrations involved seem to have little to do with the furtherance of the action, however, thematically or otherwise. One such incident involves a nobleman Theoclymenus,[42] whose story and ancestry is told partly by Homer, partly by Theoclymenus himself. The second instance is the telling of his own former history by Eumaeus[43] the swineherd: he turns out to be a prince in his own right but receives little recognition, in this particular story at any rate.

The pattern of the later books of the *Odyssey* is that adopted by the great romances which follow. The first twelve books are an exposition of the hero's wanderings during which he is made to run the gauntlet of testing experiences, is fully developed, and becomes a true hero. The swiftness of the narrative in the second half of the *Odyssey* is in stark contrast to the leisurely pace of the first. Everything seems to happen just in time, with the climactic reassumption of his throne by Odysseus and reunion with his wife and family.

It can be truly said the *Odyssey* shows the capacity of romance to express the dark and complex truths of life unavailable to realism. What strikes one as extraordinary about the *Odyssey*, in spite of its being the product of countless generations of development and burnishing, is that in this, the first, we have also the greatest romance. Its greatness consists not only in its capacity to express dark and complex truths, but also in the ingenious manner in which these truths are presented in the tale. It is little wonder that the *Odyssey*, both in its incidentals and in its overall pattern, became the model for all later romances.

THE GREEK ROMANCES

The immediate reaction of someone coming upon the Greek romances is one of surprise at their apparent modernity. The reaction of the classical scholar is usually one of amazement – that such works even exist, so seldom is reference made to them in university departments of Ancient Classics. The Greek romances seem an ancient equivalent of the 'True Romances' of recent times. One must agree, too, with the validity of Elizabeth Hazleton Haight's analogy, when she says that in the Greek romances both 'the structure and the devices used to arouse emotion anticipate the modern cinema'.[44] What the 'modernity' of the Greek romances so aptly demonstrates, is that human nature, on one level at least, has not changed in its essentials over the past two thousand years.

The following is the chronological order of the extant Greek romances, as given by Perry:[45]

1. *Ninus and Semiramis, c* 100 BC
2. Greek prototype of the *Recognitiones* of Ps.-Clement, 1st century AD
3. *Chaereas and Callirhoe*, 1st century AD
4. *Ephesiaca*, early 2nd century AD
5. *Babyloniaca c* 165 AD
6. *Daphnis and Chloe*, late 2nd century AD
7. *Clitopho and Leucippe*, mid-2nd century AD
8. *Aethiopica*, first half of 3rd century AD

This catalogue speaks for itself in many respects: it is immediately apparent, for instance, that we possess a mere eight Greek romances from over four centuries of production. In fact the number would be more accurately six, since two of the above, the *Ninus* romance and the *Babyloniaca* are only fragments of the originals. The romances numbered 5 to 8 are the ones best known in modern times, for reasons which will become apparent. There is a marked difference between the latter four romances, and the ones preceding them. The first four are usually labeled 'presophistic' romances and the final four 'sophistic'. The earliest exponents of romance in ancient times were naïve authors writing for an undiscerning readership: these authors produced what we called the presophistic romances. Later, 'sophists' became interested in romance as a means of displaying their wares, and their works are the ones labeled sophistic romances.

It is important to explain exactly what the sophistic was. It was, to put it at its simplest, a new art of Greek elocution, whose professors were called sophists. The new art, spurious as it may have been, took the literary world by storm when it began to develop after the end of the first century AD. This is how Ludwig Friedlander describes the results of the new sophistic:

> It created forms difficult to manage, hard and fast and trifling rules, even to the every form of thought, construction and rhythm: great importance was also attached to correctness of expression, which it was sought to obtain by study and perverse and pedantic imitation of ancient models, especially Attic. The chief excellence of the sophists . . . consisted to a great extent in the apparent ease with which they surmounted the technical difficulties of their art. . . . The knowledge of the technical rules of the new art of prose, gradually spreading among the educated public, sharpened the understanding, and increased the admiration of the audience. But the object of special admiration was the art of improvisation. . . . In addition to this there was a studied declamation, which only too often, like the orators' attitude, facial play and gesture, verged upon the theatrical, or closely resembled a musical performance.[46]

A little earlier, Friedlander had elaborated on the improvisation of the sophists:

> The favourite subjects for improvisation with both sophists and their hearers were taken from Greek history. 'The deeds of their forefathers were handed down by history and could be celebrated. But their speeches on numerous occasions were not so handed down. Consequently, it was possible to suggest what they might have said, and the answers that might have been made; what they would have said on occasions when they did not speak at all, if they had spoken. Some of these themes were, e.g., Demosthenes after the battle of Chaeronea; how did Demosthenes defend himself against the accusation of Demades, that he had been bribed by the Persian King with fifty talents? a speech to the Greeks after the end of the Pelopponesian war, declaring that all trophies must be destroyed, since it was really a civil war . . .'[47]

But there were topics, too, which were not historical, ones composed by the sophists to afford their students further material for debate and discussion. The Elder Seneca gives some examples of such topics in his handbook on the subject: a devoted husband

and wife vow not to survive one another; the husband, to test his
wife, sends word of his death; she throws herself over a precipice
but recovers. What should she do now? A man is captured by
pirates, falls in love with and marries the pirate chief's daughter
he is set free and returns home, whereupon he is cut off without a
penny by his father. What should he say to his father to make him
change his mind? What should the father say in defence of his
action?

The sophists – or at least some of them – seized upon the
romance as a means of exhibiting their rhetorical skills to a wide
audience. They may well have been almost ashamed, as Perry
suggests,[48] of writing a love story at all, but there is no doubt about
the major improvements which they introduced into the genre.
They also helped to gain some recognition for romance in academic
circles, but too late. It is tempting to draw a comparison between
the writers of sophistic romance and Henry Fielding. That Fielding
was 'almost ashamed' to be writing fiction is obvious from his
attempts to secure for *Joseph Andrews* a respectable academic
ancestry. And his critical essays on diverse topics are undoubtedly
the equivalent of the rhetorical displays of the sophists – though
perhaps, with much less excuse.

The art of the sophist must be understood if one is to appreciate
why specific scenes and incidents recur in all the sophistic romances. Thus, the 'trial scene', which occurs so often, gives the author
an opportunity to plead eloquently, and at length, for both the
prosecution *and* the defence. The 'death' of the heroine is another
set-piece which gives the hero (and, of course, the author), an
opportunity to bare his heart with all the eloquence he can muster
Achilles Tatius obviously believed himself particularly adept at this
scene, since the heroine 'dies' three times in all, in the course of
Clitopho and Leucippe, with three lamentations on her death by the
hero. The rhetoricians believed they could supplant poetry, and
the poetical prose of the romances seems to have its roots in this
tendency. More important for a better understanding of at least
two of the romances, is the sophists' belief that they could take
possession of the subjects of poetry also. One result of this tendency
was the development of *ecphrasis* which is 'a description of almost
anything visible – a landscape, a battle, or a person, but it often
took the form of an exegetical interpretation of a picture or a
statute . . . .'[49] *Daphnis and Chloe* is an extended *ecphrasis*, and an
ecphrasis provides the exciting force for the story of *Clitopho and*

Leucippe, with several other *ecphraseis* within the story itself.

The association between the sophists and the Greek romances has had one unfortunate result, inasmuch as the majority of critics tend to view the genre as an offshoot of the rhetoricians' schools. Not only were the rhetors or sophists themselves writing romance, but very many of the topics offered for experience in verbal acrobatics in their schools seemed to offer the skeletons of romances. But while it would be rash, and indeed inaccurate, to deny some interaction between the rhetors' schools and the romance, in its conception the Greek romance was simply *not* a rhetorical exercise: whether it could *ever* be called a rhetorical exercise, is another matter entirely. What the romance did offer the sophist was an ideal form in which he could exercise his talents. The result is an abundance of irrelevant material – descriptions of paintings, gardens, jewels; pseudo-scientific facts; long monologues and debates: indeed, anything which inspired the sophist was given the fullest possible treatment.

Allowing for exceptions at individual points in individual stories, the Greek romance follows a well-defined pattern. A young couple fall in love, and are prevented from consummating their love. This 'prevention' usually takes the form of physical separation, as they travel about the world facing one danger after another, until they are reunited, return home, are married, and live happily ever after. There are numerous incidents which recur with boring regularity in the romances – shipwrecks; capture by pirates; narrow escapes from death, rape and seduction; trial scenes; reunions; and sensational recognitions. Despite the obsessive preoccupation with chastity in the romance, one would hesitate to include it as a feature of Greek romance. Daphnis is unchaste; so are both Clitopho and Leucippe. In *Chaereas and Callirhoe*, the heroine marries again, while aware that her first husband is alive. From a study of the works, it soon becomes obvious that chastity in the Greek romances means regard for the concept rather than practice of the virtue.

Love is, of course, the exciting force of the Greek romance, yet it is a type of love which deserves some comment. Samuel Lee Wolff believes that there is no sign that love in Greek romance 'is anything but physical desire, of which the lovers are postponing the satisfaction'.[50] Later, Wolff wonders if any of the lovers are really congenial:

Are their tastes alike, or complementary, or opposite? Would they laugh at the same things, and weep at the same things? Who knows? There is not a hint of spiritual companionship between them; not a hint that the character of each is to be rounded out by that of the other; not a hint that theirs is to be a 'marriage of true minds'.[51]

One must, of course, agree with Wolff's comment on the lack of any kind of spiritual companionship in the Greek romances (with the possible exception of *Daphnis and Chloe*). It is difficult, on the other hand, to agree with his interpretation of love in the Greek romance as simply the equivalent of physical desire. Love in the Greek romance operates in two ways, providing the exciting force for the story, and a bond between the hero and the heroine. It is the innumerable attempts to break this bond which create the suspense and drama in the tale. The separation of the lovers, which always appears permanent, is regarded as a breaking of the bond, as is, obviously, the death of either hero or heroine. Fornication, rape, or adultery, is seen as another means by which the bond might be broken, if the hero or heroine is involved. Samuel Richardson was certainly not the first writer of fiction concerning 'procrastinated rape', since this is what Greek romance is all about.

Since the Greek romances are stories in which almost all the emphasis is on action, the authors are seldom interested in character development, except insofar as this is necessary for the development of the plot. And love, too, merely becomes a means towards an end. There is, therefore, little possibility of love as spiritual companionship amongst characters who are intentionally presented as pasteboard figures. *Daphnis and Chloe* is an exception, but this story is not an action-orientated tale.

'Love at first sight' may not have been the invention of the Greek romancers, but they certainly make full use of it. The formula of love at first sight is ideal for the romancer, since there is no need to show the development of this love: two people simply meet, love everlastingly there and then, and are ready to be led into their adventures. For the sophist, of course, love at first sight is a phenomenon to which he can devote pages of description and scientific analysis. One might add, indeed, that there is little point in marvelling at love at first sight in the Greek romances, when there are several instances of 'love at first hearing' – when the male simply hears a female described, and falls violently in love with her.

In spite of – or perhaps even because of his preoccupation with action – the Greek romancer is not too particular about how this action is brought about: there is seldom any emphasis on cause and effect as a means of creating or advancing action. Instead there is a total reliance on 'Fortune', 'the gods' or 'Providence' to initiate new action, or inject life into a flagging one. Despite the fact that Hellenistic man actually did regard himself as the plaything of Fortune, and despite the apparent sanction bestowed on such devices by the *Iliad* and *Odyssey*, there is no doubting the utter sterility of such a method in the romances. The use of such a method means that the author is not only released from the bonds of cause and effect, but he also has unlimited freedom to introduce a long succession of marvellous or sensational incidents at will. One can certainly never tell what is going to happen next, and this is exactly how the Greek romancer wishes it to be: it seems that this is how the reader of Greek romance wished it to be, too.

The Greek romances are not realistic works in the modern sense of the word, though realistic elements do creep in, as if by accident, now and again. It would be out of the question to object to this lack of realism in Greek romance, any more than it would be to object to lack of more complete characterisation, or absence of cause and effect in the motivation of incident. The romancers, and in particular the sophists, seemed to have a very good idea of the effects they wished to achieve and how to achieve them: one can hardly blame them for not conforming to modern theories on how fiction should be written. It is noticeable, too, that only one of the romances is set in contemporary times – that of Achilles Tatius. All the others, probably under the influence of objective poetry, as Perry claims,[52] were set in times past.

All the Greek romances have the inevitable happy ending, as well as a neat distribution of poetic justice all round, features which become part and parcel of later romances also. One can safely identify with the hero and heroine of romance, knowing that no matter what happens, all will be well in the end. It is interesting to note a modern critic claiming that the happy ending is the most important part of the legacy which *drama* bequeathed to the English novel. 'Fielding', he continues, 'must bear most of the responsibility for bringing the happy ending, without sufficient regard to the logic of character, from the realm of the dramatic comedy, into the novel'.[53]

Ninus and Semiramis

This, the earliest extant Greek romance, was written in 100 BC, approximately. It consists of only three fragments, which in themselves are severely mutilated. Ninus and Semiramis were well known in the ancient world as the heroes of an Assyrian national saga, and it is apparently on this saga that the romance is based. The author simply chose two famous personages from past history and wrote about their lives *as adolescents*, first as lovers, then as man and wife. The story is not a total fabrication, since the author is shrewd enough to refer to the well-known campaigns of Ninus at various points, even in the extant fragments. The method adopted by the author of this romance is one which has been brought to a fine art by the historical novelist of modern times. The creative artist inevitably finds himself cramped if he chooses to deal with well-known historical personages or events, since these will be well documented, and leave little scope for *plasma*, or invention. One solution to the problem is to choose minor or insignificant characters of whom little or nothing is known, about whom to reconstruct past characters and events. Another method – one adopted by Xenophon in his *Cyropaedia*, and followed by the author of *Ninus and Semiramis* – is to take the youth of the person involved and write about it. Such a work will have to be almost entirely plasmatic, since little is usually known of the youth of historical personages.

In the story of *Ninus and Semiramis*, the only historical facts seem to be the names of the heroes, and references to military campaigns. The Ninus of the saga, indeed, is quite the opposite of the one pictured in the romance. In the saga, as related by Diodorus, Ninus takes Semiramis away from her rightful husband by force, threatening to blind him if he doesn't comply. At this stage of his career, Ninus was not seventeen years old, but had spent seventeen years conquering Western Asia and Egypt. The Ninus of the saga also has his harem, to which he continually adds by seizing any woman who takes his fancy, no matter what her condition in life.

Even within the limited remains of the original romance, there are sufficient indications that it is setting or following – at least in its incidentals – the pattern of the typical Greek romance. In the pening scene of what is generally regarded as the first, in hronological order, of the fragments, Ninus seriously upsets emiramis for some unknown reason, but manages to calm her by elling her he is not the man she takes him to be, and then takes n oath. (Or at least mention is made of an oath, here.) The ndications are sufficient to suggest, from what we know of later Greek romances, that Semiramis believed herself to be in danger f, at worst, rape, and, at best, seduction by Ninus. The oath will lmost certainly, then, be a vow of chastity – never to make an ttempt on the virtue of Semiramis (plus other, unnamed females?), vithout her consent. This interpretation of the oath seems borne ut by an incident in the second fragment, where Ninus comes to peak to Semiramis's mother, and says:

It is with my oath kept true that I have come into your sight, and to the embrace of my most charming cousin [Semiramis]. This let the gods first of all know, as indeed they do know it, and as I shall doubtless prove by what I am now saying. I have overrun so much territory and have made myself master of so many nations, both those who were subdued by my own spear, and those who pay me homage and bow down to me on account of my father's power, that I could have indulged myself to satiety with every carnal pleasure; and had I done so, perhaps my passion for my cousin would have been less. But now that I have come back pure and uncorrupted, I am conquered by the god of love and by my age. I am in my seventeenth year, as you know . . . up to now I have been only a boy, a child; and if I were still unaware of Aphrodite's power, I should feel happy in my firm strength. But, now that I have been taken prisoner by your daughter, in no shameful fashion, but agreeably to the desires of both of you, how long am I to be refused . . . I am old enough to marry . . . and how many men have kept themselves unspotted (as I have) even up to their fifteenth year?[54]

Ninus is certainly setting a high standard for the later heroes of omance to follow. Even before they are eventually allowed to narry by their respective mothers, the lovers are separated by the Armenian campaign in which Ninus must take part. When they lo marry, the inevitable sea journey, and even more inevitable atastrophe occurs – the ship is wrecked and Semiramis is carried

off, captive. The fragment ends at this point, but it requires ver
little imagination to guess what happens next, and next, an
next . . . .

In spite of what was said earlier about the place of Fortune i
ruling the affairs of Greek romance, it comes as a major surpris
to discover that in the three fragments of the Ninus romance
Fortune is alluded to three times, and in much the same way as
will be referred to in later examples of the Greek romance. In hi
address to Semiramis's mother, part of which was quoted earlie
Ninus says:

> Let us wait two years, you may say, but supposing we do wa
> patiently, mother – will Fortune (Τύχη) also wait? I am a morta
> man engaged to a mortal maid, and I am exposed not merely t
> the ordinary hazards of life, such as diseases and the ill Fortun
> (Τύχη) which often destroys even those who remain peacefull
> at home by their own firesides; but *sea-voyages are waiting for me*
> and wars after wars . . . . Let also the fact that we are each c
> us the only offspring of our parents be anticipated and provide
> for, so that, if Fortune (Τύχη) plans any calamity for us, w
> may at least leave you some pledge of our affection.[55]

It is reasonable to assume that Fortune was subsequently onl
too willing to bring the premonitions of Ninus to fulfilment. O
the basis of the little evidence we have, it would be fruitless t
speculate further on the quality of the Ninus romance, either i
form or content. In spite of being such an early extant example c
the Greek romance, it can be said, however, that it display
remarkable similarities, even within the few extant pages, with late
examples.

Clitopho and Leucippe

Achilles Tatius' *Clitopho and Leucippe*, is, in many ways, the mos
enigmatic of the Greek romances. To the modern reader it seem
a particularly inept piece of work, while at the same time it can b
shown that Achilles Tatius made a revolutionary innovation in hi
romance, and it can be argued that the very ineptitude of the wor
was consciously cultivated by the author.

To demonstrate in what way the work is inept is relativel
simple. It would be an exaggeration to say that the innumerabl

irrelevances in the romance tend to eclipse the story, but it is true to say that they retard and impede the narrative to a very considerable extent. Some of these irrelevances are other narratives, which have no bearing on the main plot, narratives such as the story of Clinias and Charicles[56] or that of Menelaus.[57] Apart from these, we are treated to descriptions of the elephant,[58] the phoenix,[59] the Nile Horse,[60] and the crocodile.[61] We learn about Tyrian dye,[62] the magnet and the iron,[63] and the palm tree and its mate.[64] We read, also, a lengthy invective against women,[65] by a homosexual, and are treated, later, to a comparison of boys to women as sexual partners.[66] And these are just a few of well over one hundred digressions, which cause the present-day reader such frustration.

Nor is the ineptitude confined to digressions: within the actual story there is ample evidence also – soliloquies which are intended as expressions of intense feelings, and end in bathos; and verbiage which all but smothers the story. Take, for example, the very first lamentation in the book, but not by any means the worst – that of Charicles' father, on the death of his son, in a riding accident:

> My son, in how different a state hast thou returned from that in which thou didst leave me! Ill betide all horsemanship! Neither hast thou died by any common death, nor art thou brought back a corpse comely in thy death; others who die preserve their well-known lineaments, and though the living beauty of the countenance be gone, the image is preserved, which by its mimickry of sleep consoles the mourner. In their case, death has taken away the soul, but leaves in the body the semblance of the individual: in thy case, fate has destroyed both, and, to me, thou hast died a double death, in soul and body, so utterly has even the shadow of thy likeness perished! Thy soul has fled, and I find thee no more, even in body! Oh my son, when shall be now thy bridal day! When, ill-starred horseman and unwedded bridegroom, when shall be the joyous nuptial festivities? The tomb will be thy bridal bed, death thy partner, a dirge thy nuptial song, wailing thy strains of joy! I thought, my son, to have kindled for thee a very different flame, but cruel fate has extinguished both it and thee, and in its stead lights up the funeral torch. (i,365,366)

The very ineptitude of Achilles Tatius has led some critics to believe that *Clitopho and Leucippe* is 'too bad to be true', as it were, and quite unbecoming an educated author, as Achilles Tatius was. The supposition is that the author could have written a much better work, and that this one must obviously be a parody of the excesses of Greek romance.[67] But a major element in the success of parody is that the parodist must either explicitly or implicitly make his intentions clear, and there is no such clarity in this story. *Clitopho and Leucippe* seems not so much a parody as a more absurd version of the typical romance. Achilles Tatius' ineptitude can possibly be explained by the author's own attitude towards the romance. It seems very likely that he simply was not interested in the story *qua* story but rather in the enormous readership the romance would bring him: he could then use the story to display his many and varied sophistical wares. Achilles Tatius simply exploited the romance form for his own purposes to a greater degree than any of his contemporaries. A careful distinction must, therefore, be made between *our* impression of his story, and Achilles Tatius': we, rightly, consider it inept as an adventure story, while the author would obviously feel he had succeeded admirably in his task, viz., to demonstrate his competence and his ingenuity as a sophist.

In spite of its shortcomings, *Clitopho and Leucippe* does, however, have one remarkable innovation. The setting of the story is not in the dim and distant past, as in the other romances, but in contemporary times. This seemingly unimportant fact could have had major repercussions on the development of prose fiction in ancient times, but it came, alas, too late. Achilles Tatius presents *Clitopho and Leucippe* as a story told to him by Clitopho himself, and therefore the scene is set in his own lifetime, and that of Clitopho. The significance of this innovation is remarked on by Ben Edwin Perry: 'by it', he says, 'all the essential difference in form and potentiality between the ancient and the modern novel is bridged'.[68] Achilles Tatius did, in *Clitopho and Leucippe*, exactly what Samuel Richardson was to do in *Pamela* almost 1500 years later. Both posed as recorders of 'true histories': if either had told the story on his own authority there would have been no difference whatever – in narrative method at any rate – between their stories and the stories of today. Perry attributes a second innovation to Achilles Tatius which is a little more difficult to accept. He suggests that Achilles Tatius had grafted 'the comic or picaresque tradition of epic narrative . . . onto the ideal, thereby greatly widening the scope of the genre romance and its capacity as an artistic medium for the criticism or interpretation of life in all its aspects'.[69] In this respect, Perry suggests, Achilles Tatius can be compared to Henry Fielding, who effected a similar fusion of comic and serious in his eighteenth-century novels. Perry bases his remarks about Achilles Tatius on the contemporaneity of *Clitopho and Leucippe*; and since contemporaniety was inevitably associated in the ancient world with the comic, he suggests *Clitopho and Leucippe* is comic. This is hardly sufficient evidence on which to base a suggestion that Achilles Tatius made as great an impression on the ancient novel – at least in one major respect – as Fielding did on the modern. Perry does, admittedly, allude to episodes in *Clitopho and Leucippe*, 'many of which border on the burlesque, and are thought by some to have been intended as parody . . . ,'[70] but this is nowhere substantiated.

The narrative method and structure of *Clitopho and Leucippe* is relatively uncomplicated. Upon arriving one day in Sidon, the author meets a young man named Clitopho, who tells how severely he has suffered from the caprices of love. Not unnaturally, Achilles Tatius' curiosity is aroused, and he asks the young man to relate his full story. Clitopho is reluctant to do so: 'You are stirring up a whole swarm of words', he says; 'mystery will sound like a fable' (i,352). Achilles demands that he gratify his curiosity, 'however fabulous may seem your tale', and adds: 'this spot is in every way agreeable, and exactly suited for a love story' (i,352,353). Clitopho agrees to tell his story, and proceeds to do so. There are, of course, great disadvantages as well as advantages associated with a first-person narrative. The major disadvantage is the inability of the narrator to be always where the action is, with a consequent too-great reliance on reportage. This method would seem to be particularly inadequate for the Greek romance, a staple ingredient of which is separation of hero and heroine: indeed, in this romance, Clitopho and Leucippe are separated for six months. But Achilles Tatius – or Clitopho – overcomes this problem by simply pretending it doesn't exist, because Clitopho is never at a loss for information, with no indication whatever as to how he came by it. He not only gives us facts, of which he could not be aware,[71] but can also tell us how people looked, or the long speeches they made, at various times. When Thersander comes to rape Leucippe, for instance, 'grief and fear were plainly depicted on her countenance' (vi,463), Clitopho tells us, though he was not present. It may well be that Achilles was aware that he was 'breaking the rules', since he refuses to bring us back to the beginning of the story at the end, viz., when the story ends, so does the book, and no reference whatever is made to Achilles Tatius sitting in a grove in Sidon, listening to a young man called Clitopho telling a love story. It seems quite likely that Achilles Tatius was shrewd enough to realise that such an ending might simply highlight the contradictions and improbabilities in his narrative. The author of *Clitopho and Leucippe* had it both ways in effect – retaining the advantages of immediacy and contemporaneity which a first-person narrative gives, without any of the concomitant disadvantages. And it is extremely doubtful that his contemporary readers would have noticed any incongruity.

Apart from the anomaly noted above, the plot of *Clitopho and Leucippe* is singularly uncomplicated. There is very little retrospective narration, for instance: Leucippe, in less than a page, relates her experiences over six months in the hands of pirates, and as a slave of Melitta. Her adventures, during another separation from Clitopho, are narrated, not by Leucippe herself, but by Menelaus and Satyrus. The longest retrospective narration in the work involves the largely irrelevant subplot of Callisthenes and Calligone, and is another Greek romance in miniature. The commencement of this story is directly narrated. Callisthenes, a wealthy profligate, falls in love with Leucippe upon hearing her described. Having been refused her hand in marriage he resolves to carry her off, and lays elaborate plans to do so. Not unnaturally, since he has never seen Leucippe, he carries off the wrong girl – Calligone – as Clitopho is about to marry her. The remainder of this incidental story is told by Sostratus at the end of the main tale: Callisthenes soon realised his mistake, we are told, but fell in love with Calligone, yet refused to take advantage of her helplessness. Callisthenes, through the 'power of love', soon became a reformed man, won Calligone's respect and love, and eventually married her.

It is noticeable how strictly Achilles Tatius attends to his time scheme in *Clitopho and Leucippe*. It is quite possible, for instance, to trace the development of the action day by day throughout the book, if allowance is made for the six-month interval during which Leucippe is presumed dead, and Clitopho wrestles with his grief. Homer had set a very good precedent in the matter of time, since almost all of Odysseus' adventures can be assigned their positions in time: some, mostly the earlier ones, to a specific year; the remainder to a particular day. Few of the other romancers were as careful as Achilles with their time schemes, but one must remember that the narrative method he chose, with its imposition of contemporaneity, helped to formulate a coherent time sequence: all the other romances were in the distant past, where time was not of much consequence.

In the typical Greek romance, there is usually very little relationship between character and plot: in *Clitopho and Leucippe* there is even less. Fortune dominates this romance to a much greater extent than it does any of the others, and the results are obvious. Fortune becomes an extremely useful narrative device, of course, since the author is nowhere obliged to account for any action, or to have character and action dependent on each other: all can be attributed to Fortune. As Samuel Lee Wolff so aptly remarks of *Clitopho and Leucippe*: 'To recount the activity of Fortune in this story is to recount the story itself'.[72] There is no basis, for example, for the initial elopement of Clitopho and Leucippe, an elopement which leads to all their subsequent perilous adventures. The flight is attributed to Fortune, which delayed a letter: if the letter had arrived on time the couple would not have been tempted to elope. The assumption must be that since Fortune delayed the letter, Fortune *forced* the couple to elope: this is strange reasoning, but nevertheless, typical of Achilles Tatius. The characters themselves accept that their lives are ruled by Fortune. Even Leucippe's father, Sostratus, who has every reason to be angry with Clitopho, because of the dangers, both moral and physical, into which he has led his daughter, forgives all, since the 'grief and vexation' which he (Sostratus) has endured 'is to be attributed to Fortune not to you' (viii,491), he tells Clitopho. There are only two incidents of any significance in the story which are *not* controlled by Fortune. One is the intervention of the goddess Diana, who asks Leucippe to dedicate her virginity to her, in which case her marriage to Clitopho will be assured.[73] It is notable that in his attempt to make love to Leucippe just prior to the revelation of the dream, Clitopho actually cites the 'lull in Fortune' as the reason why they should grasp the opportunity offered.[74] On the second occasion of which we spoke, Clitopho had just got into bed with Leucippe when her mother was awakened by a prophetic dream, and went to her daughter's room.[75] It is not made clear whether this dream was inspired by Diana or Fortune. While Fortune may not have played a part in either of these situations, it is worth remarking that neither does character.

For obvious reasons, it is quite difficult to comment on the characters in *Clitophoe and Leucippe* since they are merely puppets in the hands of Fortune, with one exception. When Clitopho and Leucippe are eloping, for instance, they throw themselves aboard the first boat which happens to be leaving the port of Berytus when they arrive.[76] They don't even ask what the destination of the boat is, and the assumption must be that they consider it irrelevant, anyway, since Fortune is in such undisputed control. Each person in the story does, fortuntely, have one or two characteristics, besides his name, by which he can be distinguished from his fellows. We can say that Clitopho is a coward, for example, since he allows himself to be kicked and beaten – twice by the bully Thersander, and once by Sostratus. He is on the point of committing suicide three times, and has to be prevented from doing so on each occasion. He is involved in numerous and varied other situations in the course of the work, but on each occasion his character is simply manipulated by the author to suit the situation in question.

Leucippe is probably the least prominent of the heroines of Greek romance, since Achilles Tatius gives her little to either do or say. When she is on the defensive, as in Book II, when her mother accuses her of complicity in the attempt on her virtue, we find her quite defiant, and lying her way out of trouble. Her only other scenes of note are with Thersander, when he tries to rape or seduce her: here, she is brave, defiant and caustic. Otherwise, she appears simply as an appendage to the hero. It is difficult to say why Achilles Tatius neglected Leucippe so much: it is hardly because of his narrative method, since this did not restrict him in other ways. A good example of this restriction and the author's general attitude towards Leucippe is illustrated in the scene where she is rescued after a pseudo-death. She has had to take part in a mock-sacrifice, and afterwards lie for hours in a coffin, covered with sheep's blood. Yet it is Menelaus and Satyrus who tell of her ordeal: Leucippe does not utter a single word, then, or later, even to say she is glad to be alive. Nor does the author suggest that she is unable to speak after her ordeal – she seems, simply, to have been forgotten. Even within the limits assigned to her, Leucippe could not be described as a character of any significance.

Yet, the most significant character-sketch in Greek romance occurs, ironically, in *Clitopho and Leucippe*. This is the sketch of the young, beautiful, and wealthy widow, Melitta, who falls violently

in love with Clitopho. Not to detract from the achievement of
Achilles Tatius, it is understandable why he should have succeeded
with this character. Melitta is a minor character who is not needed
by the author for involvement in a variety of adventures, but for
just one situation. He can, therefore, allow himself to elaborate on
this sketch without unduly restricting himself later. This is, of
course, true of minor characters in all adventure stories – it is they
who *can* become three-dimensional while the hero remains flat:
not all authors, however, have the ability to develop any or all of
their minor characters. Melitta is a significant three-dimensional
character. She is quite humorous, someone who always has a quip
ready: when she and Clitopho marry, and he refuses to make love
to her, she claims she has often heard of a Κενοτάφιον (Cenotaph)
but never, till then, of a Κενογάμιον a 'cenogam' or 'empty
marriage'.[77] Melitta, later, tells Leucippe she (Melitta) has fallen in
love with a 'statue, not a man' (v,454). Mention has been made of
Achilles Tatius' failure to present intense feeling in his monologues
or soliloquies, but he does succeed in at least one instance, and,
again, it is Melitta who is involved. When she discovers a letter of
Leucippe's to Clitopho, Melitta is immediately forced to the
realisation of how hopeless her love for Clitopho must always
be; and Achilles Tatius gives a very accurate and sympathetic
description of her state of mind.[78] Another side of her character is
shown in her spirited and cunning defence against the accusations
of Thersander, in which she shows a masterly ability to fuse fact
with fiction to give an overall impression of truth and sincerity.[79]
It is notable that in spite of being – by the standards of Greek
romance – grossly unchaste, Melitta is a warm, sympathetic and
human character.

   Chastity, and its place in *Clitopho and Leucippe*, deserve special
mention, as, indeed, in the case in all the Greek romances. Achilles
Tatius treats the subject in various ways, and the best exponents
of the virtue are not Clitopho and Leucippe of the main plot, but
rather Callisthenes and Calligone of the subplot. Callisthenes is
actually reformed by the power of his love for Calligone, a harbinger
of things to come in later love-literature. Despite having Calligone
at his mercy, he not only does not rape her, but refrains from even
'soliciting her virtue'.[80] Clitopho and Leucippe have a double
standard of chastity – one for each half of the book. Before their
elopement, they twice attempt to have sexual intercourse, but are
prevented from doing so on each occasion. The first occasion

actually occurs a few days before Clitopho's proposed wedding to another woman, Calligone. He has smothered Leucippe in kisses, and they are 'about to proceed to other familiarities' when they are interrupted.[81] Later, Clitopho decides he needs something more 'substantial' than kisses, and gets Leucippe to agree to allow him into her bed that night. Again they are interrupted, this time by Leucippe's mother. The couple do not have a further opportunity of consummating their love for quite some time, and when they do, Diana intervenes to prevent it. The prevention of consummation, it should be noted, has nothing whatever to do with the characters of the people involved – nor, for that matter, has their subsequent chastity.

Clitopho does, subsequently, make love to the widow Melitta, which he describes as the 'administering of relief to a love-sick soul' (v,459), and the easing of her 'pains'. This love-making takes place on the floor of Clitopho's prison, and at about the only point in the story that it should not. Prior to this, Melitta and Clitopho had known each other for four months during which time Clitopho presumed Leucippe dead, and Melitta presumed her husband, Thersander, dead. Despite the assaults of Melitta, who is in love with him, Clitopho refuses to make love to her, and continues in his resolve even after they are married. It is only when his fiancée and her husband both arrive back from the 'dead' that he finally capitulates. The author's attitude towards chastity is ambiguous, to say the least. Yet, there is nothing ambiguous about Leucippe's chastity once she has made her vow. 'I will submit to everything but the loss of my chastity' (vi,473), she tells Thersander, and has already seen herself a martyr for chastity, when she says:

> You little think how your unblushing cruelty will redound hereafter to my praise; you may kill me in your fury, and my encomium will be this: 'Leucippe preserved her chastity despite of buccaneers, despite of Chaereas, despite of Sosthenes, and crown of all (for this would be but trifling commendation), she remained chaste despite even of Thersander, more lascivious than the most lustful pirate; and he, who could not despoil her of her honour, robbed her of her life'. (vi,474)

Love is, in this romance, identical with that in the others. It occurs at first sight, which is again a great help to the author, since he need not be concerned with delineating the development of that love. Callisthenes falls in love with Leucippe from merely hearing her described, which is an innovation: sight is obviously more influential than sound,˙ however, since he changes his allegiance immediately on seeing Calligone. Achillles Tatius celebrates the part played by the kiss, in love, to a very great degree. Clitopho utters two long eulogies[82] on the value of the kiss, and refuses to have his kisses 'adulterously dallied with' (iv,425), by having anyone but he kiss Leucippe. One of these eulogies is worth quoting to demonstrate both the significance of the kiss and the author's method generally:

> I still felt the kiss upon my lips as though it had really been something of a corporeal nature; I zealously guarded it as a treasure of sweets, for a kiss is to the lover his chief delight; it takes its birth from the fairest portion of the human body – from the mouth, which is the instrument of the voice, and the voice is the adumbration of the soul; when lips mingle they dart pleasure through the veins, and make even the lovers' souls join in the embrace. Never before did I feel delight comparable to this; and then for the first time I learnt that no pleasurable sensation can vie with a lover's kiss. (ii,377)

One does not need to be a student of Jung or Freud to interpret the many dreams of *Clitopho and Leucippe*. When Leucippe has just received Clitopho into her bed, for instance, her mother is awakened by a 'fearful dream'. In the dream she sees a robber who, '. . . armed with a naked sword seized and carried off her daughter, after which, laying her upon the ground he proceeded to rip her up, beginning at her private parts' (ii,389). There is hardly any need for elaboration of the sex symbolism here, and neither is there for an earlier dream of Clitopho, where he dreamt he had 'coalesced with, and *grown* into, the person of a maiden, as far as the middle, and that from thence upward we formed two bodies' (i,353). Later again, when Leucippe refuses to have intercourse with him, Clitopho recalls a dream he had the previous night:

> I thought . . . I saw the temple of Venus, and could discern the statue of the goddess within; upon approaching it with the design of offering up my prayers, the doors were suddenly closed, and while standing there in a state of disappointment, a

female strongly resembling the statue of the goddess appeared
to me and said: 'It is not permitted thee to enter the temple now;
but if thou wilt wait for a short period I will not only open to
thee its doors, but will constitute thee my priest'. (iv,420)

One could construct a more elaborate scheme of imagery, based
on the theme of chastity, than the above, but only at the risk of
being charged with overreading. Such a scheme would have its
basis in the many *ecphraseis* of the story, and on the many myths
which are related. Among the pictures described are those of the
rape of Europa and the rape of Philomela; among the myths are
those of Pan and Syrinx, and the myth of the Stygian Fountain. In
view of Achilles Tatius' ambiguous attitude towards chastity, and
his general lack of concern for the actual story, it is extremely
doubtful that he went to any pains to work out an elaborate scheme
of imagery for his romance: it is much more probable that these
ecphraseis and myths were simply one more way of exhibiting his
extensive knowledge, as well as his rhetorical skill.

Clitopho and Leucippe is one of the most unrealistic of the Greek
romances, for obvious reasons. The part played by Fortune, for
example, is so great, that events which might, if handled differently,
be regarded as possible, are made to look absurd by Achilles Tatius'
method. There are, of course, incidents in the romance which no
degree of expertise could render plausible, and such are the three
'deaths' of Leucippe. One of these deaths is particularly gruesome,
and is described in detail by the author. A pirate band, having
captured Leucippe, decides to sacrifice her and eat her entrails:
Clitopho is a spectator at this event, and describes it as he sees it.
First the pirates place Leucippe upon the ground, and linch her to
four wooden pegs, and then a young man, 'drawing a sword
plunged it into her heart, and drawing the weapon downwards
laid open all her belly so that the intestines immediately protruded;
then they removed and laid them upon the altar, and when roasted
they were cut into portions and partaken of by the pirates' (ii,411).
But it is not Leucippe's entrails Clitopho has seen: Menelaus and
Satyrus have tied a sheepskin bag full of sheep's entrails and blood
to Leucippe's stomach and it is this, not Leucippe, they cut open.
To do the cutting, and also to stab Leucippe in the heart, Menelaus
and Satyrus use a magician's sword with a retractable blade – a
sword which had conveniently floated ashore from a ship.[83] The
lamentation of Clitopho after this particular death is his most

absurd as he ponders on the 'joint grave' or Leucippe – her bowels on the altar, her body in the coffin, and her entrails in the pirates.[84]

Mention must be made, finally, of the trial scenes in *Clitopho and Leucippe*. The trial scenes in Greek romances gave the sophists an opportunity of showing their brilliance on both sides of the argument, for the prosecution and defence. Achilles Tatius siezes the opportunity eagerly, and not content with one, gives us two such scenes,[85] the second of which takes over ten pages to describe.

The *Aethiopica*

That Heliodorus was the most conscious and able author amongst the Greek romancers is evident from even a cursory study of his work, the *Aethiopica*, sometimes known as *Theagenes and Chariclea*. But while he effected many improvements in the Greek romance, these were within the confines already established, and Heliodorus cannot be credited with making any radical changes in the general pattern of the genre: and because of the obvious ability of the author of the *Aethiopica*, it is unfortunate that he did not decide to break new ground. Heliodorus was an author with more of a mission than the typical rhetor, and it is very probable that the pattern of the romance, already well established, suited his purposes adequately without the need for any significant change. One aim of the *Aethiopica* is certainly to celebrate a cult of the sun-god Apollo, and Eros, for a change, has to play second fiddle. Eros is undoubtedly ailing in the *Aethiopica*, yet Heliodorus is sufficiently shrewd not to let it die, since this is the sugar-coated pill he needs to lure an audience.

The sun-god Apollo is very much the presiding deity of the romance, and it is tempting to interpret the name of the author symbolically, despite the seemingly authentic pedigree given at the end of the book. In Greek 'helios' is the sun, and 'doron' a gift, so the words combined mean either a 'gift of Apollo', or 'gifted by Apollo'. It is worth noting that in the final paragraph of the *Aethiopica*, Heliodorus says he is 'a Phoenician of Emesa, in Phoenicia, *of the race of the Sun* [my italics] – Heliodorus, the son of Theodosius.'[86]

Apollo, sun-god, is the god of reason and enlightenment, and the *Aethiopica* can be viewed as the triumph of light over darkness, of reason over unreason and passion, and of civilisation over ignorance and barbarism. The triumph of reason over passion is

easily illustrated from the work, in the characters of Theagenes
and Chariclea, whose chastity is the result of reason triumphing
over sexuality. In Book IV, for instance, Theagenes swears by
Apollo and Diana that he will not try to 'obtain any favours' which
Chariclea is not 'disposed to grant', till she is restored to her family
or becomes his wife: Eros has certainly become subservient to
Apollo. Theagenes, it should be noted, is a priest of Apollo, and
Chariclea is, appropriately, a priestess of Diana (twin sister of
Apollo). Indeed, the hero and heroine are much more devoted to
their priestly callings than to each other.

The predominance of Apollo is manifest at every stage of the
story. Chariclea may be a priestess of Diana, but it is Apollo who
presents her with his priest, Theagenes, as a lover, and the 'reason'
with which to preserve her chastity. The pair fall in love at Apollo's
shrine, and it is Apollo's Delphian oracle which proclaims their
adventures and their eventual triumph over misfortune. When
Theagenes and Chariclea are about to be sacrificed by the Ethiopians, fittingly, he to Apollo, she to Diana, we discover that
Hydaspes, King of Ethiopia, is a priest of Apollo, while his Queen,
Persina, is a priestess of Diana.[87] Though he is not concerned with
showing that Apollo is the presiding deity of the *Aethiopica*,
Samuel Lee Wolff offers further evidence of the extent to which
the Apollo cult is celebrated in the story:

> One 'effect', at once pathetic and spectacular, occurs so often in
> the 'Aethiopica' that it seems to deserve special notice. I mean
> what may be called 'hieratic epiphany'. The disguised and
> wandering sun-god in old myths is from time to time made
> manifest, confounding his enemies and rejoicing his worship-
> pers; and finally, his trials done, throws off his disguise for good
> and all, and reveals himself in splendor. So it is with the
> wandering hero, who, returning in beggar's weeds upon Apollo's
> holy day – the day of the New Moon after the winter solstice –
> stands forth from his rags, and smites his enemies with arrows
> inevitable as the arrows of the Far-Darter himself. And so it is
> too with the wandering priest and priestess of the sun, likewise
> disguised as beggars and pilgrims, who yet from time to time
> show themselves for what they are, and strike the beholders
> with admiration, awe, pity and fear. No less than six times does
> Heliodorus make use of this hieratic epiphany. (179,180)

Allied to 'hieratic epiphany' in the *Aethiopica* is what Wolff calls 'hieratic control', and he explains what he means by this term:

It is the gods . . . that have controlled, through Fortune as their instrument, the whole of that triple chain of seeming coincidences which brought Calasiris, Theagenes and Chariclea together at Delphi. An examination of these occurrences will show their hieratic character. Charicles, a priest of Apollo, had received Chariclea from the priestly Sisimithres; Chariclea has become a priestess of Diana; Theagenes has come to Delphi upon a religious mission, and first sees Chariclea at the sacrifice; Calasiris, himself a priest of Isis, has been providentially warned of the dangers of his further stay in Memphis, and has appropriately retired to Delphi, where, now, Apollo and Diana by dreams and oracles expressly place him in charge of the hero and heroine, bid him return with them, and predict for them a happy destiny. Thus Theagenes and Chariclea are passed from one priestly hand to another; even the sudden death of Calasiris which throws them into the power of Arsace, has been foreseen, and ironically foretold by the oracle; till at the end they are saved by the appearance of the priest Charicles, and their restoration turns into a religious festival. The final emphasis is distinctly hieratic . . . this hieratic control, with its assertion of divine guidance, must not be forgotten. It quite decidedly makes for that general elevation of tone and distinguishes Heliodorus. (112,113)

Because of the manifestly religious quality of the *Aethiopica*, it is little wonder that later ages presumed that a Christian bishop of Trikka, in Thessaly, called Heliodorus, was the man who had, in his earlier years, written this romance. The popular rumour that the author of the *Aethiopica* and the bishop were one and the same man, was reported, Perry says, 'by the ecclesiastical historian Socrates, writing as follows in his *Hist. Eccl.* V 22 . . . "The first to institute this custom in Thessaly (the custom of requiring celibacy of the clergy) was Heliodorus who became bishop there, and who is said to have been the author of a love story in several books when he was young and to which he gave the title Aethiopica"'(108). It is certainly not beyond the bounds of possibility that the romancer and the bishop were the same man: after all, celibacy is a major feature of the *Aethiopica*, too, and the ailing of Eros has been noted in conjunction with this celibacy.

Apart from all this, however, there is something peculiarly

Christian about the *Aethiopica*. Take the role assigned to Apollo, for example. He is no Pallas Athene, appearing whenever the 'going gets rough', but is unseen, and makes himself and his designs known through omens, oracles, visions and dreams.[88] The hero and heroine see themselves as 'children of the gods', in whom they trust, and who will take care of them. There is, of course, the usual railing against Fortune in time of trouble, but the overriding impression is that events are in the hands of the gods, who have an ordered design, no matter how disordered it might seem at times. The gods in the other romances are usually regarded as synonymous with (ill) Fortune, capricious and interfering, with little concern for the welfare of the lovers, who become happy almost in spite of them.

As the title of the *Aethiopica* implies, the story of Theagenes and Chariclea will deal with the history of Ethiopia, in epic form. And the epic design which Heliodorus chose as his model is clearly the *Odyssey*. Indeed, the elevation of Apollo over Eros in the *Aethiopica* follows a precedent established by the *Odyssey* rather than the one set by the later examples of romance. To make quite sure that his readers will recognise his model, Heliodorus actually makes Odysseus the 'Poseidon' of his story. Odysseus appears in a dream to the priest Calasiris, and tells him that he, Theagenes, and Charicle, will suffer shipwreck and danger because they sailed past Cephalene without paying due respect to his memory. And he continues:

> But you shall soon suffer for this negligence; and shall experience the same calamities, and encounter the same enemies, both by sea and land, which I have done. But address the maiden you have with you in the name of my consort; she salutes her, as she is a great patroness of chastity, and foretells her at last, a fortunate issue to all her troubles. (v,120)

Chariclea, rather than Theagenes, is the 'Odysseus' of the *Aethiopica*; she is the one with royal blood; only she, literally, returns home, after seventeen years in the wilderness, and only she succeeds to a throne rightfully hers. Apart from these features of the story, Chariclea is by far the more dominant of the two main characters. Theagenes is continually encouraged by Chariclea to bear up under their misfortunes, and it is she who has the guile with which to extricate them from difficult situations. There is one particular scene in the work which serves two purposes – to confirm her superiority over Theagenes, and, at the same time, to bring Odysseus specifically to mind in the scene where he battled with the suitors. The scene in the *Aethiopica* is the one in which opposing pirate factions battle for possession of Chariclea. The battle takes place at night, and Chariclea, from the safety of a ship, 'shot her arrows . . . sparing only Theagenes. She herself did not join either side, but aimed at the first fair mark she saw, herself being all the while concealed, but sufficiently discovering her enemies by the light of their fires and torches: they, ignorant of the hand which smote them, thought it a prodigy, and a stroke from heaven' (v,129). The hieratic epiphanies so prominent in the *Aethiopica*, immediately recall the epiphanies in the *Odyssey*, and in particular the final one, where, on Apollo's holy day, Odysseus discards his beggar's rags and reveals himself to the suitors. Chariclea's final epiphany is also in conjunction with a feast of Apollo, on the day of her return home. The important part played by Apollo in both stories has already been touched upon.

The structure of the *Aethiopica* clearly owes a lot to that of the *Odyssey*. Any defects in the plot of the *Aethiopica* seem the result of an attempt to improve on Homer, or at least be more elaborate than he was. The *Aethiopica* opens in *mediis* as one might expect, but the looping narrative pattern of the *Odyssey* is preserved also by Heliodorus. Reference to the plot diagram of the *Aethiopica* in Appendix II will clarify what is meant. The *Aethiopica* opens with the slaughter of a band of pirates, and after five books and very many pages of retrospective narrative we find ourselves back, once again, with the opening scene. The *Odyssey*, as we saw, opened with Odysseus on the isle of Ogygia, and his narration of his adventures ends with an account of his arrival and stay on Ogygia, in Book XII. It is notable that at exactly the mid-point of both works, we have, as it were, returned to the beginning.

There are, as was noted previously, two main types of retrospective narration in the *Odyssey*, the major one where Odysseus narrates his adventures, and the minor one(s), in which various characters narrate events from the past. These events from the past as told by various narrators did not always, at first glance, seem relevant to the plot, but they, in fact, served to body out the narrative and provide a composite character sketch of the hero, even before we met him. Heliodorus was one of the first, but certainly not the last to presume that these minor retrospective narrations in the *Odyssey* were mere padding, and he set about providing some of his own, 'after the manner of Homer'. With the exception of sections 5 (all), 6 and 8 in the diagram of the narrative structure, all the remaining retrospective narrations seem to have nothing whatever to do with the advancement of the plot, thematically or otherwise. These narrations, which form a significant portion of the text, involve two sets of people, and two stories, the first concerning Cnemon and Thisbe, the second, Calasiris, Thyamis and Petosiris. It seems plausible, also, to suggest that the retardation of the final dénouement in the *Aethiopica* was inspired by that in the *Odyssey*. Homer, however, handled his dénouement with infinitely more skill than does Heliodorus. Odysseus, when he arrived in Ithaca, revealed his identity to some, and was recognised by others, in a progressive exposition. Not until the final few pages, however, did he reveal himself to all. Heliodorus in a very obvious attempt to sustain suspense towards the end of the *Aethiopica*, has Chariclea revealed as the daughter of Hydaspes, king of Ethiopia, at the end of a long and tedious scene in which information is revealed piecemeal. Then follows an even longer and more tedious scene, in which Theagenes is saved from death and acknowledged by Chariclea as her betrothed. In his attempt to prolong suspense after the manner of Homer, Heliodorus effectively destroyed it altogether.

The *Aethiopica* contains all the stock ingredients of Greek romance. Chastity receives due treatment, though there is one exceptional circumstance involving chastity in this romance. Chariclea suggests twice within the space of a few pages that Theagenes make love to Arsace; on the first occasion[89] to prevent their being harshly treated, and on the second, to prevent her (Chariclea) being forced, by Arsace, to marry an unwanted suitor.[90] Such a suggestion is perfectly in keeping with the character of Chariclea, which, as we shall see, is one of the most devious of characters, male, or female, in the Greek romances. Love, and all its paraphernalia is well presented by Heliodorus. All the 'fallings in love' are at first sight, or, as in the case of Oroondates, at first hearing. Every eligible male falls in love with Chariclea, every eligible female with Theagenes.

There are also the requisite number of set-piece soliloquies in the *Aethiopica*. Two of these, like those in *Clitopho and Leucippe*, are soliloquies by the hero on the death of the heroine; but Chariclea is not dead on either occasion. Separation from each other gives

Theagenes and Chariclea several opportunities to pour forth their souls in soliloquies also.

Dreams, visions, oracles and omens are prominent in the *Aethiopica*, also, but do not seem in any way extraneous, or even incredible, when one considers the part played by Apollo in the romance, and also the fact that there are so many priests and priestesses in the story. All of these visions, dreams, oracles and omens become an acceptable method of divine intervention in the affairs of men – as acceptable, one presumes, as the actual presence of the gods was in Homeric times.

Mention must be made of the very many letters which are one of the more remarkable features of the *Aethiopica*. All of these letters play their part in the advancement of the plot. Elizabeth Hazleton Haight[91] cites a few of the more important ones, viz: the letter in the dead Thisbe's hand,[92] which is of prime importance in the sub-plot in announcing the death of Thisbe's mother. There are also the business letters of Mithranes to Oroondates,[93] of Oroondates to Arsace,[94] to the eunuch Euphrates,[95] and those of Hydaspes to the Supreme Council of Ethiopia[96] and to Persina.[97] The letter of Oroondates to Hyaspes[98] in the final book prepares the way for Charicles' final explanation of his relation to his foster-daughter, and his own recognition of Chariclea. Under this heading, too, one could include the fillet exposed with Chariclea, which has inscribed on it a statement by Persina, furnishing the indisputable evidence of Chariclea's parentage. Students of the epistolary method in fiction could well begin their study with the Greek romance.

Another aspect of the *Aethiopica*, and one which reminds us of the novels of Henry Fielding is Heliodorus' dramatic conception of his story. Take, for example, the author's continual reference to the stage, and comparisons between incidents in the *Aethiopica* and ones on stage. 'You started as from a demon on the stage' (ii,35), says Cnemon to Theagenes, and Cnemon later says to Calasiris: 'it is time to bring your piece upon the stage' (ii,49). When Calasiris is reunited with Chariclea, Nausicles wonders 'what this could be which had the air of a recognition on the stage' (v,110). The story itself is talked of in dramatic terms: the sudden appearance of Calasiris at Memphis is spoken of as 'a beginning for another drama' (vi,154), and a little further on we are told that amidst all the successes at Memphis, 'the love scene of the drama triumphed' (vii,156). Earlier, Chariclea has spoken of the 'tragedy of her misfortunes' as having been 'prolonged beyond example' (v,139). It seems quite clear, too, that Heliodorus conceived his romance as a series of theatrical tableaux, the more obvious of which include the beginning of the adventure at Delphi;[99] the first turn of fortune towards evil, in the capture by pirates;[100] the reunion scene at Memphis;[101] and the happy ending.[102] All of these scenes are important points in the narrative, and Heliodorus shows his rhetorical training to the full in his lavish – but relevant – descriptions. None is better handled than the scene at Memphis which is, as Wolff says,[103] a 'notably structural' scene, marking, as it does, the transition from one main set of adventures – those caused by storms, brigands and pirates – to the other main set – those due to intrigue and illicit passion. In his depiction of the scene at Memphis, Heliodorus' method and general outlook are manifestly theatrical: there is an audience, regarded as an audience at a stage presentation, standing on the walls of Memphis, watching the 'drama' being enacted on the plain beneath. And what a drama it is, commencing with a pseudo-duel between two brothers, one of whom runs away and is pursued three times around the walls of Memphis. Then the aged father of the two sons, who has been absent for many years, reappears, but is unrecognised until he discards his beggar's rags and stands forth in priestly splendour. There is also the joyful reunion of Theagenes and Chariclea, after Theagenes has actually struck Chariclea and thrown her from him as some ragged beggarwoman. This is the 'love scene of the drama' which Heliodorus claimed triumphed over all others. And as for the conflict between the two brothers – 'the tragedy which had threatened blood', says Heliodorus, eventually 'passes into a comedy' (vii,155).

It is very significant that the *Aethiopica* should be 'dramatic' in so many ways. We noted earlier, for instance, that when drama went into decline that romance was one form which took its place. The romance also adopted the principal artistic aims and sanctions of drama, the chief of which sanctions was plasmatic licence, which allowed an author to invent as he wished. In Heliodorus the process of 'dramatisation' of prose narrative has been taken one step further. Heliodorus tends to view the whole world as a stage and consciously proffers his work as a theatrical presentation, but in prose narrative form.

There is very little to be said about characterisation in the *Aethiopica*, since Heliodorus, so far as one can gather at any rate, made no attempt to present a significant personality. Calasiris is perhaps the best-drawn of the characters, though very far from being a fully-rounded one, and he dies quite early on in the story. Wolff objects to Heliodorus' presentation of both Calasiris and Chariclea as cheats and liars,[104] and asks us, the readers, at one point,[105] to blame Heliodorus, the author, and not Chariclea for her cheating. Elizabeth H. Haight tries to explain this quality in the two, by quoting Calderini in support of the premise that 'cleverness and deception were valued traits in those times'.[106] Apart from this explanation, however, there is no doubt whatever about the value of this cheating and lying trait for Heliodorus' scheme, and this is really why the characters act as they do, and is the only explanation which should concern us. Take, for instance, Chariclea's first piece of deception. Here,[107] she states that Theagenes and herself are a brother and sister from Ephesus in Ionia, and that they had been on their way to Delos to offer sacrifice when they were involved in sundry perilous adventures, an account of which she gives. She then promises to marry Thyamis as soon as they reach Memphis. Following the normal processes involved in reading fiction, we accept this story at its face value, quite unaware that the whole thing is a total fabrication, invented by Chariclea on the spur of the moment. We have no information whatever, at this point in the story, on which to base a suspicion that the narration of Chariclea might be untrue: neither, at this time, are we aware of the cheating ability of Chariclea. The net result of this narration is that we are led completely astray – and the important fact to remember is that it is exactly this that the author intends. Chariclea's deceptive trait is, therefore, a great 'complicating device' for Heliodorus. Chariclea's final piece of deception works on another level, and shows once again how useful Heliodorus found her deceitfulness. This time we are not only aware of the truth of what has happened, but are aware also of what is going to happen, since all romances 'end happily'. But Heliodorus refuses to pander too quickly to our expectations and uses Chariclea to upset our calculations, continually putting off the dénouement, until we are almost ready to throw the book down in frustration. All Chariclea has to do is say that she and Theagenes are betrothed, and the story will end happily: but she will not. At least Heliodorus has the good grace to show that it is not only the reader who is frustrated, when he has Hydaspes remark:

How do ye O gods, mingle blessings and misfortunes! and mar
the happiness ye have bestowed upon me! Ye restore, beyond
all my hopes a daughter, but ye restore her frenzy-stricken! for
is not her mind frenzied when she utters such inconsistencies?
She first calls this stranger [Theagenes] her brother, who is no
such thing; next, when asked who the stranger is, she says she
knows not; then she is very anxious to preserve him, as a friend,
from suffering; and, failing in this, appears desirous of sacrificing
him with her own hands; and when we tell her that none but
one who is wedded can lawfully perform this office, then she
declares herself a wife but does not name her husband. (x,245,246)

Little does Hydaspes realise that Chariclea's 'frenzy-stricken'
state is her normal one. Heliodorus can only be evaluated correctly
in the light of what his intentions were, and no matter how
we may object to his manner of handling the dénouement, he
undoubtedly achieved his aim. Almost all of the deceptions
practised by Calasiris and Chariclea in the course of the *Aethiopica*
aim at similar effects – the complication or retardation of the action.

Since the *Aethiopica* is an adventure story, its success or failure,
in the final analysis, must be evaluated in terms of plot and
structure. Evaluated in this way the *Aethiopica* is a resounding
success, having one of the most intricately plotted stories of all the
Greek romances. We have already discussed the looping narrative
pattern of the story and the use of sub-plots, in relation to the
Odyssey, but there are several other aspects to be taken into
consideration.

A study of Heliodorus' use of some minor characters is a good
indication of how consciously he plotted his narrative, since he
shows great economy without the use of implausible coincidences.
The three minor characters, Oroondates, viceroy of Egypt, his wife
Arsace, and his viceroy Mithranes, will show Heliodorus' method
perfectly. Arsace is a pivotal character in the plot, having played a
part in the very early stages, unknown to us, and being ultimately
the cause of Chariclea's return home. It is she who causes the exile
of Calasiris from Memphis – thus putting him in the way of
Chariclea – and causes the feud between his sons Thyamis and
Petosiris. This feud results in the exile of Thyamis, who becomes
leader of a pirate band, capturing, in time, Theagenes and Chariclea. Arsace later causes the lovers great problems when she falls

in love with Theagenes, and uses every means at her disposal in order to make him become her lover.

Orrondates, who appears only once, in person, in the story, learns of his wife's infatuation for Theagenes from one of his men, and resolves to put an end to the affair. On hearing Chariclea described by Achaemenes, he falls violently in love with her, and sends a band of his men to Memphis to bring both Theagenes and Chariclea to him. It is when the hero and heroine are on their way to Oroondates that they are taken by a band of Aethiopian soldiers on an expedition against the viceroy. Chariclea's homecoming is thereby assured. The politicking which engages Oroondates and Hydaspes affects most of the other characters in one way or another. It is because of a dispute between the two, for instance, that Chariclea is parted from her guardian Sisimithres in the first instance, and it is the same dispute which actually causes her restoration.

Mithranes, viceroy of Oroondates, tries to earn a little extra money for himself by putting his troops at the disposal of his friend Nausicles, and thus becomes entangled in the plot in many ways. Nausicles is a friend of Calasiris, and, conveniently enough, Calasiris happens to be staying with Nausicles when he has lost contact with Theagenes and Chariclea for a few days. Nausicles is also in love with a girl called Thisbe, who has fallen into the hands of Thyamis. It is in an effort to regain Thisbe that Nausicles uses his troops of Mithranes against Thyamis. It is Theagenes and Chariclea Nausicles captures instead, but he is quite pleased to have Chariclea as a substitute for Thisbe. Mithranes holds on to Theagenes, intending him as a slave for Oroondates, or the Great King. Theagenes is very quickly rescued by Thyamis. The capture of Theagenes by Mithranes later becomes important, because when Arsace discovers this fact, she reduces Theagenes to his proper station, that of a slave to Oroondates, and therefore to herself. She presumes that as a slave Theagenes will be more cooperative. Chariclea, who is also a 'slave', having also been taken by Mithranes, is offered to Achaemenes in marriage. And it is as slaves of his that Oroondates sends for them both, eventually. These three minor characters are, therefore, major links in the chain of the plot, links and characters which have been well thought out in advance by Heliodorus.

The dispute between Oroondates and Hydaspes over the emerald mines of Philoe is an excellent example of Heilodorus' plotting.

This dispute, which seems so insignificant, at first, is, in effect, the 'exciting force' of the story, and also a major element in the dénouement. Sisimithres, guardian of Chariclea, is sent by Hydaspes as an ambassador to the viceroy of Egypt about the emerald mines. Sisimithres, rather undiplomatically, ruffles the viceroy by forbidding him to meddle any further with the emerald mines, which, Sisimithres claimed, belonged exclusively to Ethiopia. The viceroy had Sisimithres thrown summarily out of the city, forcing him to leave Chariclea, whom he had taken with him on the journey, behind. Very many years later, King Hydaspes of Ethiopia, in an attempt to settle the dispute over the emerald mines of Philoe once and for all, sets off on a major expedition against Oroondates. It is on this expedition that Chariclea, who is being taken to Oroondates, is captured by her own father, and returns home. This is a coincidence, certainly, but one which is very probable, having been so well prepared.

Another excellent example of Heliodorus' method occurs in Calasiris' retrospective narration in Books II and V of the *Aethiopica*. The intention of Heliodorus is to give a chronological narration of the previous history of Theagenes and Chariclea, and he uses Calasiris as narrator. Within the retrospective narration of Calasiris, a character called Charicles is introduced, who proceeds in turn to indulge in a retrospective narration: and in the course of this retrospective narration, a character called Sisimithres is introduced who also gives a retrospective narration. Homer did have a story within a story,[108] but Heliodorus certainly takes the idea one step further, giving us a story, within a story, within a story.[109] Heliodorus is not content, either, to allow Calasiris to finish his story at one sitting; instead, he must (as Odysseus did) take two turns. In the meantime, Heliodorus adds a further complication: between the two sections of Calasiris' narrative he, as omniscient author, tells us what has happened to Theagenes and Chariclea since last we saw them, and, of course, between the two sections of the narrative, contemporary events are proceeding and being related by the author. Heliodorus is therefore making very great demands on a reader – demanding that he, (a) grasp the details and implications of Calasiris' narrative, which spans seventeen years, (b) assimilate and integrate with this, the story of Theagenes and Chariclea over the past four or five days – both what we have seen ourselves, and what the author has retrospectively narrated –

and, (c) pay attention to and assimilate current events. Intense cerebral activity at all times is necessary for a full grasp of the plot of the *Aethiopica*. When these difficulties are added to those involved in the assimilation of sub-plots also, in which the same methods are used, then one can better appreciate what is involved in the plotting of this work. The reader is asked to keep, not just one or two, but four or five different time schemes in his head, all at the one time. T. S. Eliot accused John Milton of introducing deliberate complications into his sentences: Heliodorus can fairly be accused of introducing deliberate complications into his plot. And it can be argued that he did this to suit his own purposes. The *Aethiopica* has such an involved plot, that even the attentive reader could not be expected to grasp all the implications on a first reading. This was not a story which could be read and forgotten, but one which could be read two, or even three times, with some new revelation for the reader on each occasion. Remembering that one aim of the work was to celebrate a cult of the sun god, the intricate plot could be regarded as a means of ensuring that the lesson was learned, by forcing a close and detailed attention to the text at all times.

In spite of overelaboration and some carelessness, it can be said that in the *Aethiopica* plot has come of age in prose narrative. This is no haphazard work, but rather one which has been consciously plotted. The irrelevant sub-plots do detract from the unity of the work, and it seems very likely that Heliodorus included them in a misguided attempt to emulate Homer, or to satisfy a fashion. It is almost certain, too, that Heliodorus himself was aware of their irrelevance, to judge from remarks of the characters themselves: 'Enough of buccaneers, and viceroys and kings', shouts Cnemon at Calasiris during his narrative, 'your discourse is wandering from the point. . . . This episode has nothing to do with the main plot.' (ii,50) A little later in his tale, as if to get revenge on Cnemon for his outburst, Calasiris passes over the details of a religious ceremony. When Cnemon objects, Calasiris retorts that these details 'have nothing to do with the principal end of my narration' (iii,62).

The best place to end this study of the *Aethiopica*, is, perhaps, at the beginning, i.e. with the opening scene: how many adventure stories, or works with pretensions to be more than adventure stories, can match this opening?

The day had begun to smile cheerily, and the sun was already gilding the tops of the hills, when a band of men, in arms and appearance pirates, having ascended the summit of a mountain which stretches down towards the Heracleotic mouth of the Nile, paused and contemplated the sea which was expanded before them. When not a sail appeared on the water to give them hopes of a booty, they cast their eyes upon the neighbouring shore; where the scene was as follows: a ship was riding at anchor, abandoned by her crew; but to all appearances laden with merchandize, as she drew much water. The beach was strewn with bodies newly slaughtered; some quite dead, others dying, yet still breathing, gave signs of a combat recently ended. Yet it appeared not to have been a designed engagement; but there were mingled with these dreadful spectacles the fragments of an unlucky feast, which seemed to have concluded in this fatal manner. There were tables, some yet spread with eatables; others overturned upon those who had hoped to hide themselves under them; others grasped by hands which had snatched them up as weapons. Cups lay in disorder, half fallen out of the hands of those who had been drinking from them, or which had been flung instead of missiles; for the suddenness of the affray had converted goblets into weapons.

Here lay one wounded with an axe, another bruised by a shell picked up on the beach, a third had his limbs broken with a billet, a fourth was burnt with a torch, but the greater part were transfixed with arrows; in short, the strangest contrast was exhibited within the shortest compass; wine mingled by fate with blood, war with feasting, drinking and fighting, libations and slaughters. Such was the scene that presented itself to the eyes of the pirates.

They gazed some time, puzzled and astonished. The vanquished lay dead before them, but they nowhere saw the conquerors; the victory was plain enough, but the spoils were not taken away; the ship rode quietly at anchor, though with no one on board, yet unpillaged, as much as if it had been defended by a numerous crew, and as if all had been peace.

Daphnis and Chloe

In both style and technique, *Daphnis and Chloe* is the best of the Greek romances. This one differs from the other Greek

omances more than in the quality of the workmanship, however.
t is the only Greek romance – so far as can be ascertained – which
s placed entirely in a pastoral setting. It differs, too, from the other
omances, in being an extended *ecphrasis*, as Longus himself tells
us, in so many words, in the prologue to the story:

> When I was hunting in Lesbos, I saw, in a wood sacred to the
> Nymphs, the most beautiful thing that I have ever seen – a
> painting that told a love story. The wood itself was beautiful
> enough, full of trees and flowers, and watered by a single spring
> which nourished both the flowers and the trees; but the picture
> was even more delightful, combining excellent technique with a
> romantic subject. . . . In it there were women having babies,
> other women wrapping them in swaddling clothes, babies being
> exposed, sheep and goats suckling them, young people plighting
> their troth, pirates making a raid, enemies starting an invasion.
>
> After gazing admirably at many other scenes, all of a romantic
> nature, I was seized by a longing to write *a verbal equivalent to
> the painting* [my italics]. So I found someone to explain the picture
> to me, and composed a work in four volumes as an offering to
> Love and the Nymphs and Pan.[110]

It seems very likely that Longus conceived *Daphnis and Chloe*
purely as an artistic creation of his own, presented for its own
sake, and that the prologue is simply a formal claim to literary
respectability. There is no further reference, implicit or explicit, in
the course of the romance, to the *ecphrasis*.

To claim that *Daphnis and Chloe* was influenced to any extent by
the pastoral poetry of Theocritus, is to detract from the achievement
of Longus. There is little doubt that the idea for placing *Daphnis
and Chloe* in a pastoral setting was suggested by pastoral poetry,
but in every other respect Longus must be regarded as an innovator.
Individual works of art do not simply grow out of one another,
and, anyway, there is fundamental difference between, say, the
Idylls of Theocritus and *Daphnis and Chloe*.

It may seem strange to suggest that *Daphnis and Chloe*, which
seems to differ in almost every respect from the conventional Greek
romance, follows the same basic pattern. The inability of the hero
and the heroine to consummate their love could be regarded almost
as the *sine qua non* of Greek romance. This inability arose through
lack of opportunity in many cases, because the hero and heroine

were separated by storms, shipwrecks or whatever: in other case
the lovers – or at least one of them – had taken a vow of chastity
which was not to be broken until marriage; in such a cas‹
the author ensured that marriage proved a difficult proposition
Longus' genius is evident in his ability to adhere to, yet transform
this aspect of Greek romance. Daphnis and Chloe are unable t‹
consummate their love, and this inability *is* due to separation, bu
this separation is both a literal and a figurative one. The hero an‹
heroine have every opportunity of consummating their love, an‹
grasp every opportunity in an attempt to do so, but fail, however
because of their utter ignorance of basic human physiology. It doe
mean that they join the protagonists of the other romances in thei
frustration. Daphnis eventually gets a lesson in sexual intercours‹
from a lady called Lycaenion in the third Book, but is too frightene‹
to try out his new-found knowledge on Chloe, because Lycaenio›
has warned him that if he does, Chloe will 'scream and burst int‹
tears, and lie there streaming with blood as though you murdere‹
her' (iii,81). Daphnis does not wish Chloe to scream at him 'as i
he were an enemy', and is 'particularly frightened of the bloo‹
and he assumed that bleeding must mean a wound' (iii,82). An‹
so the 'separation' continues.

Prior to this, there was what is best described as a 'psychologica
separation' between Daphnis and Chloe. Each fell in love with th‹
other, but neither was aware that it *was* love, nor could they explai›
why they felt so peculiar. Their relationship was actually unknow›
to either, a very strange state of affairs, and the antithesis of th‹
situation in the typical romance. It is only when Phileta‹
comes along and informs Daphnis and Chloe that their feeling‹
are normal, and the result of love, that the lovers becom‹
aware of what is happening. Philetas also tells the couple wha
the 'remedies' for love are, but – unfortunately for the lovers – h‹
is no more explicit than to suggest that they indulge in 'kissin‹
and embracing and lying down together with naked bodies' (ii,48)
which, the pair discover, is no remedy.

Although the lovers are separated when each is abducted, h
by Tyrian Pirates, she by the Methymnaeans, the separation o›
each occasion is of no more than a few hours' duration. A mor‹
lengthy separation is caused – fittingly enough in a pastora
romance – by Winter. Longus remarks that Winter was worse fo
Daphnis and Chloe than the war with the Methymnaeans ha‹
been, because they cannot see one another (ii,70). The final instanc

of separation takes yet another form. When Daphnis is discovered to be of noble birth it is immediately presumed that marriage to a mere shepherdess is a remote possibility: all ends well, however, when Chloe is proved Daphnis' equal. They marry almost immediately and that night 'Daphnis did some of the things that Lycaenion had taught him' (iv,121).

It would be wrong to view *Daphnis and Chloe* simply as a love-story, however sophisticated, since it operates on quite another level also, which involves Longus' philosophy of nature. Nature does not merely provide a decorative setting for the story but is ingeniously interwoven into the framework. Daphnis and Chloe are children of nature not just in the figurative sense, since she has been saved from death and weaned by a ewe, he by a she-goat: we are informed, in addition, that after being found, Daphnis is entrusted to the she-goat to be nursed. It is interesting to note also that Lamon, when he comes on Daphnis first, is tempted to ignore the baby and go off with tokens of his identity: but he does not do so, because he 'felt ashamed to show less humanity than a goat' (i,20). Likewise, Dryas, when he finds Chloe, is 'taught by the ewe's example to pity the child and love it' (i,21). Daphnis and Chloe almost become creatures of nature themselves in every respect, even going so far as to 'imitate the sights and sounds' of nature:

> Hearing the birds singing they burst into song, seeing the lambs gambolling they danced nimbly about, and taking their cue from the bees they started gathering flowers, some of which they dropped into their bosoms, and the rest they wove into garlands . . . (i,23)

Mentally and physically, Daphnis and Chloe are at one with nature. Their love evolves over two season cycles, commencing in the Spring of one year, consummated in the Autumn of the following one. And the evolution reflects the developments in the seasons quite beautifully. They first meet in the Spring when their love is in its springtime, and, come Summer, it has ripened considerably. 'What inflamed them more', says Longus, speaking of their love, 'was the time of year. It was now the end of spring, and the beginning of summer' (i,34). Their love reaches its first maturity with Autumn, when Philetas tells them of their love, and the remedies to be applied. Winter, fittingly, puts their love into hibernation, almost, and they 'look forward to the Spring as to a resurrection from death' (iii,71). With Spring 'their hearts melted away at what they saw, and they too felt the need for something more than kisses and embraces' (iii,77). In Summer Daphnis asks Chloe to be his wife; marrying her, eventually, in Autumn.

The love of Daphnis and Chloe for nature is not simply a one-sided affair. Nature not only saves them from death in infancy, but continues to watch over and guide them through their lives. Pan and the Nymphs represent nature, in this function, to a very great extent. When Chloe is abducted by the Methymnaeans, Pan sends them a terrifying dream and forces them to set Chloe free: when Daphnis is captured by the Tyrian pirates, he is freed when the cattle on the ship answer the call of the pan-pipe and jump overboard, capsizing the vessel: Daphnis gets ashore by seizing the horns of two cows. At two moments of crisis in the story,[11] the Nymphs come to Daphnis to reassure him – indeed, on the second occasion to do even more than simply reassure him, since they supply him with three thousand drachmas as a dowry for Chloe, thus preventing her marriage to any other. Although Daphnis and Chloe are the best and most obvious exemplars, the whole work is a manifestation of the special relationship between those who love nature, and those whom nature, in turn, loves. Daphnis means a laurel, Chloe, a green shoot, and the names of the other characters too, are taken from natural objects: Dryas, an oak tree; Dorcon, a gazelle; Myrtale, the myrtle. Their lives are regulated by the seasons of the year as is the love of Daphnis and Chloe. Nature reciprocates human sympathy with nature by showing her sympathy when it is needed: the cows moo pitifully and run wildly about, on the death of their master Dorcon, which even the shepherds themselves presume to be 'the cows' way of mourning for their departed herdsman' (1,41); and, later, when Lampis destroys the garden of Lamon, the bees buzz continuously over the battered and broken flowers 'as if they were mourning for them' (iv,100).

Longus is not simply content to put the case for the country – he is also concerned to state the case *against* the city. The most obvious example of this is the visit of the Methymnaean youths to the country. They are rich young men with lots of servants, and belong to the leading families in the town of Methymna. When the youths arrive in the countryside of Mytilene they go hunting in fields not designed for hunting, and cause a great upheaval in the natural order of things. Daphnis describes the hounds as behaving 'like a pack of wolves' (ii,54), and they are out of the control of their masters. The Methymnaeans are punished by the loss of their yacht and all their belongings: fittingly, it is the goats they have chased to the sea-shore that send the yacht to its destruction. When the youths arrive home they demand vengeance from their fellow townsmen, without stating what actually happened in Mytilene. The Methymnaeans launch ten ships and commence to ravage the Mytilenean seaboard, carrying off a great many sheep, as well as corn and wine. They eventually raid the fields of Daphnis and Chloe, seizing everything they can lay their hands on. Chloe sees them coming and rushes for sanctuary to the Nymphs, and begs her pursuers to spare both her animals and herself:

> But it was no use, for the Methymnaeans jeered contemptuously at the images of the Nymphs and not only carried off the animals but actually drove her along with them, treating her exactly like the sheep and goats and lashing her with switches of willow. (ii,56)

Quite soon after having boarded ship the Methymnaeans are, aptly, thrown into panic by dreadful sights and sounds. They realise they are being punished by Pan, but cannot understand why, since 'no temple of Pan's had been looted' (ii,60). But it is soon made quite clear that the countryside is Pan's temple. In a dream, Pan appears to Bryais, the Methymnaean general, and says to him:

> 'You impious and ungodly wretches, how dare you behave in such a lunatic fashion? You've filled the countryside that I love with fighting, you've stolen herds of oxen and goats that are under my care, you've dragged away from the altar a girl whom Love has chosen to make a story about, and you've shown no reverence either for the Nymphs who witnessed the crime, or for me.' (ii,61)

Pan threatens the Methymnaeans with death by drowning if they fail to release Chloe and all the animals. They comply with his request quite readily. The attack on Mytilene by Tyrian pirates is a variation on the same theme. They too carry off everything they can lay their hands on; they, too, view Daphnis as plunder, only 'worth more than plunder from the fields' (i,38). This is civilised perversity, and it reaches a climax when they kill Dorcon. Dorcon's cattle, obeying the call of the pan-pipe, jump overboard and capsize the boat, causing all the pirates to drown: only Daphnis and the cows are saved.

While quite some space has been devoted to an analysis of the part played by Pan and the Nymphs in *Daphnis and Chloe*, it is, in fact, Eros who is the presiding deity of the romance. This is as it should be, since the education of Daphnis and Chloe in love is the main subject of the story. Dryas and Lamon, foster parents of Chloe and Daphnis, have identical dreams[112] one night, when Daphnis is fifteen, Chloe thirteen years old. In the dream, they see the Nymphs handing Daphnis and Chloe over to Eros, who strikes each with an arrow and orders that Daphnis should in future be a goatherd, Chloe a shepherdess. Here, and henceforth in the story, Eros occupies the position usually occupied by Fortune in the Greek romance, i.e. Eros dominates the story. 'Love made something serious flare up' (i,24), we are told, soon after Daphnis and Chloe have gone into the fields for the first time. The 'something serious' referred to, is Daphnis' falling into a deep pit, dug to trap a she-wolf. It is when Daphnis, with the aid of Chloe, washes the mud from his body that she 'falls in love' with him, on seeing him naked for the first time. Philetas is the one who informs Daphnis and Chloe that they 'are dedicated to Love, and Love is looking after you' (ii,47). He knows this, he says, because Eros has told him. Later, when Daphnis bursts into tears at having been rejected, he feels, by Chloe's foster-mother, as a suitable husband for her foster-daughter, he asks the Nymphs for help. They reply that Chloe's marriage 'is the business of another god' (iii,88), and imply that such a matter is outside their jurisdiction. This does not prevent them from pleading, later, with Eros, to give his consent to the marriage of Daphnis and Chloe. Eros agrees, and gives Dionysophanes (father of Daphnis) instructions on what to do to discover Chloe's parents. When Chloe is discovered to be the daughter of a leading citizen, Megacles, her marriage to Daphnis is assured. All of these incidents are ones in which Eros himself appears, but even when he is absent, the passion of Love which he initiated between Daphnis and Chloe on his very first appearance, continues to occupy the centre of the stage.

An important distinction must be drawn between Eros, in

Daphnis and Chloe, and Fortune in the typical Greek romance. As Samuel Lee Wolff notes, in *Daphnis and Chloe*, 'causation resumes its sway in a measure quite unknown to Heliodorus or Achilles Tatius'.[113] This statement is certainly accurate, but it would be quite wrong to presume, therefore, that the plot of *Daphnis and Chloe* advances under the law of cause and effect, since this is not really so. Eros initiates almost all the action in *Daphnis and Chloe*, but Longus ensures that all such incidents are prepared for, and worked out in purely human terms. The examples Wolff gives are adequate to show how Longus operates. In one incident a she-wolf has been carrying off lambs, so shepherds dig a deep pit which they conceal with brushwood: meanwhile, two of Daphnis' goats fight, the victor pursues the vanquished, and Daphnis runs after both, falling into the pit where he becomes badly soiled: on being rescued he must wash. On another occasion, when the Methymnaeans go hunting, a farmer steals their mooring rope because the rope which held his grape-crushing stone has broken. When the Methymnaeans discover that their rope has gone they twist a long green withy into a sort of rope, and with this they secure their yacht to the land. Later, when they go hunting, their hounds drive Daphnis' goats to the seashore, where, finding no other food, they eat the green withy. The yacht floats away; the Methymnaeans beat Daphnis, and are themselves beaten, in turn, so they incite their countrymen to make war on Mytilene. In modern fiction such incidents would be attributed to coincidence: in *Daphnis and Chloe* it is to Eros that they are attributed. It must be strongly emphasised that Fortune and coincidence are not synonymous in the other Greek romances, where the authors never bother to augment the operations of the supernatural with plausible preparations on the human level: Fortune simply intervenes without warning to effect whatever changes the author deems necessary to the plot.

The inclusion of Philetas, the cowherd, in the story of *Daphnis and Chloe* was one of Longus' more ingenious moves. By the time Philetas has finished telling the story of his life, the full implication of his tale dawns on us. Philetas tells of his love for Amaryllis, whom Eros gave to him: he talks also of his days as a cowherd: 'Many's the song I've sung to these Nymphs here', he says, 'and many's the tune I've piped to Pan over there, and many's the herd of cows I've led by music alone' (ii,45). Philetas has come to talk to Daphnis and Chloe, because that morning he had met Eros himself, who explained that he has looked after Philetas and Amaryllis, in the past, but 'now it's Daphnis and Chloe that I'm looking after' (ii,47). Much later, Philetas presents Daphnis with his pan-pipe, which he can play 'better than anyone except Pan (ii,64), and he begs Daphnis to leave the pan-pipe to 'an equally worthy successor' (ii,67). The abiding impression the reader receives – and it seems more than likely that it was just such an impression Longus sought to create – is one of an unending succession of ideal loves and lovers, all of them under the care and guidance of Eros, ably aided by Pan and the Nymphs. The subject of this romance is simply that of one such pair of lovers, but Philetas and Amaryllis were the previous 'Daphnis and Chloe', and Daphnis has undertaken to pass on the pan-pipe to a 'worthy successor', who, we presume, will be the 'Daphnis' of the next ideal relationship between a boy and girl. *Daphnis and Chloe* thus becomes, not just an isolated story of a single, ideal love, but a representation of ideal, pastoral love in all ages, and in all places.

Longus, like his fellow sophist-romancers, cannot resist parading his sophistical wares, but in this regard he is the least culpable of all the sophists. He gives us individual accounts of how both Daphnis and Chloe felt, when they fall in love. This analysis of 'symptoms', with its neat rhetorical antithesis is the hallmark of the sophist, and *Daphnis and Chloe* bears such a hallmark. It is important, however, to note that, in Longus, verbiage does not smother or strangle the feelings which the author intends to convey to the reader; nor, once he has commenced, does Longus forget when to stop, in his enthusiasm for his own rhetorical acrobatics. This is how Chloe talks of her love:

> 'There's something wrong with me these days, but I don't know what it is. I'm in pain, and yet I've not been injured. I feel sad, and yet none of my sheep have got lost. I'm burning hot, and yet here I am sitting in the shade. How often I've been scratched by brambles and not cried! How often I've been stung by bees and not screamed! But this thing that's pricking my heart hurts more than anything like that. Daphnis *is* beautiful, but so are the flowers. His pipe does sound beautiful, but so do the nightingales – and I don't worry about them. If only I *were* his pipe, so that he'd breathe into me! If only I were a goat, so that I could have him looking after me! You wicked water, you made Daphnis beautiful, but when I tried washing it made no

difference. Oh Nymphs, I'm dying – and even you do nothing to save the girl who was nursed in your cave. Who will put garlands on you when I'm gone? Who will rear the poor lambs? Who will look after my chattering locust? I had a lot of trouble catching her, so that she could talk me to sleep in front of the cave – and now I can't sleep because of Daphnis, and she chatters away for nothing.' (i,27/28)

Descriptions of gardens or natural scenery were very attractive for the sophist – indeed Achilles Tatius spends over two long pages on one such description. Longus describes several similar scenes, among them the gardens of Philetas and Lampis. But there the comparison ends, since the *ecphraseis* of Longus are relevant in a pastoral romance, and he keeps himself in check in this instance, also. Another good example of Longus' restraint is in his pastoral court scene. The court scene is a recurring feature in Greek romance, and, in particular, the sophistic, since it gives the sophist numerous opportunities to display his skills: Achilles Tatius is a case in point here, also, since one of his court scenes takes over ten pages to describe. In *Daphnis and Chloe*, however, things are different: Philetas is the judge, and the Methymnaeans, who are the plaintiffs, decide to use 'clear and concise language in view of the fact that they had a cowherd for a judge' (ii,53). Their case is put in seven sentences, and Daphnis answers them in ten, which is a far cry from the typical, sophistic court scene. Even the interpolated stories, so typical of the Greek romances, are untypical in Longus. They are short, and relevant also, inasmuch as they all deal with either the Nymphs or Pan, tutelary deities of the story.

The humour in *Daphnis and Chloe* is an aspect of the work which deserves at least a mention, and it is a humour that is quite subtle. One does get the impression that Longus is being continually ironic at the expense of his characters, but if asked to show how, one would find it a difficult task. What the author's attitude will be, is indicated in the prologue, when he prays that he will be able to write his story while retaining his sanity. The most obviously humorous incident in the story is when a dog runs off with meat from Dryas' house. 'Dryas was annoyed', we are told, 'for it was his own helping; so he grabbed a stick and did what another dog would have done – dashed off in pursuit' (iii,73). Immediately after this incident, Daphnis is invited to stay the night with Dryas and his family – which includes Chloe. Chloe hoped she might be able to sleep with Daphnis but he goes off to bed with Dryas:

> But Daphnis derived some imaginary pleasure from the arrange-
> ment, for he thought it very pleasant even to go to bed with
> Chloe's father – with the result that he kept embracing Dryas and
> kissing him, dreaming that he was doing it all to Chloe. (iii,75)

The remainder of the humour in the story is confined to one-
line comments: Chloe in love is like a cow 'stung by gadflies' (i,27):
when unable to have sexual intercourse with Chloe, Daphnis
complains that 'any sheep knew more about love than he did'
(iii,78): Dorcon decides to rape Chloe, and to do so dresses up as
a wolf: and when he had 'done his very best to make a beast of
himself' (i,32), he lies in wait for Chloe.

The most intriguing aspect of *Daphnis and Chloe* is that it contains
every one of the features, in one form or another, which we
associate with Greek romance, and yet the work is unique. It is,
as has already been stated, the best of all the Greek romances,
from whatever point of view one may wish to view it. This does
not, however, acquit it of one major defect – that of being, perhaps,
too artificial and idealised.

THE LATIN ROMANCES

The so-called Latin romances consist of only two works, the
Satyricon of Petronius, and *The Golden Ass* of Apuleius. These are
comic romances, which immediately places them in a category
quite distinct from the typical Greek romance, which is ideal or
serious in intent. There is very little that can be said about the
origins and development of the comic romance, since each work
is *sui generis*. Perry sums up the situation perfectly when he states:
'The origins and *raison d'être* of comic romances, whether ancient
or modern, have to be explained far less with reference to literary
traditions and precedents than to the special purposes of their
individual authors. The first mentioned of these two factors is
trivial and insignificant, but the latter is decisive.'[114] Perry is very
perceptive also in his analysis of the type of person who writes a
comic romance – an analysis which seems quite accurate when
applied to either ancient or modern authors of comic romance:

The spirit that prevades a comic or satirical novel, such as the *Satyricon* of Petronius, the *True History* of Lucian, or the *Metamorphoses* of Apuleius, presupposes an author with a sophisticated and critical outlook on the world; and the authors of this kind of book who are known to us are all highly educated men with reputations for achievement in other fields than prose fiction. The intellectual world to which they belong, and whose formal and aesthetic standards they acknowledge is that of literature and learning on the high level of classical and academic tradition, which dominated the literary scene both after and before the birth of the ideal sentimental novel, and was unaffected by the latter.[115]

It is notable that there is no ideal Latin romance extant, nor is there any indication that one was ever written. The reason for this seemingly anomalous state of affairs is not difficult to discover, however; Greek, not Latin, was the common language of the Roman Empire, and there would, therefore, have been no mass readership for a Latin romance. Since there was no great demand for Latin romance, no new breed of writers in Latin, independent of tradition and patronage, was brought into being, and the old order held sway. In such a situation, the only type of fiction permissible was the comic. Comedy tended by its nature to be beyond criticism, and even acceptable within the dominant classical tradition. If either Petronius or Apuleius had written a romance along the lines of, say, *Chaereas and Callirhoe*, he would have created an upheaval in the literary world. In fact, Apuleius does not include *The Golden Ass* in a list of his works, and Tacitus, in his pen-picture of Petronius, makes no reference to the *Satyricon*.

The *Satyricon*

The *Satyricon* is without doubt the most significant work of prose fiction written in ancient times. The extent of its significance is indicated by the fact that it took western civilisation well over fifteen hundred years to produce a work on a par with it. Ironically, the *Satyricon* is, relative to its importance, the most neglected of works of fiction: the inordinately long intermission of fifteen hundred years between itself and *Don Quixote* may be one reason for this neglect. The *Satyricon* has, of course, been studied in great detail by classical scholars from a 'classical' point of view. It affords the scholar innumerable examples of vulgar Latin, providing plenty of food for speculation, and it is also a study in Menippean satire. It seems particularly strange to find Ben Edwin Perry describing the *Satyricon* as a mere 'container', into which Petronius could pour 'all the wealth of literary, philosophical, and artistic expression that was welling up within his fertile genius and demanding an outlet'.[116] If Perry's analysis is correct, then the status of the *Satyricon* as a work of fiction is significantly reduced. It is hoped that Perry's suggestion will be shown to be inaccurate; in the meantime, it is sufficient to point out that the *Satyricon*, for the classicist, is simply a mine of literary, philosophical, and philological lore.

The major difficulty confronting any student of the *Satyricon* is that a large portion of the text is missing, having never been rediscovered. There is general agreement that the extant portion of the *Satyricon* covers part of Book XIV, and all of books XV and XVI, with minor omissions. Perry estimates that since books XV and XVI total ninety-six pages in one text, the original work could have been up to eight hundred pages long – a staggering thought. There may, of course, have been a book, or books, following the sixteenth, even.

The title of Petronius' work deserves an explanation, if only because of the numerous misleading ones which have been offered, and, indeed, accepted as accurate. '*Satyricon*, with which one understands the noun *libri* or books', says Perry, 'is the Greek genitive plural of σατυρικός which is used by Plutarch and by Pliny the elder, contemporary authors, in the sense of "satyr-like" or "lascivious"'.[117] P. G. Walsh adds[118] the illuminating information that the word σατυρικός also bears the additional sense of 'derisive'. An accurate subtitle for the *Satyricon*, then, would be 'A Derisive Account of Lascivious Behaviour'. Much of the confusion over the title has arisen because of the similarity between the Greek word σατυρικός, and the Latin *satirae*, meaning 'satires'. The adjective *satiricus* is not found, in any case, before the fourth century AD, and there is no connection whatever, etymologically, or in any other way, between the two words.

The pen-picture given by Tacitus of Petronius – generally agreed to be the same Petronius as wrote the *Satyricon* – is worth quoting. If, having read the *Satyricon* carefully, one were asked to draw a pen-picture of the author, the end product, one feels, would not be essentially different from the one drawn by Tacitus:

Petronius deserves a word in retrospect. He was a man who passed his days in sleep, his nights in the ordinary duties and recreations of life; others had achieved greatness by the sweat of their brows – Petronius idled into fame. Unlike most who squander their substance, he was never regarded as either debauchee or profligate, but rather as one highly skilled in the art of luxurious living. In both word and action he displayed a freedom and a sort of self-abandonment which were welcomed as the marks of a forthright and unsophisticated nature. Yet, in his proconsulship of Bithynia, and later as consul elect, he showed himself an able and capable administrator. Then came the relapse; his genuine or affected vices won him admittance into the narrow circle of Nero's intimates, and he became the Arbiter of Elegance, whose sanction alone divested pleasure of vulgarity and luxury of grossness.

His success aroused the jealousy of Tigellinus against a possible rival – a professor of voluptuousness better equipped than himself. Preying on the emperor's lust for cruelty, to which all other lusts were secondary, he bribed a slave to turn informer, charged Petronius with his friendship for Scaevinus, deprived him of the opportunity of defense, and threw most of his household into prison.

At this time, it happened, the court had migrated to Campania; and Petronius had reached Cumae when his detention was ordered. He disdained to await the lingering issue of hopes and fears; still, he would not take a brusque farewell of life. An incision was made in his veins; they were bound up under his directions, and opened again, while he conversed with his friends – not on themes of grave import nor in the key of the dying hero. He listened to no discourses on the immortality of the soul or the dogmas of philosophy, but to frivolous songs and playful verses. Some of his slaves tasted of his bounty, others of the whip. He sat down to dinner, and then drowsed a little; so that death, if compulsory, should at least be natural. Even in his will, he broke through the routine of suicide, and flattered neither Nero nor Tigellinus nor any other of the mighty; instead he described the emperor's enormities; added a list of his catamites, his women, and his innovations in lasciviousness; then sealed the document, sent it to Nero, and broke his signet ring to prevent it from being used to endanger others.[119]

Perry, as we have seen, thought that Petronius was urged to write because of the 'welling up' of his fertile genius, and that the *Satyricon* is the container. He suggests, further, that Petronius chose comedy as 'a shield against the suspicion that he was engaged in anything other than tomfoolery'.[120] These statements cannot be substantiated from the *Satyricon*. From what we know of the author, and from the work itself, none of the poetry, or the discussions on literature, are intended, as original contributions, to be taken seriously. Nor is it likely that Petronius needed a shield: we are only too well aware of the antagonism of Nero towards contemporary authors, and the results of such antagonism: but it must be stated that this hostility was directed mostly against authors of political and literary eminence. It is doubtful that Petronius would have had anything to fear from Nero, or that any such apprehensions dictated the form his work was to take. One must take some account, too, of the fact that the *Satyricon* seems exactly the type of work Petronius would write, from what we know of him. Indeed, Perry tends to contradict his own thesis, anyway: he gives his own pen-picture[121] of the type of person who writes a comic romance, and produces an identikit of Petronius, Apuleius, Lucian, or, indeed, Fielding: yet there is no suggestion, in any case other than Petronius' that they were forced into writing comic romances as a 'shield against the suspicion' that they were 'engaged in anything other than tomfoolery'.

It is possible, with evidence based on references within the text to antecedent events, references in the fragments extant, as well as references in contemporary and later authors familiar with the *Satyricon*, to gain some information about the missing section of the work. It seems quite likely that the tale opened in Marseilles,[122] in the south of France, with Encolpius, the hero, in love for the first time with a girl called Doris. Not unlike many of the heroes of romance, Encolpius leaves his native home and begins his wanderings because of a dream or oracle which states:

> Hero, leave your home for newer worlds
> For you now dawns a mightier day;
> Be strong, and the Danube, that last boundary,
> The icy North and the peaceful Egyptian realms,
> The nations of the rising and setting suns,
> Will all greet you by name: Ithacan descend
> A greater Ithacan, upon those foreign sands. (176)

From the text, we gather that one of his first encounters has been with Lichas and his wife Hedyle, with whom he becomes very friendly. Encolpius seduces Hedyle, and Lichas and he fight as a result. (114) Another encounter is with Tryphaena, and it seems likely that Giton was her slave, before he was taken away by Encolpius. (113) The fragments contain a reference to a court case, (168) which may or may not be connected with Tryphaena's complaint about having her reputation as a decent woman publicly blackened. (114) Having been prosecuted for some crime or other – possibly associated with Giton and Tryphaena – Encolpius may have given an account of Tryphaena's sexual proclivities, and fled. By the time we meet them, Encolpius and Giton have reached the Bay of Naples and have yet another character in tow – Ascyltus. The major episode preceding the extant section of the *Satyricon*, involves a priestess of Priapus called Quartilla, whom our characters observe performing rites in honour of that God. A major section of the extant work takes place in a city on the bay of Naples, moving eventually to the town of Croton.

Any analysis of the *Satyricon*, as fiction, must begin by acknowledging that the work is a parody of ancient romance, and intended as such by its author. This parody takes two forms, a parody of the *Odyssey* in particular, and a general parody of the body of Greek romance written after the *Odyssey*. The parody of Homer's epic is quite obvious in the *Satyricon*, because of the numerous references to Odysseus or his adventures: on each occasion Petronius' intention of parodying the original is clear. The dream or oracle which, we presume, urged Encolpius to leave his home and go on a journey, refers to him as a second Odysseus, promising him similar, if not greater glory than Homer's hero: 'Ithacan, descend a greater Ithacan, upon those foreign sands' (176). Encolpius' subsequent adventures are a travesty of those of Odysseus. Poseidon, the vindictive and implacable revenger of the *Odyssey* is replaced, in the *Satyricon*, by Priapus. Although the similarity between the part played by these gods in their respective stories is quite clear, Petronius dispels any doubts we might have, when he has Encolpius soliloquise as follows:

Others have been hounded by gods and implacable fate
Not I alone.
Hercules hounded from Argos,
And propping heaven on his shoulders.

Impious Laomedon
And those two angry immortals:
He paid the price of his offences.
Pelias felt the weight of Juno.
Then there was Telephus –
He took up arms in his ignorance
Even Ulysses went in fear of Neptune's power
Now I too take my stand among these –
Over land and white Nereus' sea, I am hounded
By the mighty rage of Priapus of Hellespont. (160)

The choice of Priapus as a Poseidon-equivalent for the *Satyricon* was a masterstroke on the part of Petronius. As well as being a powerful and sinister god, Priapus was also a somewhat absurd deity,[123] so that his obscene comicality dovetailed perfectly with Petronius' design for the story. Like Poseidon, Priapus, too, was connected with the sea, being the patron of sailors and fishermen: even more pertinent is his patronage of all those who were undertaking a journey.[124] The *Satyricon* presents this absurd god in a complete inversion of his normal role. His role as patron of sailors is shown, however, when he appears to Lichas in a dream, and warns him that his enemy Encolpius is on board his ship. Priapus looms grotesquely over the *Satyricon*, and has a part in every major incident in the work. It is he who delivers the heroes over to Quartilla, delivers them to Lichas, and renders Encolpius impotent with Circe. From the extant section of the *Satyricon*, we know that Encolpius has offended Priapus twice: on the first occasion he profanes the shrine of Priapus by spying on Quartilla as she performed the sacred rites of the god; on the second occasion he kills Priapus' darling goose. One can only presume that these are but two of the many blundering offences against the god. The major, and continuing offence against Priapus, because of his generative function, is, quite probably, the homosexual relationship between the hero and Giton. Because of this relationship, Encolpius rejects all heterosexual activities, and when the lovely Circe does arouse his passion for the opposite sex once more, Priapus makes him impotent, in revenge.

The Circe episode in the *Satyricon* is relevant not only for the implication of Priapus. Petronius intends us to recall the Circe episode in the *Odyssey*, a suggestion borne out not only by the name of the female involved with Encolpius, but also by the pseudonym adopted by the hero – that of Polyaenus, a Homeric epithet for Odysseus. Odysseus succeeds, sexually, with Circe, Encolpius fails with his. Odysseus' men are turned into animals, Encolpius too is 'unmanned', but farcically so. It is subsequent to his failure with Circe that Encolpius attempts lopping off his genitals, a farcical attempt, made even more so by being described in the exalted language normally attendant on major events in epic poetry:

> Three times I took the mur'drous axe in hand,
> Three times I wavered like a wilting stalk
> And curtsied from the blade, poor instrument
> In trembling hands – I could not what I would
> From terror colder than the wintry frost, it took asylum far
>   within my crotch,
> A thousand wrinkles deep.
> How could I lift its head to punishment?
> Cozened by its whoreson mortal fright
> I fled for aid to words that deeper bite. (150)

By the time Encolpius has finished addressing his offending member:

> She held her eyes averted and downcast
> Nor altered aught her face at this address
> Than supple willow or drooping poppyhead. (150

Encolpius begins to regret having spoken to his member, and 'bandying words with a part of the body that more dignified people do not even think about' (151). But he absolves himself from blame when he considers that he has a famous precedent: 'didn't Ulysses have an argument with his heart . . . ?' (151), he says.

Earlier in the work, Encolpius has his room raided by a policeman and Ascyltus, who are searching for Giton. When Encolpius sees them coming, he orders Giton under the bed, and bids him tie his hands and feet to the webbing to stay out of the clutches of the searchers. 'Giton was not slow and in a moment he inserted his hands in the fastenings and beat Ulysses with his own tricks' (105) – a reference to Odysseus' hiding himself under the shaggy belly of the Cyclops' ram to escape detection. Giton escapes detection at first, in spite of the policeman's pushing a rod under the bed to see if anyone was hiding there. As in all the best farces, however, sneezes, which shake the bed, reveal the whereabouts of Giton. When Ascyltus pulls back the mattress, 'he saw our Ulysses, and even a hungry Cyclops would have had pity on him' (107). Later, when Encolpius and Giton find themselves on the ship, at sea, of their greatest enemy, Lichas, they compare themselves with Odysseus and his men trapped in the Cyclops' cave. (110) Perhaps the most farcical incident of all in the *Satyricon* which is compared with a scene in the *Odyssey* is the recognition scene on board Lichas' ship. Encolpius has taken great pains to hide his identity – not by clothing himself in beggar's weeds – but by shaving his head completely, eyebrows and all, and having the inscriptions of runaway slaves put on his face. Giton's true identity is discovered by his voice, and Lichas immediately suspects that his fellow-slave may be Encolpius. Encolpius describes how Lichas:

> ran to me, and without considering my hands or face but immediately stretching out an investigating hand to my private parts, he said: 'How are you Encolpius?' Will anyone now be surprised that Ulysses' nurse after twenty years found a scar sufficient identification when this shrewd man so cleverly went straight to the one thing that identified the runaway? (114)

What is so distinctive about Encolpius' private parts, or why Lichas should be so familiar with them is a matter for speculation only. The lost part of the *Satyricon* would obviously hold the answer. The 'Odyssean' analogy is what is important here, however.

The parody of the general body of Greek romance in the *Satyricon* is, as one might imagine, much less precise than the parody of the *Odyssey*. There is no reference by name – in the extant section at any rate – to any Greek romance, and there is only one reference to the romance in general, when Quartilla accuses Encolpius, Ascyltus, and Giton of behaving like the 'brigands of romance'.[125] But the total inversion of the typical romance plot and general situation, in the *Satyricon*, is far too obvious to ignore. The normal heterosexual relationship between the hero and heroine of Greek romance is travestied by the homosexual relationship between Giton and Encolpius, for instance. This pair of 'lovers' mock the lovers of Greek romance at almost every point in their 'love affair'. They have problems of infidelity and even rape: every male Giton encounters, covets him as a sexual partner of his own, and this is true of even the aged Eumolpus. Ascyltus is a case in point. He begins by trying to rape Giton, and when the boy objects he tells him: 'If you're playing Lucretia you've met your Tarquin' (33). He eventually manages to seduce Giton, and when Encolpius finds the pair in bed together, a brawl develops. The combatants eventually agree to allow Giton choose his lover. Encolpius gladly agrees because he is convinced, as all true lovers are, that his loved one will be true to him: contrary to all his expectations, however, Giton opts for the rapist. Having recovered his loved one, eventually, Encolpius finds the problem of Giton's chastity still gnawing at him, much later in the story: 'Tell me, dear', he says to him, 'That night Ascyltus stole you away from me, did he stay awake and do anything bad to you or was he content with a lonely and honourable night?' (151). Giton reassures Encolpius that his chastity has been preserved. Far from being preoccupied with chastity – except for that of the other partner in the relationship – the lovers are always on the lookout for fresh, sexual exploits. In effect, complete and utter debauchery is a hallmark of the whole of the *Satyricon*, and the suggestion seems to be that there is no such thing as virtue: even the interpolated story of the Matron of Ephesus bears this out.

The *Satyricon* has most of the incidentals of Greek romance also – shipwreck (123), apparent death (103), attempted suicide (100). It also has the stock reunion scene; when Giton and Encolpius meet after being separated, this is how Encolpius describes the scene:

> I rushed to take him in my arms and press my cheek to his tearful face. For a long time neither of us recovered voice. The boy's lovely breast heaved with a succession of sighs. 'Oh this shouldn't happen,' I said, 'for me to love you though I was deserted, and for there to be no scar on my heart after this great wound. What have you to say after giving yourself to another lover?' (100)

When Giton goes off with Ascyltus, Petronius takes the opportunity of having Encolpius pour forth his heart like the typical hero of Greek romance. This soliloquy, while reminding one of the typical soliloquy of the Greek romance, is yet an inversion of all the sentiments normally expressed in such soliloquies:

> 'Why couldn't that earthquake have swallowed me up? Or the sea, such a menace even to innocent people? Did I escape the

law, did I outwit the arena, did I kill my host, only to end up,
despite my claims to be a daring criminal, just lying here, a
beggar and an exile, abandoned in a lodging house in a Greek
town? And who brought this loneliness upon me? An adolescent
wallowing in every possible filth, who even on his own admission
had been rightly run out of town, who had known freedom and
respectability only in contexts of vice, and who had been hired
as a girl even by someone who knew he was a man. As for the
other one! Putting on women's clothes the day he became a
man, talked into effeminacy by his mother, doing only woman's
work in the slave pen, and after he couldn't meet his debts and
had to change his sexual ground, he abandoned the claims of
an old friendship and – in the name of decency! – sold out
everything like a whore on the strength of a one-night stand.
Now the loving pair lie clutching each other every night and
perhaps when they are worn out by their love-play, they laugh
at my loneliness. But they won't get away with it. As sure as
I'm a man and not a slave, I'll wipe out the insult with their
guilty blood.' (91)

All this is forgotten, however, when Giton returns, and quite
soon the pair find themselves floating together in stormy seas,
their ship having been wrecked; they utter the typical complaints
of lovers about to die:

Clasping Giton to me with a cry, I wept and said: 'Did we
deserve this of heaven – is death alone to unite us? But our cruel
luck does not allow it. Look, the waves are already overturning
the ship. Look, the angry sea is trying to break our affectionate
embraces. If you [Giton] ever really loved Encolpius, kiss him
while you can and take this last pleasure from the jaws of death.'
    As I said this, Giton took off his clothes and, covered in my
tunic, brought up his head for a kiss. And in case the envious
waves should drag us apart even when clinging together like
this, he tied his belt round both of us and said:
    'If nothing else, we will float longer if we are tied together in
death, or if out of pity the sea is likely to throw us up on the
same shore, either some passing stranger will throw stones over
us out of common humanity, or, as a last favour that even the
angry waves cannot refuse, the drifting sand will cover us'. (124)

In spite of the fact that Priapus dominates the action of the *Satyricon* – and is acknowledged by Encolpius as doing so – Fortune too, in keeping with the tradition of Greek romance, is given its share of the action. Fortune is mentioned on at least six occasions, and in terms very much akin to those in which Priapus is referred to. It is Fortune, for instance, that Encolpius blames (108), for putting them on the same boat as Lichas and Tryphaena, and he acknowledges later that Fortune has defeated him.[126] When Lichas' ship is wrecked, and Giton and Encolpius are in the water together, Encolpius views the storm as simply obeying the commands of Fortune. The most interesting references to Fortune come while Encolpius and company are in Croton. Everything is going so well for Encolpius, that he presumes Fortune – not Priapus – 'had taken her eyes off me' (142). Later, when legacy-hunters have been drained dry, and are beginning to cut down on their liberality, Encolpius presumes that Fortune 'is beginning to have her regrets again' (162). This distribution of the action between Priapus and Fortune seems a clear indication of Petronius' double purpose in the *Satyricon* – to parody both the *Odyssey* and Greek romance.

Modern critical opinion still insists on viewing the picaresque novel as having originated in sixteenth-century Spain, in spite of the existence of the *Satyricon*. This confusion may be due, in some sense, to the origin of the word picaresque, which is a Spanish one coined specifically to describe the realistic rogue fiction of Spain. But just as the word 'romance', coined in the Middle Ages, can be used, retrospectively, to describe ancient Greek fiction, so, too, can 'picaresque' be used to describe works like the *Satyricon*. It is interesting to note, in parenthesis, that the *Satyricon*, the text of which had been lost for almost a thousand years, was rediscovered and published in Milan in 1482: *Lazarillo de Tormes*, regarded as the first of the Spanish picaresque novels, was printed in 1553. By any standards – even those of the Spanish picaresque – the *Satyricon* is undoubtedly a perfect example of the genre. The word 'picaro', from which picaresque is derived, means a rogue or knave. The picaro is 'an offender against the moral and civil laws; not a vicious criminal such as a gangster or a murderer, but one who is dishonourable and antisocial in a much less violent way'.[127]

This description fits Encolpius and his friends perfectly. They are the first anti-heroes of fiction, and follow a completely antisocial path of theft, sacrilege, seduction, perversion, and sadism. The people they encounter are seldom much better; their antisocial bias simply has a more sophisticated exterior. The heroes of the *Satyricon*, exactly like their counterparts 1500 years later, are continually on the move: they must be, if they are to escape the clutches of individuals or the law, which is always a few steps behind. The whole object of the picaresque novel, Edwin Muir says, 'is to take a central figure through a succession of scenes, introduce a great number of characters, and thus build up a picture of society'.[128] This, too, the *Satyricon* does. Nor is this elaborate picture of society in the days of Nero an accidental by-product of the narrative method adopted. Even in the extant section of the *Satyricon*, Petronius' intent is very obvious – to satirise the money-grabbing mentality so predominant at the time, and to show the inevitable results of such a mentality – the production of people like Trimalchio, the degradation of people, even to cannibalism, and the inevitable catastrophic consequences, for culture and the arts. It is rather a difficult task, sometimes, to decide whether a work is unified or not: in the case of the *Satyricon* the task is a particularly hazardous one, since the bulk of the work is missing. It seems quite likely, however, that the money-grabbing theme and its consequences was one of the main unifying themes of the work. Even the opening scene of the extant work is a harbinger of things to come, and an indication of what has passed. Encolpius is in the process of denouncing the whole system of education as practised in the rhetorical schools. The schoolteacher Agamemnon replies, saying he must give his students – or rather their parents – what they want, otherwise he will be out of a job. He continues:

> When spongers are trying to get a dinner out of their rich friends, their main object is to find out what they would most like to hear. The only way they will get what they are after is by winning over their audience. It is the same with a tutor of rhetoric. Like a fisherman he has to bait hooks with what he knows the little fishes will rise for; otherwise he's left on the rocks without hope of their biting. (30)

Agamemnon goes on to blame the parents for the whole crisis in education, in their demand for instant success for their children:

they sacrifice everything, even their hopes, to their ambition. Then in their overeagerness they direct these immature intellects into public life. They will tell you that there is no mightier power than oratory and they dress up their boys as orators while they are still drawing their first breath. If only parents would not rush them through their studies! (30)

Later, Eumolpus echoes this same view when he gives his reasons for 'the present decadence, when the loveliest of the arts were dying out, not least painting, which had vanished without the slightest trace' (96): 'Financial greed has caused this revolution', he says; 'in former days when mere merit was still sufficient, the liberal arts flourished and there was great competition to bring to light anything of benefit to posterity' (96). Eumolpus goes on to list the great artists of the past: the distinctive common bond between those he names is the avoidance of even the society of men. Lysippus, for example, was so preoccupied with the lines of one statue that he died of starvation. Times have changed says Eumolpus, and he relates how:

But we . . . daren't study even arts with a tradition. Attacking the past instead, we acquire and pass on only vices. What has happened to dialectic? Astronomy? Or the beaten road of wisdom? Who has ever gone into a temple and prayed to become eloquent – or to approach the fountainhead of philosophy? People do not even ask for a sound mind or body, but before they touch the threshold one man immediately promises an offering if he can arrange the funeral of a rich relation, another if he can dig up some treasure, another if he can come into a safe thirty million. Even the senate, the standard of rectitude and goodness, habitually promises the Capitol a thousand pounds of gold, and to remove anyone's doubts about financial greed, tries to influence even Jove with money. So don't be surprised that painting is on the decline, when a lump of gold seems more beautiful to everybody, gods and men, than anything those crazy little Greeks, Appelles and Phidias ever made. (97)

Trimalchio is the perfect incarnation of all that is worst in the *nouveau riche*. He has risen from slavery to immeasurable riches and he is obviously typical of very many of the ever-increasing number of *nouveaux riches* in the empire. He has made his money through trade and commerce, like the majority of the new middle classes, and is now investing his money in land. The extent of his wealth is indicated at many points: 'There's more silver plate lying in his porter's cubbyhole than any other man owns altogether' (52), says one of his friends, who goes on to doubt whether one in ten of Trimalchio's servants knows who his master is. (52) Later, the events of one day, 26 July, on his estates is read out: there have been 30 males, 40 females born; 500 000 pecks of wheat have been threshed and stored; 500 oxen have been broken in; 10 000 000 sesterces have been deposited in the strongroom. (65)

Trimalchio's culture is in inverse proportion to his wealth: he must still rank, even today, as one of the greatest of all fictional philistines. He has pretensions to learning, for instance, and talks of Homer narrating 'the twelve labours of Hercules and the story of Ulysses – how the Cyclops tore out his thumb with a pair of pincers' (62): later, he speaks of Hannibal taking Troy (62), and later again of Cassandra killing her sons (62), and Daedalus shutting Niobe in the Trojan horse. (62) Trimalchio's lack of culture on every other level is quite remarkable also. When Encolpius first meets him (45), he is urinating, in public, into a silver chamber pot. At the meal, he treats the guests to a disquisition on his constipational problems and their remedies, as well as giving his guests advice on how to relieve similar problems. (61) His silver plate has, we find, the weight of the silver enscribed on the rims (48), and at the meal he sends for a weighing scales to prove that a bracelet of his weighs ten pounds. But the ingenious climax to the meal comes when Trimalchio goes through the arrangements for his own funeral. He wants a nice tomb and a monument:

> After all it's a big mistake to have nice houses just for when you're alive and not to worry about the one we have to live in for much longer. . . . I'll make sure in my will that I don't get done down once I'm dead. I'll put one of my freedmen in charge of my tomb to look after it and not let people run up and shit on my monument. (82)

Trimalchio, in his own epitaph, sums up everything Petronius has been trying to represent in him:

A SELF-MADE MAN
HE LEFT AN ESTATE OF 30 000 000
AND HE NEVER HEARD A PHILOSOPHER   (83)

To emphasise that Trimalchio is not an exception, Petronius gives him plenty of company at the meal. Agamemnon, the schoolteacher is there – ironically, in view of his earlier analogy between someone who wished to cadge a dinner, and a schoolteacher. And he obviously knows well what Trimalchio would most like to hear, he is so adept at flattering him. One of Agamemnon's neighbours at the meal is a good example of the type of parent the schoolteacher spoke of. The father has killed his son's three goldfinches because they were distracting him from his studies; and he believes the lad has 'done enough dabbling in poetry and such like' (60). He has bought his son some law books for some legal training because 'there's a living in that sort of thing' (60). He tells how he took the son aside and 'gave it to him straight':

Believe me, my lad, any studying you do will be for your own good. You see Phileros the solicitor – if he hadn't studied, he'd be starving today. It's not so long since he was humping round loads on his back. Now he can even look Norbanus in the face. An education is an investment, and a proper profession never goes dead on you. (61)

In a few deft strokes, the characters and histories of the other characters at the meal are accurately communicated. Their histories have one thing in common – they involve either the making or losing of money. Chrysanthus 'started out in life with just a penny, and he was ready to pick up less than that from a muck-heap, if he had to use his teeth. He went up in the world . . . was certainly Fortune's favourite – lead turned to gold in his hand' (56,57). Diogenes was 'humping wood on his back not long since. They say . . . he stole a hobgoblin's cap and found its treasure' (52). Proculus, on the other hand, 'had a million in his hands, but he slipped badly. I don't think he can call his hair his own. Yet I'd swear it wasn't his fault. . . . Some dirty freedmen pocketed everything he had' (53). Another slave-turned-millionaire, Hermeros, is proud to say he 'didn't learn no geometry or criticism and such silly rubbish, but I can read the letters on a notice board', he says, 'and I can do my percentages in metal, weights, and money'. (70)

As Trimalchio is the person, so Croton is the place in which the money-grabbing mentality is incarnated. This is revealed even before Encolpius and company reach the city of Croton, when they meet a farmer who first describes the city, and then continues:

> My dear sirs . . . if you are businessmen, change your plans and look for some other source of livelihood. If, however, you are a more sophisticated type and you can take incessant lying, you are following the right road to riches. You see, in this city no literary pretensions are honoured, eloquence has no standing, sobriety and decent behaviour are not praised and rewarded – no, whatever people you see, you must regard as divided into two classes. Either they have fortunes worth hunting or they are fortune-hunters. In this city no one raises children, because anyone who has heirs of his own is not invited out to dinner or allowed into the games; he is deprived of all amenities and lives in ignominious obscurity. But those who have never married and have no close ties, attain the highest honours – only these have real courage, or even blameless characters. You are on your way to a town that is like a plague-ridden countryside, where there is nothing but corpses being pecked and crows pecking them. (127)

Our heroes, instead of turning aside from Croton, are actually attracted to the place by this description, and decide to take advantage of the Crotonians in order to line their own pockets. They hatch up a story as follows:

> Eumolpus had buried his son, a young man of great oratorical abilities and high promise, and . . . the unhappy old man had therefore left his native city so that he should not have daily cause for tears at the sight of his son's followers and friends or his tomb. Shipwreck was next added to his grief, in which he had lost more than twenty million sesterces. But he was not worried by the loss, except that being deprived of his servants, he did not see about him what was proper to his rank. Besides, he had thirty million invested in Africa, in farms and loans . . . (128)

The fortune-hunters of Croton believe every word of this fiction, and are soon vying with one another in putting their financial resources at Eumolpus' service.

The events at Croton are an important variation on the money theme of the *Satyricon*. The meal at Trimalchio's was an exhibition of the *nouveaux riches*, the people who had progressed from slavery to immeasurable wealth: Croton, on the other hand, exhibits the aristocracy, but an aristocracy which has degenerated beyond recognition. The members of this class are unwilling to join the rat-race of trade to prevent the erosion of their fortunes; instead, they prey on their fellow men – those who have fortunes to leave when they die. The securing of a legacy or legacies is the object in life of the fortune-hunters, to the exclusion of all other aims. Petronius pursues this 'man-eat-man' syndrome to its logical conclusion, by having Eumolpus demand that those who benefit from his will shall cut up his corpse 'and eat it in front of the citizens' (162). Eumolpus even gives examples of cannibalism, to urge them on – the Sanguntines, for instance, 'who ate human flesh when they were hard pressed by Hannibal – and they weren't expecting a legacy. The Petelians did the same in the last stages of a famine, and all they were after in eating this dish was to avoid dying of starvation' (163). The lesson to be learnt from the examples is obvious enough: it is more beneficial to eat another human being to gain a legacy than it is to eat one merely to stay alive. The text of the *Satyricon* ends soon after Eumolpus' demand, and we don't know, and perhaps never shall, what happened. But we do know that the fortune hunters were prepared to comply with the demand: 'The enormous reputation of his money blinded the eyes of the poor fools. Gorgias was ready to carry out the terms' (163). It is very likely that Eumolpus' demand was part of a strategem to enable him to make a quick exit from Croton; yet, it is doubtful if Petronius would have refrained from extending his theme to its logical conclusion: this would mean that the fortune-hunters would eventually eat the corpse of Eumolpus or a pseudo-Eumolpus. If this was so, then the Croton incident certainly marked the end of the *Satyricon*, since Petronius could hardly have amplified the theme further. It is worth noting, finally, that the effect of the rise of the nobodies, and the declension of the aristocracy is exactly the same in each case – the rejection of any kind of culture. Croton is a city in which 'no literary pretentions are honoured, eloquence has no standing, sobriety and decent behaviour are not praised and rewarded' (127). The net result is simply an overwhelming cultural crisis, a crisis which had actually arisen in Neronian times, the evidence for which is widely available in contemporary writings. Petronius was not, therefore, positing a hypothetical situation.

The most significant feature of the *Satyricon* for the modern reader is, undoubtedly, its realism. This realism was the intentional, yet somewhat accidental result of Petronius' attempt to parody ancient romance. Like Cervantes and Fielding, at two later, all-important stages of the development of fiction, Petronius realised that the only really effective way to deflate romantic pretensions was to have them collide head-on with the so-called 'facts of life'. The inversion of the typical romance quest, becomes a picaresque-type quest – in the *Satyricon*, the question for money. With the *Satyricon*, *Don Quixote*, and *Joseph Andrews* as evidence, there is every reason for arguing that realism, and therefore the novel, is, in its origins, a direct result of parody, and that it is, in particular, parody of romance, which brought realism and the novel into being. This is one of the essential links between the novel and the romance, a link clearly obvious in the *Satyricon*, the first work of realistic fiction in European literature.

There are some, of course, who query the quality of realism in the *Satyricon*, and John Sullivan is one of them. Among his arguments against the realism of the Satyricon are the following:[129] (a) Petronius does not aim at verisimilitude; (b) there is an aside to the reader; (c) there are various expressions of the author's own taste and views; (d) there is a large element of fantasy; (e) the realistic elements are placed in a highly literary framework; (f) the use of verse. It is difficult to know what reply to make to the charge that Petronius did not aim at verisimilitude, except to suggest that it would have been impossible, almost, for him to do so in the year 60 AD. But whether realism is dependent on whether one aims for verisimilitude or not, is a debatable point. If Petronius is unrealistic because of an aside to the reader, Fielding and George Eliot are among two of the later band of novelists who must be convicted of being even greater transgressors. Almost every novelist who ever wrote must be convicted of the next charge – that of expressing his own taste and views. The 'large element of fantasy' in the *Satyricon*, according to Sullivan, is the incident of the legacy-hunters at Croton, and Eumolpus' narration of a homosexual experience: one can only reply that Sullivan is being slightly

ridiculous here. As for the final two charges: Henry Fielding can
be convicted on both these grounds, since all his novels, by his
own admission, have a literary framework, and Petronius' verse,
intended usually as a parody of epic style is much more 'realistic'
than Fielding's attempts at similar effects. There seems little point
in making a scene-by-scene analysis of the *Satyricon*, pointing out
the many aspects of realism to be found therein, or to discuss the
many magnificent character sketches in the work: P. G. Walsh has
done just this in his book, *The Roman Novel*, singling out the 'Cena
Trimalchionis' for special study, in a separate chapter.

There are a few remaining aspects of the *Satyricon* which deserve
mention, not least of which is that of the self-conscious narrator,
believed by most critics to be a development which came over
fifteen hundred years later, in fiction. But Petronius did originate
this aspect of fiction also, in spite of the fact that there is only one
extant instance of an address to the reader, in the work. This is
what he has to say on that occasion:

> The Censor frown and knits his brows,
> The Censor wants to stop us,
> The Censor hates my guileless prose,
> My simple modern opus
> My cheerful unaffacted style
> Is Everyman when in his humour,
> My candid pen narrates his joys,
> Refusing to philosophize
>
> Find me any man who knows
> Nothing of love and naked pleasure.
> What stern moralist would oppose
> Two bodies warming a bed together?
> Father of Truth, old Epicurus
> Gave philosophy a soul
> And taught, his followers assure us
> Love is Life's sovereign goal. (151)

Since this is, perhaps the single most important statement in the
whole of the extant *Satyricon* it is, perhaps, instructive to consider
a prose translation of Petronius' verse, which is given by Michael
Heseltine in the Loeb translation of the work:

Why do ye, Cato's disciples, look at me with wrinkled foreheads,
and condemn a work of fresh simplicity? A cheerful kindness
laughs through my pure speech, and my clear mouth reports
whatever the people do. All men born know of mating and the
joys of love; all men are free to let their limbs glow in a warm
bed. Epicurus, the true father of truth, bade wise men be lovers,
and said that therein lay the crown of life.[130]

This statement is, beyond question, a defensive one. Petronius is,
it seems, anticipating a charge of obscenity and over-preoccupation
with sexuality, which might be levelled against the *Satyricon*. And,
intriguingly, the defence he offers is, essentially, that offered by
the realistic movement of modern times, viz., 'letting the facts
speak for themselves', and stressing the ordinary aspects of
experience. Petronius says he 'reports whatever the people do'.
The second half of the statement is simply an elaboration on what
the people actually do: *all* men born know of mating and the joys
of love; *all* men are free to let their limbs glow in a warm bed. One
would not wish to seem to be exaggerating the importance of
Petronius' statement: one can only reiterate that the *Satyricon* is a
realistic work, and that the author had formed an inchoate theory
of realism as it applied to that work.

The *Satyricon* has numerous short anecdotes and one short story
incorporated into the extant section of the text. This is in line with
precedent established in both the *Odyssey* and Greek romance
generally. Nor do the interpolations follow any set pattern or serve
to adumbrate any single theme. The most famous of the tales, that
of the Matron of Ephesus,[131] fits in with one of the main themes of
the work, that all virtue, sexual or otherwise, has its price: such
a coincidence in themes seems purely coincidental, however
Eumolpus' tale of his affair with the son of his host in Pergamum,
is one of the more disreputable stories in the work. (94ff.) The
remaining interpolations concern werewolves (73,74), and magical
occurrences of one kind or another. Letters too, are swapped
between Circe and Encolpius (147,148), and a final interesting item
is the very numerous references[132] to drama, and mime in particular
in the course of the story.

The *Satyricon* is undoubtedly – even in its truncated form, a great
and unique work – one which has never received its due acclaim
as realistic fiction and as a significant landmark in the history of
prose fiction.

The Golden Ass

Apuleius, author of *The Golden Ass*, was born in or around the year 120 AD in Madaura, a town in the northern province of Roman Africa. His father was a man of some distinction in the area, and when he died, Apuleius was left comfortably well off. The profession of Apuleius at the time was that of writer and lecturer, and in each of these capacities he became famous in Africa during his own lifetime. One specific incident in his life is worth recounting as illustrative of a major aspect of *The Golden Ass*. Apuleius married a wealthy widow called Pudentilla, and her relatives brought a legal action against Apuleius, charging him with using magic in order to gain her consent. A consequence of the charge and his acquittal was the composition of the *Apologia*, in which he shows how absurd the whole incident was, yet demonstrating, at the same time, his conversance with the theory if not the actual practice of magic. The net result of the Pudentilla incident and the *Apologia*, was that Apuleius acquired a reputation as a magician, a reputation further fostered by the publication of *The Golden Ass*. It is instructive to note that while *The Golden Ass* contributed to Apuleius' reputation as a magician, the author's prior repute as a magician possibly contributed to the acceptance of the work as a true account of an actual experience.

The Golden Ass is based on a lost Greek work entitled Μεταμορφωσεις, invariably ascribed nowadays to Lucian. There is, however, an extant work in Greek entitled *Lucius the Ass* which is generally considered to be 'an epitome or syncopated edition of the Μεταμορφωσεις'.[133] Both these works, *The Golden Ass* and *Lucius the Ass*, are, it is generally agreed, independently derived from the original Μεταμορφωσεις. But *The Golden Ass* is certainly not just a translation into Latin of Lucian's work: while Apuleius retains the basic plot of the original, he expands the narrative considerably, in various ways, not least of which is the introduction of numerous additional tales. One presumes that the *Satyricon* exercised at least some influence on Apuleius, but it is difficult to single out any particular aspect of *The Golden Ass* to support such a view. Indeed, it is a much more simple task to point out the dissimilarities between the two works. There is no realism in *The Golden Ass*; Apuleius is not concerned to depict the real world of his time. The situations and characters in the work are, as Walsh says, 'almost as stylised as those in Grimm's *Fairy Tales*'.[134] Neither can *The Golden Ass* be described as a satirical work, nor even picaresque, in spite of the wanderings of the hero. Lucius is no picaro, as a human being or as an ass. Any roguery that occurs is invariably reported in the interpolated stories. Ideal Greek romance contributed something to *The Golden Ass*, but only in incidentals such as the use of Fortune, the trial scene,[135] and, possibly the religious climax of the work. The Milesian Tales, mannered stories of 'bizarre adventure or sexual encounter',[136] have obviously been a major influence on Apuleius, particularly in the anecdotes.

Ben Edwin Perry has no very high opinion of *The Golden Ass*, believing it to be 'primarily a series of mundane stories', and continues:

> The contrast in mood and nature of subject matter between the last book of the *Metamorphoses* [*The Golden Ass*] and the ten that precede it is no sharper than that which marks the transition from one story or group of stories to another in the first ten books. Love of variety and the tendency to pass in rapid succession from the contemplation of one wonderful thing to another, with a minimum of logical connection, is profoundly characteristic of Apuleius in all his literary activity.[137]

Perry's judgement seems, at first glance, to be quite accurate: *The Golden Ass* is an extraordinary *mélange*, in which Apuleius provides almost every kind of love and adventure in a host of seemingly incompatible stories. Walsh[138] provides particularly damning evidence from the text to support the view that Apuleius was quite unconcerned about consistency in the narrative, as far as details are concerned, at any rate. There are, however, consistencies of a higher nature than those of 'logical connection' and 'consistency of detail', and it is an overriding thematic consistency that Apuleius tried to give *The Golden Ass*. Apuleius had set himself a difficult task, his stories were so many and diverse, but he was quite aware of what he was doing, as can be seen from his address to the reader:

> In this Milesian tale I shall string together divers stories, and delight your pleasant ears with a kindly history; if you will not scorn to look upon this Egyptian paper written with a ready pen of Nile reeds – stories of men's forms and fortunes transformed into different shapes, and then restored again in due sequence

back into their selves – a true subject for wonder.[139]

Apuleius claims he is going to string together diverse stories – tories of men's forms *and* fortunes transformed into different hapes and then restored, and this is what he does in *The Golden* \ss. He was obviously aware of the thematic connections between is varying stories, and wrote with these in view: his difficulty vas in blending so many types of love and metamorphosis into a vork of logical connections and consistent details – and in this he vas not particularly successful. It is a moot point, indeed, whether e even tried to provide his work with any such consistency. With he aid of hindsight, it seems obvious to us that the answer to \puleius' problem was not to borrow Lucian's tale as a basis for he narrative he wished to write: he should have either borrowed more congenial plot or else constructed one himself. It is hardly ɔ Apuleius' discredit, however, that he failed to create a new and evolutionary form of fiction, two thousand years ago.

William Adlington, who translated *The Golden Ass* in 1566, not 'nly accepted Apuleius' statement of his aim, but went on to show ow the general outline of the work accorded with the author's im. Having described Lucius' transformation into an ass, he ontinues:

Verily under the wrap of this transformation is taxed the life of mortall men, when as we suffer our mindes so to bee drowned in the sensuall lusts of the flesh, and the beastly pleasure thereof (which aptly may be called the violent confection of Witches) that wee lose wholly the use of reason and vertue, which properly should be in man, and play the parts of brute and savage beasts. By like occasion we reade, how divers of the companions of Ulysses were turned by the marvellous power of Circe into swine. And find we not in Scripture, that Nabuchadnezzar the ninth King of Babylon, by reason of his great dominions and realmes, fell into such exceeding pride, that he was suddenly transformed of Almighty God into an horrible monster, having the head of an oxe, the feet of a Beare, and the taile of a Lion, and did eat hay as a Beast. (xx)

Adlington's reference to Circe and Odysseus' men is particularly pposite, since it was indeed lust of the flesh which resulted in heir transformation into swine, while retaining, as Lucius does,

human minds. In the course of *The Golden Ass* itself, Lucius (180)
compares the wisdom he has gained through his adventures to
that gained by Odysseus – an acknowledgement that Odysseus
problems are basically sexual ones, and it is these which cause hi
lengthy wanderings. Adlington elaborates on the statement quoted
above, by saying that 'metamorphosie of Lucius Apuleius may b
resembled to youth without discretion, and his reduction to age
possessed with wisedome and virtue' (xx). Later again, he describe
the book as 'a figure of man's life' (xx).

The Golden Ass is the story of physical and intellectual lust and
its consequences, and the first three Books of the work are part o
the elaborate preparation for the eventual transformation of Lucius
Within a few pages of the opening, a traveller called Aristomenus
whom Lucius chances to meet on his way to Hypata in Thessaly
tells a strange tale of witchcraft. The story (29ff.), concerns one
Socrates, who, having been beaten and robbed by thieves, hap
pened to come to the house of an old woman called Meroe. Mero
entertained him and made 'good cheer'. Socrates is eventuall
'pricked by carnall desire' and Meroe takes him to her bed chamber
where they lie together. Too late, Socrates discovers that Meroe i
a witch who specialises in changing men who cross her, into
animals. No such moderate punishment awaits Socrates, however
who meets his death in a macabre fashion. This tale is the first o
many warnings for Lucius not to dabble in witchcraft. And th
parallel between his case and that of Socrates is very notable
Socrates' initial mistake is his sexual association with Meroe
whereby he is trapped with her magical arts. Lucius lusts afte
sorcery, and witchcraft and sexuality is his avenue of access. H
decided, initially, to pursue the witch Pamphile's maid, so that h
might be initiated into witchcraft and sorcery. His pursuit of Fotis
instead of being merely a means, becomes an end in itself, to such
an extent that he forgets all about witchcraft and sorcery. It is onl
after the incident of the wine skins, indeed, that he remember
his original purpose in pursuing Fotis. Both cases, that of Socrate
and Lucius, involve a primary sexual association, or lust of th
body, leading to a secondary association with witchcraft. The en
result for Socrates was death, but Lucius disregards the warning.

The second warning comes in a quite different form, yet on
which the reader accustomed to the *ecphraseis* of Greek romanc
would tend to overlook as another one of the pointless rhetorica
digressions so common in Greek romance. The warning i

expressed in the relief sculpted over the gates of his aunt Byrrhena's house, and depicts Diana being spied on by Actaeon. Diana herself is first described at length, and then, eventually, the lower part of the relief containing Actaeon:

> Behind the back of the goddesse was carved a stone in manner of a Caverne, environed with mosse, hearbes, leaves, sprigs, green branches and bowes . . . Moreover, amongst the branches of the stone appeared the image of Actaeon: and how that Diana (which was carved within the same stone, standing in the water) because he did see her naked, did turn him into an Hart, and so he was torn and slain of his own hounds. (49)

The story of Actaeon is merely a variation of the Socrates story – lust, magic, and death – since the legend represents lust tearing a man to pieces, when he has been magically transformed into an animal. It is worth noting that each of these two warnings involves the death of the lustful male: the death of Lucius is a metaphorical one, ending in his rebirth.

Following directly upon the warning contained in the relief, comes the most explicit warning of all to Lucius, from his aunt Byrrhena. Significantly, she commences her statement by swearing 'by this goddesse Diana, that I do greatly tender your safety' (49,50). Byrrhena goes on to warn him against Pamphile, who is 'accounted the most chief and principall Magitian and Enchantresse living' (50). The warning is couched in sexual terms, and describes the consequences of association, or refusal to associate sexually with Pamphile – transformation into 'stones, sheep, or some other beast' (50). The effect on Lucius is quite the opposite to that intended by his aunt, and he 'willingly determined to bestow . . . his money in learning of that art of witchcraft and now wholly to become a witch' (50). It is at this point, also, that he decides to use Fotis in his attempt to again access to the world of sorcery and witchcraft. Nor are the warnings completed, as evidenced by the fate of Bellepheron, who dared consider himself equal to the powers of magic and paid the price (59ff.): the incident of the wineskins (66) is actual proof of the grotesque powers of Pamphile, but Lucius is again deaf to the warning.

At the end of the third Book, Lucius is eventually turned into an ass, a state of body befitting his state of mind in meddling with magical powers. He pays for his lust not simply in the

transformation but in diverse ways in the remaining five Books
His seemingly interminable wanderings and vicissitudes begin, a
he becomes a prey to both animals and men.

Most of the stories interpolated into that of the wanderings o
Lucius, as an ass, involve the theme of sexuality in one form o
another. There is the story of the servant who loves a harlot anc
drives his wife to kill their child and herself: the servant, a
punishment has his body coated with honey and is eaten alive by
ants (166,167). Another story (205ff.) concerns the love of a
stepmother for her son, which results in her banishment, and the
death of a conniving servant; while a third (211ff.) tells of a woman
who murders, amongst others, her husband, daughter and sister
in-law. At the very end of Book Ten, a pageant is presented
depicting the Judgement of Paris, wherein Paris, Lucius says, 'sold
his judgement for a little pleasure, which was the cause afterward
of the ruin of all his progeny' (217).

The story of Cupid and Psyche, which extends over two Books
of *The Golden Ass*, deserves special mention. This short story is, as
Walsh notes, the centrepiece of *The Golden Ass*, 'deliberately shaped
to stress the connexion between the maiden's error, suffering
and redemption and the similar experiences of Lucius'.[140] Walsh
suggests that 'Cupid and Psyche' is the projection of Lucius
pilgrimage into the world of myth, but he warns against the
presumption that every situation and every character in the short
story has a correspondence in *The Golden Ass* as a whole.[141] I
should be said, at this point, that 'Cupid and Psyche' is invariably
chosen by the critics of Apuleius as a perfect example of the
author's inclusion of a tale, interesting in its own way, but quite
irrelevant to the advancement or unity of the plot. Yet, at the very
least, 'Cupid and Psyche' must be acknowledged to represent one
example of 'men's . . . fortunes transformed into different shapes'
as promised by Apuleius at the opening of the book. Psyche's
fortunes certainly do undergo great transformations: first she is
taken to be a 'new Venus' (100), but no one comes to woo her.
Next she is married to a 'serpent dire and fierce' (103), her wedding
taking the form of a funeral. It is, in fact, Cupid she marries, but he
deserts her soon afterwards, for breaking his injunctions to her.
She wanders aimlessly through the world trying to find him, but
cannot. Venus has her 'scourged with rods and whips' (124), and
gives her impossible tasks to perform, until she is rescued by
Cupid. Jupiter, having been entreated by Cupid, decrees that the

marriage of the two is lawful, and forbids Venus to interfere further: he then takes a 'pot of immortality' and has Psyche drink from it 'that she might be immortal and love her husband everlastingly' (131). The resemblances between the story of Lucius and that of Psyche are obvious enough. She, too, is given warning after warning not to meddle with the unknown, but she succumbs to temptation and is punished. She, too, like Lucius, wanders the world looking for her type of salvation – the return of her husband. Her tests under Venus are akin to Lucius' trials under Isis. Both tales dramatise a journey of the soul through the world until it is finally united with a divinity. Coming, as it does, in Books Four and Five, the tale of Cupid and Psyche predicts the eventual redemption of Lucius.

It would be artistically satisfying to have Lucius eventually redeemed from lust by a show of chastity, and from witchcraft by religious conviction. Such a scheme would clearly manifest the maturity gained by Lucius through his experiences on two levels. But while Lucius' relationship with Isis can be regarded as a redemption from witchcraft and sorcery, Apuleius does seem to blunder in having Lucius, as an ass, copulate with a matron of Corinth, quite close to the end of Book Ten: one must conclude that Lucius has not matured sexually, and Apuleius would seem to have blundered somewhat in stating this so explicitly and in such close proximity to Lucius' religious maturity. This incident is not, indeed, untypical of Apuleius' tendency to expand specific scenes at the expense of his overall scheme. Walsh notes this, too, saying there is a 'central ambivalence' in the romance, 'a tension between Milesian ribaldry and Platonist mysticism'.[142] Walsh warns,[143] however, against the typical presumption that the Milesian ribaldry and Platonist mysticism are exclusive alternatives – a presumption, he says, that has vitiated a great deal of criticism of *The Golden Ass*. The main theme of *The Golden Ass* remains quite clear: profane love has turned a foolish young man into an ass; sacred love not only restores to him his manhood but makes a priest of him also. Strange as it may seem, Apuleius' work greatly resembles the *Odyssey*, at least in its externals. In *The Golden Ass* there is a lone hero, like Odysseus, in search of himself; and it is this spiritual odyssey which is the central experience of the work. The adventures of Lucius the ass project Apuleius' view of the crucial experience of man's life, his fight to achieve maturity: at the start of the tale Lucius is a foolish youth, at the end a mature

man and priest. All of this was adequately expressed just over fou.
hundred years ago by William Adlington when he described *Th*
Golden Ass as a 'figure of man's life' from 'youth without discretion
to 'age possessed with wisedome and vertue' (xxi).

This brief analysis of *The Golden Ass* completes an examinatior
which sought to demonstrate the origins and development o
ancient fiction extending over a period of almost four hundrec
years, from 100 BC to 300 AD. The Greek romance came into being
with the 'open' society of ancient Greece, which had replaced the
age-old 'closed' one: Alexander and his exploits can be creditec
with the destruction of the old order. In its origins, the Greek
romance was, seemingly, developed specifically for the rising
middle classes or their sons and daughters, either or both of which
groups were looking for love, adventure and sensation in their
fiction. From its inception, Greek romance was independent o
academic tradition and was, therefore, free to develop as it wished
many writers of romance, in an effort to evade the prejudice o
the academics, did, however, claim to be writing 'history', a claim
which fooled no one at the time, but which has created quite some
confusion since. Drama was an important influence on ancient
fiction. The decline in drama at the time in question created a void
which was effectively filled by the rise of fiction. Drama, too,
supplied many of the techniques and much material for the new
genre.

   The few extant Greek romances examined show an extraordinary
variety of theme and treatment, ranging from the wanderings of
an individual in search of himself, as in the *Odyssey*, to the
wanderings of a loving couple in search of each other as in *Theagenes*
and Chariclea; from the wanderings of an ass in *The Golden Ass*, to
the static situation of *Daphnis and Chloe*. The treatment, too, is as
varied, ranging from the sublime as in the *Odyssey*, and perhaps,
Daphnis and Chloe, to the ridiculous, as in *Clitopho and Leucippe*. The
most significant work of ancient fiction was written in Latin, the
Satyricon. Its author was a well-educated man, and his work was
an educated man's reply to romance. The result of his reaction to
romance has left us with the only work of realistic fiction from
ancient times, and its importance cannot be exaggerated.

   The failure of ancient fiction to attain the intellectual and artistic maturity of the modern novel, must be accounted one of the greatest non-events in the history of literature. With some qualification, it can be stated that ancient fiction had, at its demise, attained the same stage of development as the modern novel had in the eighteenth century. Petronius is the Fielding of the ancient world, and the *Satyricon* is his *Shamela*. Petronius did not, unfortunately, go on to write a *Tom Jones* via *Joseph Andrews*; in fact he failed to develop in any way after the *Satyricon*. It may well be that Petronius died before he had such an opportunity of development: one must repeat once more that the stranglehold of academic tradition on Petronius must have been such that any development from the *Satyricon* would have been difficult anyway – much more difficult than it was to be for Fielding. And it must be said also that Petronius' problem was the problem of all writers of ability in ancient times – prevention by belletristic snobbery from writing fiction, a form unrecognised by the literary *dicta* of antiquity. This exclusion of the most able authors from the writing of fiction must have had a deleterious effect on the development of the form. This, among other reasons, is why, in over four hundred years, ancient fiction had shown so little progress.

Another, and possibly the major factor in the failure of the novel to develop fully in ancient times was the rise of Christianity. By the time Christianity became the religion of the empire, the society for which the romance was created was no more. Nor was Christianity willing to allow romance to wilt and die naturally: it pursued the pagan, erotic romance with unrelenting vigour, and contributed greatly to its speedy demise. Nietzsche summed it all up succinctly when he remarked that Christianity 'gave Eros poison to drink; he did not die of it certainly, but degenerated to Vice'. It was not only Eros who was involved, however, but also the innumerable gods, and Fortune, who were depicted as controlling man's destiny. It is hardly a coincidence that two of the very few extant Greek romances were written by Heliodorus and Achilles Tatius, both of whom are reputed to have later become Christian bishops.

2
Medieval Romance

It is a commonplace of literary history to describe medieval romanc as the prototype of the modern novel, yet this is surely a cas where the commonplace is inaccurate. It is easy, on the other hand to recognise why medieval romance should be so regarded: th very existence of such a large body of narrative fiction woul naturally lead one to presume a connection between it and late narrative forms. And from presumption seems to have com conviction. The actual facts of the situation show, however, tha English narrative was in a state of utter moribundity in the fifteent and early sixteenth centuries, and was only rescued from imminen death by the introduction of Spanish picaresque and newly translated Greek romances. In spite of implications to the contrary a study of any of the many histories of the English novel support the suggestion that medieval romance played little or no part ir the development of the novel. Ernest A. Baker's *The History of th English Novel*, which devotes literally hundreds of pages to discussion of medieval romance, is a case in point. One continually wonders what exactly is the relevance for the English novel, of a the romances Baker discusses and analyses. It is hardly sufficien reason to discuss them simply because they exist. Only very seldon does Baker suggest why the romances he discusses are relevant he adverts to 'realistic' scenes now and again, and claims, fo example, that Chrétien de Troyes:

> was not content merely to relate love stories; he meditated and analysed and interpreted, much in the style of a modern novelist . . . Hence, through his work, and the cycles of romance that were directly or at further removes founded upon it, modern fiction is ultimately affiliated, not only to medieval poetry, but also to the oldest imaginative creations of the Aryan race.[1]

Of Malory's *Morte Darthur* he has this to say, later:

The *Morte Darthur* is not a novel, but it shows advance towards the future novel. Attention is turned more than in any of the antecedent stories that went to its making, upon the inner world of character and motive.[2]

Baker's method is quite suspect, suggesting, as it does, a teleological basis for the development of the English novel. There is also the implicit suggestion that when all these developments in individual works are added together that they will somehow produce the first novel. Margaret Schlauch's work, *Antecedents of the English Novel*, is a further illustration of the difficulties involved in dealing with medieval romance as the basis of the modern novel. Professor Schlauch talks of 'embarking on a quest for precursors of modern novels',[3] and sees the major problem in the following terms:

> Did these great innovators, Defoe, Richardson, and Fielding create in a vacuum when portraying people of their own sort, or did they operate within a tradition which was able to contribute something from an earlier time to their conception of realism?[4]

The remainder of the work is concerned with what the author so aptly describes as a quest for 'vignettes of daily existence'.[5] Professor Schlauch's method is adequately demonstrated by some quotations from the book. In *Valentine and Orson*, for instance, there is, she says, one scene which is 'described with unusual realism of detail';[6] in *Paris and Vienne*, one situation 'based entirely upon contradictions existing in the objective social environment';[7] and in *Sir Gawain and the Green Knight* the author 'shows a striking ability to place before readers and listeners a transcription of natural colloquies carried on in specifically realized settings'.[8] Professor Schlauch is probably quite correct in describing her choice of vignettes as realistic, but to deduce that a precedent for realism in fiction was thereby created is extravagant. Medieval romance *can* be shown to have played an important role in the development of the English novel, but certainly not in the way the general body of historians of English fiction would have us believe.

The intriguing title of the final chapter of R. W. Southern's book *The Making of The Middle Ages* is 'From Epic to Romance'. The title is intriguing because the final chapter which sets out 'to draw together the scattered threads of this book, and to face more directly than hitherto some of the fundamental changes of attitude, or shifts of emphasis, which have met us in every sphere of life,'[9] seems to have nothing whatever to do with epic and romance. But Professor Southern later explains the title:

> The change of emphasis [in the middle ages] from localism to universality, the emergence of systematic thought, the rise of logic – to these we may add a change which in a certain sense comprehends them all: the change from Epic to Romance. The contrast is not merely a literary one, though it is in literature that it can be most clearly seen. it is a reflection of a more general change of attitude which finds expression in many different ways.[10]

Southern's remarks immediately remind us of another era, over one thousand years earlier, in which the change from epic to romance also comprehended changes in every sphere of life, social, economic, and intellectual. Friedrich Heer, in his magnificent work *The Medieval World* completes the picture when he speaks of the Middle Ages in terms of 'open' and 'closed' societies:

> During this period [1150–1350] Europe underwent some far-reaching transformations. The continent which in the twelfth century was open and expanding by the mid-fourteenth century had become closed, a Europe of internal and external frontiers . . .[11]

Heer later goes on to describe the characteristics of the 'open' society of the twelfth century:

> The frontiers, later to become barriers, 'iron curtains' delimiting separate worlds, were still open, even fluid. There were open frontiers on Europe's eastern borders. Until the time of the Mongol onslaught and the Fourth Crusade (1204) Russia was still accessible to the West, linked to Western Europe and Germany by commercial and economic ties and by aristocratic intermarriage. In the eleventh and twelfth centuries an international trade route running from Scandinavia to Byzantium passed through the centre of Russia, by way of Novgorod.[12]

It could be argued that medieval society 'opened' much too soon from a purely literary point of view – that epic was still only developing when it was forced, by external influences, to pass prematurely into the romantic stage. Many of the defects discernible in medieval romance could possibly be attributed to this premature transformation. Neither, unfortunately, did the conditions which brought romance into being, last very long. Heer, as we saw, claimed that the 'open society' of the middle ages lasted through the twelfth and into the early thirteenth centuries: a hundred odd years is a negligible length of time in purely literary terms, and was certainly insufficient to allow medieval romance to come to full fruition. The view of the historians is borne out by that of the student of medieval romance itself: 1150 to 1250 is usually considered by the literary historian as the period of active romance-writing; thereafter it was merely a question of reworking old themes and materials.

Medieval romance can, therefore, be fully appreciated only in the light of one hundred years of fruitful development: this should be compared with the more than five hundred years during which the Greek romance was growing and developing. Even within its century of development medieval romance had few of the advantages of Greek romance, not to mention additional disadvantages. The Middle Ages did not, for instance, possess a printing press – either the equivalent of the ancient Greek and Roman one, or the modern one. One must add, of course, that the ancient 'printing press' was devised simply because it was badly needed: education had expanded to such an extent that the level of literacy had risen rapidly: this new reading public had to be catered for. The Middle Ages were not quite as 'open' as the Hellenistic age, obviously: there was no such expansion in education in the Middle Ages, and no consequent development of a reading public. Huizinga describes the retention of verse in medieval romances as an indication of one of the 'more primitive stages of literature',[13] but it also indicates a correspondingly primitive stage of development in the society for which it is written. 'Even as late as the thirteenth century', Huizinga writes, 'every subject, even natural history or medicine, seemed to lend itself to treatment in verse, because the principal mode of assimilating a written work, was still hearing it recited and getting it by heart.'[14] It was not, indeed, until the fifteenth century that prose was used in romances – and even then it was not used in the composition of new works so much as for the recasting of the old verse romances.

A distinct feature – one might say a distinct disadvantage – of medieval romance was that it was written specifically for, and almost wholly about one section of medieval society – the aristocracy. In spite of the so-called open quality of medieval society, Friedrich Heer does admit that the higher aristocracy of Europe, a single 'clan' by the beginning of the twelfth century, were a significant exception:

> The commanding position of the Norman nobility, with its offshoots spread over France, Sicily, and England, was a conspicuous example of the growing tendency towards the formation of a 'closed caste' sharply distinct both from the subordinate peasantry and from the free and unfree inhabitants of the towns. Further, in the twelfth century there were significant advances in the directions of making the aristocracy yet more exclusive.[15]

That medieval romance reflected the lives of this closed caste is indicated by the epithets invariably used to describe it, viz. romance of *chivalry*; romance of *courtly love*; *society* romance. The thought of 'all those who lived in the circles of court or castle was impregnated with the idea of chivalry'[16] writes Huizinga, who adds, later: 'The sentiments of courtly love were current only among the knightly class, and by no means extended to inferior persons.'[17] Huizinga is informative also on the whole concept of courtly love:

> The existence of of upper class whose intellectual and moral notions are enshrined in an *ars amandi* remains a rather exceptional fact in history. In no other epoch did the ideal of civilization amalgamate to such a degree with that of love. Just as scholasticism represents the grand effort of the medieval spirit to unite all philosophic thought in a single centre, so the theory of courtly love in a less elevated sphere, tends to embrace *all that appertains to the noble life*.[18] [my italics]

A. B. Taylor states the matter from a different point of view when he writes that stories of courtly love 'make no appeal to the lower classes of any country'.[19] It is very difficult to view medieval romance, then, as a democratic form of literature, since it was almost the exclusive preserve of the aristocracy.

It may seem startlingly perverse to claim that medieval romance is not true romance at all, and yet there is a great deal of truth in such a claim. The proposition could be put less startlingly, perhaps, by stating that a definition of romance which includes the medieval version needs some qualification. No one states the facts of the case so well or so succinctly as Robert Kellogg, himself a specialist in Middle English literature:

As the word romance is usually employed, the major narratives of Malory, Chaucer, Gottfried, Wolfram, and Chrétien would be called 'medieval romances', and distinguished, as such, from the *chansons de geste*, which are closer to heroic epic in spirit and poetical techniques. But as we have been using the word romance . . . it signifies a fiction composed by an individual author for esthetic ends, as opposed to traditional or historical narrative. Greek romance is romance in this sense. *Parzival* is not; it is mainly traditional, with the author figuring as embellisher and adaptor rather than as creator. No value judgement is implied here. The question is really one of a different approach to authorship. One of the original senses of the word novel is that of 'a new thing'. A traditional story is not 'a new thing'. A created fiction like *Daphnis and Chloe* is new. In Chaucer's *Canterbury Tales* the stories are traditional, and have their sources which can be located in the tradition; but the frame device of the pilgrims is quite novel, going well beyond previous known experiments in framing and dealing creatively with traditional types of character, though not abandoning them. The freer a writer is with his sources, the further he is moving away from the traditional or mythic narrative, and the closer he is coming toward creative or romantic narrative. The Greek romances are not the last word in fictional independence from myth, obviously, but they are free to name their characters, to locate their story in time and space, to vary and diversify the events in their pattern of love, separation, adventure, and reunion. An adaptor of the Perceval story or the Tristan story, is not free. And stories such as these are not the fictional creations of individual authors, but the result of slow accretions and modifications as the *mythos* passed from hand to hand in oral and written tradition.

The so-called medieval romances, then . . . are not romances but elaborate mythic narratives . . . and, as such, they derive their authority – usually quite openly – from tradition.[20]

Nathaniel E. Griffin in an article entitled 'The Definition of

Romance', written in 1923 put the case another way, when he wrote that the 'persistence of authentication – even when hardened into mere convention – is an unerring sign of incomplete romanticization'.[21]

It is important to realise that the author in medieval times would have regarded this reliance on tradition not as a defect but as one of the major excellences of his work. C. S. Lewis points this out clearly in *The Discarded Image*:

> At a conscious level everybody will no doubt agree that literature is a constructive rather than a destructive process; but it might be more difficult to convince people that in the twelfth and thirteenth centuries, more perhaps than at any other time in the history of narrative art, the measure of artistry was the ability not to invent new stories but to build up sequences out of existing ones. The aim was not 'creation' in our sense, but re-creation – the elaboration and transmission of inherited material. it was important to hand on the matter worthily. If you had asked Layamon or Chaucer 'Why do you not make up a brand new story of your own?' I think they might have replied (in effect) 'Surely we are not yet reduced to that'. . . . The originality, which we regard as a sign of wealth might have seemed to them a confession of poverty.[22]

In a later essay, Lewis explains that the 'characteristic activity of the medieval – perhaps especially the Middle English – author is precisely "touching up" something that was already there'.[23]

It is certainly ironic that the very genre which actually supplied the description 'romance' for specific types of narrative should itself be declared illegitimate as romance. Yet it is the modern critic who, having decided that romance must be a truly fictional genre, disqualifies medieval romance from inclusion. One could argue that critics of the seventeenth and eighteenth centuries were much more accurate in describing the medieval narratives as 'Histories'. Arthur Johnston points out,[24] for instance, that those who coined the epithet 'romance' had the seventeenth-century French romance in mind rather than the medieval one. These seventeenth-century French romances are useful in highlighting the so-called defect in the medieval tales. The French romances, though actually claiming always to be based on historical fact, were not: they were truly fictional, with only a thin veneer of historicity, which fooled no one. It is interesting to note that in *The Nature of Narrative*, the modern developmental equivalent of a Greek romance such as the *Aethiopica* is considered to be, not *Parzival* or *Valentine*, but rather *The Grand Cyrus*, a French romance of the seventeenth century.

The history of medieval romances subsequent to the Middle Ages is, in one sense, a history of their reduction to the nursery, i.e. to become the reading matter of children. Arthur Johnston shows in detail[25] how this reduction occurred. More important, perhaps, is his claim that, prior to the year 1760, the medieval romances were not studied in their original form, and certainly never read by the typical reader – child or adult – of the day. It was in the 1600s that the first chapbook[26] versions of the medieval romances were produced. The largest of these would have been twenty four pages long – an indication of the extent to which the originals were pruned – and featured such notables as *Valentine and Orson*, *Guy of Warwick*, *Bevis of Southhampton*, *Don Bellianis*, and *The Seven Champions of Christendom*. One can well imagine that these chapbook versions of the medieval tales had an added touch of 'romance' for people as they read about the age of chivalry which, with its pomp and circumstances, had gone forever. These chapbooks also ensured that the romances were 'democratised' at last. The subject matter remained much the same, but the audience had come to include both the vulgus and the nobility. Towards the end of the seventeenth century, better quality though still abbreviated versions of the medieval stories appeared, and these became the bases of the texts read in the nurseries (and elsewhere, of course), in both the eighteenth and nineteenth centuries. Lawrence Price published a version of *Valentine and Orson* in 1673, and John Shurley abridged and rewrote *Guy of Warwick* in 1681, *Don Bellianis* in 1683, *Bevis of Southhampton* in 1689, and *Amadis of Gaul* in 1702. Greater attention will be paid later to attitudes towards romances generally in the eighteenth century: it is sufficient to note at this point, however, that all serious thinkers in the seventeenth and early eighteenth centuries were very decidedly opposed to medieval romances, the product of a 'period of darkness and superstition'.[27] The writer of a medieval romance was generally considered to have had his judgement in abeyance 'otherwise he would have seen that his stories were full of impossibilities, that "blows which cleave a man in two", were not made any more credible by the invention of a magic sword'.[28] When one considers this attitude, as well as other circumstances, it is extremely difficult to see in what way medieval romance could have influenced the development of the English novel. One can of course argue that all the great writers of the seventeenth and eighteenth centuries were nurtured on tales such as *Valentine and Orson* and *Guy of Warwick*, and must, therefore, have been influenced by them.[29] This is undoubtedly true; indeed one could add that these romances played a major role in fertilising and developing the childhood imaginations of authors such as Richardson and Fielding. But how does one evaluate the literary influences of childhood on the adult author? One can well imagine, for instance, the difficulty in trying to ascertain the influence of the *Wizard* or *Hotspur*, or, perhaps, even the writings of Enid Blyton, on some contemporary British authors.

The object of the discussion above has not been to show the total irrelevance of medieval romance as an influence on the development of English fiction generally and on the novel in particular. The teleological bias inherent in the majority of studies of medieval romance has simply diverted attention from the true significance of medieval romance in the history of English fiction. However alien its origins, medieval romance in England developed a native tradition of narrative, and the significance of such a tradition cannot be exaggerated. It may not have been the most fruitful and influential of traditions, but it did exist and its development can be clearly traced. After, say, the year 1250 came the reworking of old themes; later, prose versions of the verse narratives; and, later again, the chapbook versions; and, finally, the abbreviated 'quality' (relative to the chapbooks, that is) versions. The significance of medieval romance lies not only in the creation of a narrative tradition; it obviously fostered first a listening, then a reading tradition in England. One wonders, for instance, what sort of foothold Greek romances and Spanish picaresque would have gained in England, if the ground had not been prepared for them by medieval romance. Medieval romance can, of course, be regarded as a major influence on the development of the novel – that is, if one regards reaction to romance rather than any development from it, as an influence. *Don Quixote,* regarded as one of the most significant works in the history of modern fiction, English and other, is an anti-romance or, perhaps, more accurately, a parody of the medieval romances. Spanish picaresque, too, can be regarded as anti-romance, though in a somewhat different way to *Don Quixote*. It is important to note, here, that with *Don Quixote* the wheel of modern fiction had turned to the same extent as had the

ancient, when it ceased: the *Satyricon* stands in the same relation
to the Greek, as *Don Quixote* does to the medieval romances.
An examination of these two parodies, ancient and modern, is
intriguing for the revealing light it throws on the distinctions
between the ancient and medieval romance, simply because Petronius' method would not have suited Cervantes, or vice versa. *Don
Quixote* is a realistic work, but realistic in a specific way, viz. the
hero is a madman – and what are the bounds of realism in such a
work if the author so wishes? It is fair to suggest, therefore, that
in *Don Quixote* the crazy world of medieval romance is most aptly
demonstrated by a 'crazy' man. The world of Greek romance could
hardly, on the other hand be described as 'crazy'. (Indeed the
modern reader would identify much more quickly and easily with
the world of Greek, rather than that of medieval romance.)
Consequently, Petronius had no need to go to such lengths as
Cervantes – a relatively simple realistic story, framed in a particular
way, suited his purpose admirably.

This discussion can be terminated by restating what seems to be
the most obvious fact of all about medieval romance, viz. that it
had little or nothing to offer narrative which had not already been
created in ancient times. One must agree with the writer in *The
Cambridge English History of Literature* when he writes that it is
'scarcely a paradox to say that the Middle Ages have influenced
modern literature more strongly through their architecture than
through their poems'.[30]

3
Pre-Eighteenth-Century Romance

ELIZABETHAN ROMANCE

The ancient Greek romances were rediscovered in sixteenth-century Europe and eventually translated into the vernacular of most countries. Their introduction into England during the second half of the century, played a major part in the resuscitation of a perfectly moribund fiction. The first romance to be translated into English was the *Aethiopica* of Heliodorus, in 1569, and it is hardly coincidental that the stirrings of native creativity began in the following decade.[1] The *Aethiopica* was an immensely popular work, appearing in ten editions during the remainder of the sixteenth century: in 1572–3 a stage play based on the *Aethiopica*, and entitled *Theagenes and Chariclea*, was performed in London. Longus' *Daphnis and Chloe* was translated into English in 1587, and *Clitopho and Leucippe* in 1597. One of the first English beneficiaries of Greek romance was, it seems, John Lyly. The influence of ancient romance on *Euphues* (1578), was an indirect one, however, as Samuel Wolff points out. The plot of *Euphues* is, Wolff claims,[2] based on a story in the *Decameron* called 'Titus and Gissippus'.[3] 'Titus and Gissippus' is, in turn, obviously based on a lost Greek romance. Although Wolff's arguments are based on conjecture as well as proof, there is little reason to doubt their validity. The style of *Euphues* seems to have very much in common with that of Greek romance, but it would be unwise to presume that Euphuism originated in ancient fiction, in spite of the similarity between passages in *Euphues*, and *Clitopho and Leucippe*. Late Greek rhetoric had been studied widely throughout the Renaissance, and Lyly, one of the new breed of university men, would undoubtedly have come into contact with it. He would have inherited the stock of 'favorite situations' and have been trained to handle these in the conventional manner. Someone once suggested, quite aptly, that the subtitle of *Euphues* could be rephrased in modern parlance as

'How to be Clever': this would be an apt subtitle for any of the sophistic Greek romances, also. The diffusion of Greek rhetoric during the Renaissance is important in showing why Greek romance, with its embodiment of the tenets of late Greek rhetoric in fiction, was so attractive to the educated author of sixteenth-century Europe. While acknowledging that Lyly was influenced by Greek romance in *Euphues*, it should be pointed out, also, that the work differs from ancient fiction in one major respect. Greek romances, as Wolff points out, 'give to plot – the mere happening of things – a place much more important than they give to character'.[4] In ancient times, as we saw, the sophists were willing to bear with the 'action' – the *sine qua non* of romance as they saw it – for the opportunities it offered for the display of rhetorical versatility. Lyly, however, refused to acknowledge the absolute necessity for action and in doing so transformed Greek romance. 'Lyly's interest in the movement of the mind suffering under the onslaught of experience, was so great', says Walter Davis, 'that he consistently subordinated narration to dialogue or soliloquy; at times, it might be more accurate to say, he buried narrative beneath dialogue'.[5] *Euphues* could, therefore, be regarded as a natural development from Greek romance, a development stunted in ancient times because of the demise of the genre.

In the case of Sir Philip Sidney's *Arcadia*, the major work of prose fiction in the Elizabethan era, there is little need for conjecture about the influence of Greek romance. 'The very opening of the *Arcadia* at once strikes the note of Greek romance',[6] says Wolff. Wolff, indeed, has done such systematic and thorough work in demonstrating the extent of Sidney's indebtedness to Greek romance, that there is little of value one can add to his research. Over sixty pages of reference and quotation, Wolff shows, for example, how the *Arcadia* partakes of 'the grandiose Heliodorean framework';[7] how more than ten specific incidents in the *Aethiopica* reappear in Sidney's work;[8] and how the *Arcadia* utilizes the general 'theatricality'[9] of the *Aethiopica*, and even its 'pathetic optics'.[10] Among the characters of the *Arcadia* are a Clitophon, a Leucippe, and a Clinias. While the *Aethiopica* obviously exerted the greatest influence on Sidney, other aspects of the *Arcadia* may have been derived from the Greek romances generally. Among these can be numbered the stock motifs, *ecphraseis*, and the widespread use of Providence, Fortune, and oracles.

Because of the innumerable particular and general parallels

between the *Arcadia* and Greek romances, Sidney's romance could be mistakenly regarded as a mere literary montage. Wolff is quick to head off any such suggestion, however, emphasising Sidney's originality at all times, even to the extent of inventing a new plot. At the end of his discussion of the *Arcadia*, Wolff states exactly what Sidney's accomplishment was: he has learned, he says, 'the very accent of Greek Romance . . . has deliberately written Greek Romance in English . . . has domesticated the *genre*'.[11]

Robert Greene, the most prolific author of fiction in the Elizabethan era, serves as a magnificent foil for Sir Philip Sidney, and adequately demonstrates the pitfalls which he avoided in the *Arcadia*. Each of Greene's works is a *mélange* of a kind: he simply plundered the Greek romances, for example, in order to supply himself with materials for fiction. As in the case of Lyly, Greene was seemingly led to the Greek romances via Boccaccio. Two tales in *Perimedes the Blacksmith* (1588), are, as Wolff shows,[12] based on two stories in the *Decameron*, stories which bear all the hallmarks of Greek romance. An intriguing aspect of Greene's borrowing is that he chose from Boccaccio 'only Greek Romance material'[13] which he used exactly as he found it. The explanation Wolff offers for Greene's choice of materials is that there was a 'distinct affinity'[14] between his talent and that of Greek romance generally. The fruits of Wolff's labour in tracing Greene's indebtedness to the Greek romance are astonishing. He can demonstrate where whole passages in the original Greek texts have simply been translated and used verbatim by Greene: numerous other passages are clearly proved to be paraphrasings of the originals. Wolff also shows innumerable incidents, scattered over thousands of pages of the Greek texts, which have been appropriated by Greene for his own works. The Greeks also – almost inevitably – supplied the general framework and narrative techniques for most of Greene's fiction. If the affinity between him and the Greek romances generally was a 'distinct' one, the affinity between Greene and Achilles Tatius was even greater still. One wonders, indeed, if it was this affinity or rather slavish imitation which caused Greene to resemble Achilles Tatius even in the worst aspects of the Greek's work. Greene never lets an opportunity for 'speechifying' go by, and the influence of Fortune in his works surpasses its influence in even *Clitopho and Leucippe*. *Arbastos Morando, Philomela, Pandosto*, and *Menaphon*, are the works of Greene in which the influence of Greek romance is most obvious. In spite of being the Elizabethan author who made most use of the Greek romances, Greene seems to have learnt little from his experiences, and had little to teach his contemporaries either, who would have been better advised to return to the originals for any inspiration. Samuel Wolff sums up Greene's failure as follows:

> Unlike Sidney, Greene never learnt to invent romances of his own . . . the nearest he can come to Greek Romance is in some of its faults – its *tychomania*, its general dearth of character, its distorted 'psychology', its labored antitheses. When he attempts the sustained elaborate oracle-guided plot of Heliodorus, he fails even with the 'Arcadia' before him as a model. When he attempts the Heliodorean setting, he fails again. The best he can do with Longus is to take over his *motifs* directly; the best he can do with Achilles Tatius is to transcribe almost verbatim his adventitious ornament.[15]

Two other authors of fiction in the Elizabethan era who came under the influence of Greek romance were Barnaby Riche, an ex-soldier, and William Warner, a London attorney. In 1581 *Riche his Farewell to Militarie Profession* appeared, and four of the tales in the book are essentially Greek romances, and invariably regarded as the first appearance of true Greek romance in England. Warner continued the trend when, in 1584, he published *Pan his Syrinx*, another full-blown Greek romance. Neither Riche nor Warner was to repeat the experiment but both were pioneers who showed what might be done in the genre, in English.

The influence of Greek romance on Thomas Lodge was a minor one. His first work, *Forbonius and Prisceria*, published in 1584, was dedicated to Philip Sidney and resembles the *Arcadia* in its use of the pastoral setting inherited from Longus. This pastoral setting was retained by Lodge in his later works. It is of interest, also, that Lodge makes the heroine of his first romance, Prisceria, a granddaughter of Theagenes and Chariclea. Walter Davis is of the opinion that Greek romance 'did infuse some of its character'[16] into Lodge's final work, *A Margarite of America*, published in 1596. It is extremely difficult, however, to demonstrate such 'character'. The last work to be written in the sixteenth century which is undeniably influenced by Greek romance is Emmanuel Ford's *Ornatus and Artesia* (1598?). This work has all the ingredients of the typical Greek romance, love at first sight, pirates, attempted rape, shipwreck, separation of hero and heroine, and the eventual happy reunion: the style of *Ornatus and Artesia* is also reminiscent of the ancient romances, but whether derived from them or not, is a moot point.

Whatever else one may say about Elizabethan fiction, it can be stated without qualification that it set a standard of achievement which was not to be reached again for almost one hundred years. The influence of the Greek romances can be seen at its best in a work such as the *Arcadia*, at its worst in the works of Robert Greene. Ancient fiction contributed much to plot structures and to what Margaret Schlauch calls 'a methodology for producing heightened intricacy in the plot'.[17] There were, of course, qualities inherent in the Greek romances which appealed to both Elizabethan writer and reader. Foremost among these were the displays of rhetorical versatility in the Greeks – a type of ancient Euphuism – which suggested to the Elizabethans how they too might display their cleverness. The opportunities, in fiction, for such display were numerous, and the Elizabethans followed the Greeks in ranging from elaborate pictorial settings, to discussions of the intricacies of love and its effect on the minds of heroes and heroines. The Elizabethans also found the concept of Fortune, as depicted by the Greeks, intriguing. Walter Davis points out that 'Fortune' in the Greek romances, 'is not adequately expressed by the medieval emblem of Fortune's wheel, with its socio-economic emphasis on rise and fall in place, but is rather a vision of man fighting for survival in a hostile universe'.[18] This vision of man struggling for survival in a hostile universe was to become the philosophy of life, almost, of the Jacobean era. Such a view was very obviously coming to the fore in the later Elizabethan era, aided and abetted, perhaps, by the Greek romances and their English imitations. In the Elizabethan era, one can still point to the mitigation of a happy ending, however. Charlotte Morgan explains the popularity of the Greek romances in the Elizabethan era thus:

> Their vogue is to be explained on the ground that they satisfied the taste of the time for the theatrical, the complex, the marvellous, the sentimental, and, to a certain extent, for the morbid. They were the product of a sophisticated and decadent civilization, but they possessed the superficial effectiveness, the fatalism, and the word painting with which to capture the fancy of the imaginative, sensation-loving Elizabethans. And at the same time they were characterized by an over-refinement and unreality

which appealed strongly to European society at the close of the Renaissance, when men were once more looking backward rather than forward, for refinement rather than strength, and seeking to escape from, rather than to cope with, the hard facts of reality.[19]

The greater part of the seventeenth century was one of the most barren periods in the history of English fiction. So barren, indeed, was this period that the historian of fiction might well argue that the thread of English fiction was cut before it had stretched very far. The reasons for this sterility are not hard to come by. The reading public of the seventeenth century was, as Philip Henderson observes, 'split up, more than ever before or since, into sharply defined and mutually antagonistic sections, each with its particular prejudice . . .'[20] The most influential of these 'mutually antagonistic sections' was undoubtedly that of the puritans. They objected to drama as well as fiction, and discouraged the middle classes from reading fiction: one could say, with some qualification, that the puritans succeeded in their aims. Another force was at work, also, however, militating against fiction: the scientific rationalists with their devotion to factual observation and analysis, were coming to the fore. This movement undermined fiction because the intelligentsia could no longer find satisfaction in dream worlds and fairy tales. During the greater part of the seventeenth century, the major developments in fiction were taking place outside England, and the history of fiction in England in this period is the history of translation and slavish imitation of foreign sources. If one accepts the concept of the broken thread of English fiction, then the tradition of fiction, and, indeed, that of Greek romance, must be traced through France whence fresh impetus and a new start was given to fiction in England.

FRENCH ROMANCE OF THE SIXTEENTH AND SEVENTEENTH CENTURIES

In the sixteenth century, prose fiction in France followed much the same pattern as in England. The translations of the Greek romances into French began much earlier than translations into English, however. The French translation of *Clitopho and Leucippe* appeared as early as 1545, the *Aethiopica* in the following year, and *Daphnis*

and Chloe in 1559. The net result of these translations was a flood
of imitation-Greek romances in French during the second half of
the sixteenth century. This flood, as George Saintsbury points
out,[21] reaches its peak in the last decade of the century. The
authors of these romances were, as Saintsbury remarks, 'nearly as
numerous as their titles, but the chief were a Sieur de Nervese . . .
and a Sieur des Escuteaux'.[22] It was not until twelve years after
the publication of *Daphnis and Chloe*, that any attempt was made
at an imitation: this was Belleforest's *La Pyrénée et Pastorale Amoreuse.*
A more original work along the lines of Longus' work appeared in
1585, entitled '*Les Bergeries de Juliette*, de l'invention d'Ollenix du
Mont Sacré',[23] written by Nicolas de Montreaux. And in 1593,
another pastoral work appeared, the *Philocalie* by Du Croset.

The history of fiction in seventeenth-century France is mostly a
history of a constant interrelationship between romances and a
particular type of social circle. Madame de Rambouillet was the
first to originate such a circle in 1608. Madame de Rambouillet was
an Italian by birth, entering the French court at the turn of the
century as the wife of the Marquis de Rambouillet. A refined and
talented young woman, she found the French court, with its
coarseness, licentiousness, and intrigue, quite abhorrent. By the
year 1608, she had retired to a dwelling designed by herself, and
began to exercise her remarkable talents in an attempt to reform
the taste of French society. Her magnificent home, the Hôtel de
Rambouillet, was soon the meeting-place of the most distinguished
persons of the day. Almost contemporary with the establishment
of the Hôtel de Rambouillet, there appeared *Astrée*, a pastoral
romance by Honoré d'Urfé. The first two books of *Astrée* were
published in 1610, and followed the pattern established by *Daphnis
and Chloe*, and continued in England by the *Arcadia*. The *Astrée*,
though hardly as artistic a creation as the *Arcadia*, was, nonetheless,
a significant improvement on previous pastoral romances in France,
and an important development in the history of French fiction.
The work contained the inevitable lovers bowing to adverse
fortune, heroic adventures, use of oracles and magnificent displays
of rhetoric. The work was an immediate and spectacular success,
and seemingly tailor-made for the people who were gathering in
the Hôtel de Rambouillet. They appreciated particularly its cultured
polish, its refinement, and its observance of all the necessary
proprieties. *Astrée*, indeed, seemed to portray quite accurately the
very type of society which the Marquise de Rambouillet hoped to

bring to pass in France. Skill in discussion, sparkle in the give-and-take of repartee was an end in itself at the Hôtel de Rambouillet, and anything, no matter how trivial, served as a basis for conversational exercise. A great deal of attention was also devoted to the passing of courtly compliment and to the devious process of formal lovemaking. *Astrée* was not the product of the Hôtel, yet, while it did not demonstrate the art of repartee to any great extent, did show skill in discussion, did feature conversation prominently, and did have love as the basis of the whole story. *Astrée* initiated a relationship between romance and social circles which lasted for almost half a century. Later exponents of the genre were either members of such circles, or wrote with them specifically in mind. These romances were, in turn, avidly read, dissected, and discussed in the *salons*, where they emphasised and encouraged tendencies already present. In the first twenty years of its existence, the Hôtel de Rambouillet, as well as the innumerable imitations which grew up all over France, did much to purify the French language, and refine the manners of the age. Around the year 1630, however, a spirit of pedantry and affectation had crept into the *salons*, and any kind of naturalness was soon excluded.

In 1621, a French-born Scot named John Barclay wrote a romance entitled *Argenis*, in the Longus, Sidney, d'Urfé tradition. *Argenis* was almost as popular as *Astrée*, parts of which were still appearing, and continued to, until 1627. In 1632 came a turning-point in French romance, with the publication of *Polexandre* by Marin Le Roy de Gomberville. John Dunlop[24] remarks on the 'striking resemblance' between *Polexandre* and a typical Greek romance: 'the disposition of incidents is similar', he writes, and 'as in the Greek romance, the events, in a great measure, arise from adventures with pirates; and the events are chiefly laid at sea or in small islands, or places on the sea coast'.[25] The exciting force of the story is provided by Polexandre himself, when, like so many heroes in Greek romance, he falls in love with the incomparably beautiful heroine merely on seeing her portrait. In *Polexandre*, Gomberville discarded the pastoral setting almost entirely, and instead substituted pseudo-historical events in remote times and nations, plus interminable wanderings: the species he initiated in France became known as 'heroic romance'.

The actual order of the chief 'heroic' authors, and their romances is as follows: Gomberville, *Polexandre* 1632; *Citherée*, 1640–2. La Calprenède, *Cassandra*, 1642; *Cleopatre*, 1648; *Faramond*, 1662.

Georges and Madeleine de Scudéry, *Ibrahim*, 1641; *Artamene*, 1649; *Clélie*, 1656; *Almahide*, 1660. Because of their seemingly interminable quality these romances came to be known as *romans à longue haleine* – 'longwinded romances'. The term 'heroic' as applied to the French romances could lead to some confusion, suggesting, as it does, that the seventeenth-century version is quite distinct from, say, the Greek. John Dunlop offers the following explanation for the use of the term:

> In romance of chivalry, love though a solemn and serious passion, is subordinate to heroic achievement. A knight seems chiefly to have loved his mistress, because he obtained her by some warlike exploit; she formed an excuse for engaging in perilous adventures, and he mourned her loss, as it was attended with that of his dearer idol – honour. In the heroic romance, on the other hand, love seems the ruling passion, and military exploits are chiefly performed for the sake of a mistress: glory is the spring of one species of composition, and love of the other . . .[26]

If Dunlop is correct, then medieval romance should be more properly entitled 'heroic', and a more accurate term for the seventeenth-century French version would be 'erotic' or 'love' romance. It is clear, too, from what Dunlop says, that there is no significant difference between Greek and seventeenth-century French romance – at least insofar as love is the spring of both.

Madeleine de Scudéry, one of the most popular of the writers of heroic romance, invariably thought of herself as a follower of Heliodorus and of Greek romance generally. In the preface to her first work, *Ibrahim*, she states her position quite clearly:

> Whereas we cannot be knowing but of that which others do teach us, and that it is for him that comes after, to follow them who precede him, I have believed, that for laying the groundwork of this work we are to consult with the Grecians, who have been our first Masters, pursue the course which they have held, and labour in imitating them to arrive at the same end, which those great men propounded to themselves. I have seen in those famous *Romanzes* of Antiquity, that in imitation of the Epique Poem there is a principal action whereunto all the rest, which reign over all the work, are fastened, and which makes them

that they are not employed, but for the conducting of it to its perfection. The action in Homers *Iliades* is the destruction of Troy; in his *Odysseas* the return of Ulysses to Ithaca; in Virgil the death of Turnus . . . and to pass from the Poem to the *Romanze*, which is my principal object, in Heliodorus the marriage of *Theagines* and Cariclia.[27]

De Scudéry later explains why she intends to make use of shipwrecks in her romances – because, as she says, 'I approve of them in the works of others, and make use of them in mine; I know likewise, that the sea is the scene most proper to make great changes in, and that some have named it the Theatre of Inconstancy'.[28] There is hardly any need to speculate on what works de Scudéry had in mind. Any possible objections to the rank of Scudéry's hero or heroine are headed off by reference to the fact that 'Theogines [sic] and Charicla [sic] are but simple Citizens'.[29] De Scudéry also expresses, in the preface, her intention of using 'ornament' in *Ibrahim*, because those romances are simply 'irksome', she says, which 'do nothing but heap adventure upon adventure, without ornament, and without stirring up passions by the artifices of Rhetorique . . .'[30] Here again, the tradition is clear. In the preface to *Cyrus*, also, de Scudéry makes it clear that Heliodorus is her model. La Calprenède, too, consciously modelled his romances on those of Heliodorus. It is hardly extravagant to say that the writers of heroic romance in seventeenth-century France regarded Heliodorus in much the same way as playwrights regarded Seneca.

Heroic romance does, as one would imagine, differ from the Greek in several ways. The most obvious difference is the change in the handling of the theme of love. Love at first sight is still predominant, with the hero 'falling' first, followed a short time later by the heroine. The love itself burns with as bright as flame as in Greek times, but – and this is the significant difference – it is now completely circumscribed by an elaborate code of behaviour, composed of a mixture of Platonism and *préciosité*, a code prominent in the love affairs of the *salons* in seventeenth-century France. The new heroines are, like their Greek counterparts, the most beautiful creatures on earth, as well as possessing qualities such as courage and loyalty. But they differ from the Charicleas and Leucippes in being conscious masters of polite conversation, as well as experts in the rules of etiquette governing their loves. The heroic romance,

in fact, legislates a strict code of behaviour for all aspects of life
from the battlefield to the boudoir. 'No matter what the emergency',
writes Charlotte Morgan, 'you may depend upon the hero to show
a judgement "natural and proper", and the heroine never to sin
against the social code. The inculcation of virtue and propriety
was, in these French romances . . . a primary object with the
authors.'[31] Another major innovation in the French romances was
the introduction of 'duty'. In Greek romance there was always, of
course, an implicit duty – the complete and utter allegiance of each
lover to the other. The 'heroic' concept of duty, explicitly stated
over and over again, was duty to one's parents and duty to one's
country. Nor does any hero or heroine question the justice of such
allegiance: they all accept, almost as a fact of life, that no matter
how passionate or overwhelming their love might be, it is subject
to the higher demands of duty. Indeed duty is of such importance
in the heroic romances that each could aptly be subtitled *Love and
Duty Reconciled*, since this is the one and only way in which a
happy ending can be brought about. If the heroine's father objects
to her lover, or if the hero is an enemy of her country, she knows
and accepts that there is only one course open to her – the dutiful
one. Luckily, the Gordian knot is invariably cut and love and duty
are, at last, reconciled.

Chastity, too, because of the complex rules of etiquette, takes on
a new complexion. Though the heroine of Greek romance almost
invariably ends up with her chastity preserved, there is always at
least the possibility that she might succumb to an 'honourable'
seducer. Indeed, Chaereas, in an exceptional situation, does succumb to the honourable Dionysius in *Chaereas and Callirhoe*. There
is, therefore, a certain element of suspense dependent on the
chastity of the Greek heroine. In the seventeenth century, the code
of conduct surrounding chastity in heroic romance is such as to
put the virtue almost beyond the control of the individual, and
reduce it to a completely artificial concept.

There are other, incidental features of heroic romance which
are not to be found in the Greek. Great emphasis is placed on the
single combat in heroic romance, as a means of settling arguments:
tournaments, too, are regularly featured, in which jousting matches
decide who is the most beautiful of ladies.

The relationship between heroic and Greek romance can, perhaps, be best illustrated by outlining the plot of a typical seventeenth-century French romance. As in all romances, hero and

heroine fall madly in love with one another. He is noble and extremely courageous, she is noble, chaste and an exemplary young lady. The romance details their numerous adventures from the time they meet until their eventual marriage and happy life thereafter. The couple are invariably prevented from marrying by one, or several reasons – parental opposition, disparity in rank, the threat of incest, the machinations of villains and the intrigues of rivals. Natural disasters such as shipwreck, as of old, contrive to keep the lovers apart, also. The romancers of the seventeenth century were sufficiently ingenious to hit upon a 'land equivalent' of the shipwreck, viz. earthquake. Eventually, all difficulties are miraculously ironed out when true parentage is discovered, or the villains reform, or characters long dead solve a seemingly insoluble problem by 'returning to life'. The incidentals, too, of the typical heroic romance bear all the hallmarks of the Greek; that is if 'incidental' can be applied to the numerous stories told of their own adventures by the minor characters, some of which extend to a greater length than the main tale. Oracles, expositions, and Fortune (though less influential than in Greek romance) all play roles in heroic romance also.

George Saintsbury's remark about heroic romance – 'produced by wiseacres for wiseacres'[32] – inevitably reminds one of the suggested subtitle for *Euphues* – 'How to be Clever'. And there is an obvious similarity in the narrative style of Greek romance, *Euphues*, and heroic romance. This similarity may be due less to the influence of the Greek romances than to the widespread diffusion of late Greek rhetoric in the latter half of the sixteenth, and early seventeenth centuries. The Hôtel de Rambouillet, for instance, one of whose professed major aims was the purification of the French language, would have eagerly grasped the 'pure' model of Greek rhetoric. The following extract, from George Saintsbury's *History of the French Novel*, is remarkable not so much for its accurate depiction of some of the peculiarities of narrative style in heroic romance, as for the perfect applicability of the same comments to Greek romance:

> When things in general are 'on the edge of a razor' and one is a tried and skillful soldier, one does not, except on the stage, pause to address the unjust Gods, and inquire whether they have consented to the destruction of the most beautiful princess in the world; discuss with one's friends the reduction into cinders of the adorable Mandane [in *Artamene*], and further enquire,

without the slightest chance of answer, 'Alas! unjust Rival! hast thou not thought of thy own preservation rather than of hers? . . . Of *mere* talk there is enough and immensely to spare; but it is practically never real dialogue, still less real conversation. It is harangue, narrative, soliloquy, what you will, in the less lively theatrical forms of speech watered out in prose . . . But it is never real personal talk . . .'[33]

The French romancers eagerly seized on the Greek *ecphrasis*. Romance after romance teems with grandiose set descriptions of gardens, armour, battles, and – an addition – of furnished apartments.

The 'grandiose Heliodorean framework' is always obvious in the heroic romances. If anything, the framework of the French romances was more grandioise and much more intricate. And when one considers that a typical heroic romance was up to five times the length of, say, the *Aethiopica*, one has some appreciation of the extent and degree of the intricacies involved. A brief outline of one of the heroic romances – *Clelia* – with most of the intricacies unravelled, and the majority of the minor ones omitted, will illustrate some of the characteristics of the genre. Porsenna, an Italian king, sends his son to Africa for safekeeping. A storm sinks the ship carrying the young boy, but he floats ashore in his cradle, where he is found by a Roman patrician whose name is Clelius. The boy is called Aronces and reared by Clelius, whose wife later gives birth to a baby girl who is named Clelia. Aronces eventually falls in love with Clelia, and she with him. Clelius objects to a liaison between his daughter and a nobody, preferring, instead, the suit of Horatius, a man equal in rank to himself. Clelia is forbidden even to see Aronces. Eventually, Aronces' true parentage is discovered and Clelius agrees to the marriage of his daughter with the prince. The happy couple are about to be married when an earthquake occurs, separating them. Horatius takes advantage of the disaster to carry off Clelia, and Aronces goes in search of her. Events have been meanwhile conspiring to create a more ominous separation between the two lovers. Porsenna has become an ally of Tarquin, bitter enemy of Rome, and therefore of Clelius. Aronces is in a quandary: his duty to his father tells him he must fight on his side, while his love for Clelia demands that he fight on the side of her father, or at *least* not fight against him. Both parents now oppose the marriage of Aronces and Clelia. Eventually,

Aronces wins Clelius over by his many and magnificent feats of valour, while Clelia has had an opportunity to winning Porsenna over by her 'valour', viz. her feminine charm. Tarquin is, eventually, defeated, and the Romans conclude a separate peace treaty with Porsenna: the way is, at last, clear once more for Aronces and Clelia to marry, and they are successful on this, their second attempt. The tale had in fact opened *in medias res* with the first marriage ceremony. This bare outline encompasses about one-third of *Clelia*. Following the lead of the Greek romancers, de Scudéry and her contemporaries wove numerous other histories of other pairs of lovers into the text. One of the most interesting of these in *Clelia* is the story of Brutus and Lucretia, which is, essentially, a reflection of the main plot, with variations. Brutus and Lucretia love one another passionately, but Lucretia, at the command of her father, marries Collatine. Her duty to her new husband ensures that she is faithful to him, though she is obviously unhappy. Sextus, son of Tarquin rapes her, and she kills herself rather than survive this infamous blot on her honour. Tarquin himself, in the course of the main plot, had attempted to seduce Clelia when she became a prisoner of his, but the attempt failed. The threat of incest also rears its head in the tale, when Clelia's brother, presumed drowned, falls violently in love with her.

One of the latest of the heroic romances, *Faramond*, written in 1662 is a veritable see-saw battle between love and duty all through: no sooner is one conflict resolved but another takes its place. The reader wonders, indeed, how the final conflict can possibly be resolved when the heroine's father, king of the Cimbres, calls her to him on his deathbed, and bids[34] her avenge the death of her brother, killed by Faramond. Her father's injunction places the heroine, Rosemonde, in an impossible position, since she and Faramond are passionately in love with each other. Love and duty are miraculously reconciled when the 'brother' of Rosemonde, killed by Faramond, is discovered not to have been a blood-brother at all. Her true brother is found, meanwhile, to be alive and well. Rosemonde is thus no longer bound by duty to seek the death of Faramond, and marries him.

HEROIC ROMANCE IN ENGLAND

The history of fiction in England during the first half of the seventeenth century presents a completely different picture to that in France. English fiction had, in effect, almost reverted to the moribundity from which it had been only lately rescued. The popularity of the *Arcadia* is some indication of the sterility affecting English fiction: between 1600 and 1642, no less than nine editions had appeared. And Sidney's work had even been added to, first in 1621, and later, in 1627, when a further book was added by Richard Beling. But Charlotte Morgan is correct when she states[3] that the *Arcadia*, in spite of its popularity, was a negligible influence on later English fiction. The dominant influence was, in fact, the French heroic romances.

As early as 1625, forces had been at work preparing the way for the reception of French heroic romance in England. In that year Charles I had married a sixteen-year old French princess named Henrietta Maria. From early childhood, Henrietta Maria's inclination had been towards the fine arts, and, though hardly submitted directly to the influence of the Hôtel de Rambouillet, she had almost certainly grown up in sympathy with much of its significance, and was well acquainted with its tenets. Soon after Henrietta's marriage to Charles, a strong current of French influence passed into England, affecting – at first at any rate – the circles of society surrounding the Royal court. There was certainly an attempt to regulate the English way of life according to the principles and practices of Madame de Rambouillet. All the paraphernalia of the *précieuses* came to England, too, of course, not least the romances. The fervid English students of the sacred French texts of heroic romance, read, as E. A. Baker remarks, 'not only for amusement but also for edification, and trained themselves to think and feel and speak and behave according to the best French standards of breeding'.[36] Coteries were established in England in imitation, as far as possible, of the Hôtel de Rambouillet. Mrs Katharine Philips – known as 'The Matchless Orinda' – is an excellent example of such a coterie leader: the Duchess of Newcastle was another, though quite different leader. Of her Pepys wrote: 'The whole story of this lady is a romance and all she does is romantic'.[37] The 'Matchless Orinda' was a leader of a bourgeois *salon* all of whose members were given fictitious names, taken from the French romances. The *salon* aimed at encouraging refined friendships between the sexes and aspirations to literary excellence.

During the exile of the English court in France, the writing of heroic romance was at its peak. Nor did the absence of the court from England affect the vogue of the romances there. The Royalist families – who would be quite unaffected, anyway, by the anti-fiction propaganda of the Puritans – regarded the French romances as a kind of repository of aristocratic values. These values they intended to uphold, even in the midst of defeat. One of the last acts of Charles I, prior to his execution, was to present the Earl of Lindsey with a copy of *Cassandra*, the heroic romance written by La Calprenède.

The heroic romances were read in England first in the original French, by a court circle which flaunted its ability to read and speak French fluently. The English translations of the French works came much later. *Ibrahim* and *Cassandra* were translated in 1652, *Le Grand Cyrus* in 1653, *Cleopatra* in 1654, *Clelia* in 1659, and *Faramond* in 1662. Soon, the inevitable imitations began to emerge, the first appearing in 1653, written by 'a person of honour', and entitled *Cloria and Narcissus, or the Royal Romance*. In 1659 another royal romance was published, entitled *Panthalia*, written in all probability by Richard Braithwaite. In 1660 George Mackenzie, a law student, had his romance *Aretina* published, and four years later John Bulteel's *Birinthia* appeared. *Pandion and Amphigenia* by John Crowne was published in 1665. Two other romances, interesting for a variation they introduced into the conventional heroic romance, were *Bentivolio and Urania* written by The Reverend Nathaniel Ingelo, DD, and the other, *Theodora and Didymus* (1687), written by the eminent physicist Robert Boyle. Both works were what could be called Christian heroic romances. Ingelo's romance is intended as a religious allegory, while Boyle's work is based on the 'true story' of Theodora and Didymus, which the author intends to 'rescue from more unskilful hands than even mine, a story that abundantly deserv'd to be well told'.[38] Based as it is on seeming fact, the author is prevented from ending his romance happily – both hero and heroine are martyred – thus, it would seem, eliminating the most obvious of all the hallmarks of romance. But this is the first of the 'Divine Romances', where the happy ending occurs not in this life but in the next: and it is on the next life that Boyle places the emphasis.

One of the most popular of all the native English romances was *Parthenissa* written by Roger Boyle, Lord Broghill (later Earl of Orrery). Boyle – a brother of Robert Boyle, the physicist – issued the first three parts of *Parthenissa* in 1654, and other parts at intervals thereafter: the six collected volumes of the romance were published in 1676. *Parthenissa* is of particular interest since it is the English work which comes nearest to the French romances in length, number of characters, or complexity. The tale was never completed by Boyle, though this hardly matters much, since all the clues that one expects of heroic, and, indeed, Greek romance, are present. When the 1676 edition finishes, Parthenissa is 'dead', having committed suicide by poison to prevent being raped by one of her many lovers, Arsaces. The hero, Artabanes, is fully intent on joining her in death, but fails to fall correctly on his sword, and lives. When we first meet him, at the opening of the work, he is in Hierapolis to consult the oracle of Venus. The oracle, when it speaks to Artabanes, foretells the 'resurrection' of Parthenissa as follows:

> *From Parthenissa's Ashes I will raise*
> *A Phoenix in whose Flames thou shalt be blest*
> *—: Wait then about this Temple a few Days*
> *And all thy Torment shall be crowned with Rest*[39]

In typical romance fashion, Artabanes, of course, fails to see the significance of the oracle, that it is a 'Juliet'-type potion, so beloved of the Greek romances, that Parthenissa has drunk.

The love-versus-duty theme appears, as might be expected, in *Parthenissa*, but the English version is not quite the same as the French. Artabanes, violently in love with Parthenissa and she with him, is ordered by his father to begin courting the princess Zephalinda with a view to marrying her. 'Madam', says Artabanes to Parthenissa, 'that my father is resolved to be obeyed is not more certain than that I am determin'd the contrary, for in this case obedience is a crime . . .' (l,iii,68). The true hero of heroic romance should never even think such thoughts, let alone express them. At any rate, Artabanes effects a reconciliation between love and duty by the simple method of cheating his father into believing that the chosen Zephalinda will refuse to have him.

It can be stated, with very little qualification, that *Parthenissa* reads almost like a translation of a lost Greek romance though much inferior in quality. Fortune, for instance, is regarded as the ruling force of the story by the characters and is described as 'blind' (l,i,6). She soon beings to show her ill will towards the lovers, an ill will so grievous, indeed, that Artabanes presumes she has declared 'an irreconcilable hatred to me, in which she has been so firm, that I admire from whence she merited the name of Inconstant' (l,iii,76). Very soon Artabanes rides away from his former life, wherever 'Fortune would conduct' him (l.iii,79). Before long, the ship on which he is travelling is attacked by pirates and a savage battle follows in which the hero is grievously wounded. In his despair at the infidelity of his loved one, Parthenissa, he would have preferred to die of his wounds, but even in this situation, Fortune is contrary. As Artabanes says to his friend, Simander: 'Yes, *Simander*, I live, Fortune is yet too much my Enemy to end my miseries' (l,iii,84). Fortune is similarly blamed, later, (l,iii,87), when hero and heroine are delivered to slavery. The enmity between Artabanes and Surena, which is at the heart of the story, is attributed to Fortune, and when the two resolve to be friends, at last, Fortune is found to be planning a renewed enmity (l,iii,567).

Without going into too-great detail, it is possible to demonstrate that *Parthenissa* shares most of the characteristics of the typical Greek romance. The work has an intricate structure; there are numerous apparent deaths; stories are interpolated at will; the lovers are separated for three years because of a misunderstanding; hero and heroine vow on several occasions that neither will outlive the other; there are attacks by pirates and storms at sea; every eligible male falls in love with Parthenissa; she in turn is ever-loyal to Artabanes; Arsace, king of Parthia, makes numerous attempts to rape the heroine, but she foils all attempts – the final one by commiting 'suicide'. The narrative style of *Parthenissa* is typically heroic, or Greek, also. There are numerous set descriptions, long monologues, soliloquies, and a generally artifical rendering of emotional climaxes. A good example of just such a climax is the soliloquy, given below, which is spoken by Artabanes on learning of the death of Parthenissa. With a change of names, the passage could easily pass for an extract from a Greek romance:

> You are dead, fair Princess, you are dead! And you died for *Artabanes*: Ah too great, and too ungrateful heart, which canst know this, and yet canst live after it; but I will punish thee for needing any help but thine own to act thy duty; yes, ungrateful heart, thy debt to my Princess shall be paid, though not by thee; my Resolution shall have the glory of that performance, since thou hast declined it, or at least art so long in acting it . . . Divine *Parthenissa*! what you have done, leaves the miserable *Artabbanes*

[sic] nothing to do, but to admire and follow you: the first he has still performed, and the last he now performs. (4,iv,601)

Similar in tone and style to the above extract, are the dull, theatrical monologues exchanged by the so-called passionate lovers, when they meet again after a separation of three years (4,i,493).

The ungrecian emphasis on the conflict between love and duty in heroic romance has already been noted, but there are other features, also, which are not to be found in the Greeks. Jousting matches, for instance, are quite common in all the heroic romances. In *Parthenissa*, such a match gives Artabanes a legitimate method of demonstrating the extent of his love for Parthenissa. Later again in the same work, an Arabian prince appears in Parthia, on a tour of the world, to prove that his sweetheart Mizalinza is the most beautiful lady in the world. He has had twenty-four jousting matches before his arrival in Parthia, won all of them, and has twenty-four portraits of ladies to prove his assertion. In the twenty-fifth match, Artabanes inevitably relieves the prince of those twenty-four portraits, as well as that of the 'fair Mizalinza'. The *punctilio* in the conduct of love affairs, which was introduced into heroic romance by the French is also very well illustrated by an incident in one of the interpolated stories in *Parthenissa*. The hero, Artavasdes, is so carried away by the force of his love for the heroine Altezeera, that he actually *suggests* that he loves her. Altezeera is upset at this breach of decorum, and censures Artavasdes as follows:

Ah Artavasdes, I have been too patient, and by not suppressing your first inconsiderateness, have thereby authoriz'd what you have since committed, yet I give this presumption to your services, but let me have no repetitions of it, least you force me against my inclination to become your Enemy . . . (l,ii,39).

On their next meeting, when Altezeera fears a repetition of the previous incident is imminent, she is quick to prevent it by saying to Artavasdes: '. . . the first time you speak to me of your Passion, it shall be the last . . .' (l,ii,43).

As the seventeenth century drew to a close, the vogue for heroic romance diminished greatly in England for several reasons. The French anti-romances had highlighted the absurdity and affectation of the heroic romance, commencing as early as 1651 with Paul Scarron's *Roman comique*. This was soon followed by Molière's

Précieuses Ridicules in which he castigated and ridiculed the devotees of heroic romance. Another effective blast against the heroic romance was delivered in 1666 by Antoine Furetière in *Le Roman Bourgeois*, which depicted a middle-class girl making herself absurd by affecting the grandiose airs and ideals of the heroines of heroic romance – a type of female Quixote, in fact. All of these French anti-romances found a ready sale when later translated into English.

Ioan Williams believes the rejection of heroic romance to have been a typically English rejection of the neo-classicism upon which the French had founded their prose fiction.[40] But there were less academic forces at work, also, which affected the reception of heroic romance in England. To appreciate these forces, one must first take a wider view of fiction in England during the seventeenth century. A distinction must first be drawn between literary and popular fiction: 'The former was written for a limited aristocratic public by authors consciously conforming to recognized canons in order to attain certain artistic ends. The latter, i.e. popular fiction, was written regardless of rules, to catch the fancy of readers at large.'[41] Each of these fictional strains had developed side by side in the seventeenth century, yet with little interrelation between them. Towards the end of the century, the new, prosperous middle classes began to make a return to the arts as it were, and their effect on fiction as well as drama was soon felt. The chapbooks, and, indeed, the vast majority of popular literature, with the exception of works such as *The Pilgrim's Progress*, was not to their taste, and neither, as might well be imagined, was the heroic romance. The *Athenian Mercury* 17 December 1692, reflects the feelings of the middle classes towards heroic romances. The *Mercury*, edited and published by John Dunton, was designed primarily to answer readers' questions, and, in the course of a reply to the question, 'Whether 'tis lawful to read Romances?' stated that romances 'are not at all convenient for the Vulgar, because they give 'em extravagant Idea's of practise . . . Add to this the softening the mind by Love . . . and the fooling away so many hours, and days, and years, which might be much better employed, and which must be repented of . . .'[42]

The rise of the middle classes coincided with – indeed could itself be said to have brought about – the revolution in the writing and publication of fiction. The patronage system had all but collapsed, and authors began to depend on the public for their livelihood: the bookseller/publisher became the middleman between writer and public, and saw to it that the middle classes were given what they wanted – or at least what the bookseller/publisher presumed they wanted. But the tastes of the aristocracy had changed, too, by the turn of the century: they were satiated with the bulk and complication of heroic romance, and were looking for something new. It can be said, therefore, with some qualification, that at the end of the seventeenth century the fictional tastes of both the middle and upper classes had coincided, and there was, at last, not two reading publics in England, but one.

The typical English reader considered the interminable length of heroic romance to be its major flaw. Mary de La Riviere Manley believed the English had 'naturally no Taste for long-winded Performances, for they have no sooner begun a Book but they desire to see an End of it . . . .'[43] The objections to length were easily overcome, and there was, suddenly, an abrupt shortening of prose fiction. Publishers needed a name for the new works with the intention of distinguishing between them and the long romances: the term they chose was 'novel'. The word thus adopted the connotation of a short romance. Mrs Manley talks of these 'little Pieces' as opposed to the 'Prodigious length of the Romances'.[44] 'A Novel', the Earl of Chesterfield wrote to his son, 'is a kind of abbreviation of Romance . . . .'[45] And George Canning wrote in The *Microcosm* that novel-writing had 'by some late authors been aptly enough styled the younger sister of Romance. A family likeness indeed is very evident; and in their leading features, though in the one on a more enlarged and in the other on a more contracted scale a strong resemblance is easily discoverable between them.'[46] In no sense can these 'novels' be regarded as realistic works, in spite of great advances on the realism of heroic romance. Yet, very many critics have seized upon the preface to *Incognita* (1692), by William Congreve, as evidence of an acknowledged relationship between the 'novel' and 'realism'. The extract below is the one at the centre of the controversy:

Romances are generally composed of the Constant Loves and invincible Courages of Hero's, Heroins, Kings and Queens, Mortals of the first Rank, and so forth; where lofty Language, miraculous Contigencies and impossible Performances, elevate and surprize the Reader into a giddy Delight, which leaves him flat upon the Ground whenever he gives of, and vexes him to think how he has suffer'd himself to be pleased and transported, concern'd and afflicted at the several Passages which he has Read, viz. these Knights Success to their Damosels Misfortunes, and such like, when he is forced to be very well convinced that 'tis all a lye. Novels are of a more familiar nature; Come near us, and represent to us Intrigues in practice, delight us with Accidents and odd Events, but not such as are wholly unusual or unpresidented, such which not being so distant from our Belief bring also the pleasure nearer us.[47]

This is the passage which critics have regarded as one of the first critical statements on the distinction between novel and romance, where 'novel' implies 'realism', 'romance', impossibilities and implausibilities. If one pauses for a moment to consider that a novel, for Congreve, would have implied an abbreviation of long-winded romance, then the latter half of his statement takes on a whole new complexion. The suggestion throughout is that it is not only the length, but the impossibilities and implausibilities of romance which are *modified*. Note, for instance, that novels are only *more* familiar than romances, that novels continue to use *accidents and odd events* which are not *wholly* unusual or unprecedented and therefore are not *so* distant (as romances) from our belief. Congreve's claims in his preface put him, ironically, in exactly the same camp as the French writers of heroic romance. Almost without exception, the prefaces to the heroic romances stated what Congreve's preface does. The French romancers continually prided themselves on the *vraisemblance* of their works, in contrast to the *histoires fabuleuses des ancien chevaliers*. Madeleine de Scudéry talks, for example, of romances 'which set before us monsters, in thinking to let us see Miracles; their Authors by adhering too much to wonders have made Grotesques, which have not a little of the visions of a burning Feaver. . . . As for me, I hold, that the more natural adventures are, the more satisfaction they give.'[48] The dichotomy between theory and practice in the heroic romances is so great, that one is tempted to believe that in the case of each romance there were two authors involved, one to write the preface, the other the story, and no liaison whatever between them. Such seems to be true, also, of Congreve in *Incognita*, unless one appreciates what he means by a novel: then it is apparent that he has given himself plenty of latitude, and makes use of his freedom. *Incognita* is a short romance, but not one in the Greek mode, except, perhaps, in the use of Providence. It is, as Congreve explains in the preface, the story of an 'intricate armour', where two friends Aurelian and Hippolito, fall madly in love – at first sight, naturally – with two girls they meet at a masque. After one impossible tangle after another has occurred, the problems of the quartet are solved. It is apparent both from the tale itself and the preface, that Congreve is much more interested in the 'Design, Contexture and Result of the Plot',[49] than in any attempt to achieve any standard of realism. His leanings towards the stage are very obvious in this story, since he has set out to imitate 'Dramatick writing', and all his talents are directed to this end. One must, finally, draw attention to the subtitle of *Incognita*, which is *Love and Duty Reconciled* – a subtitle which immediately suggests the heroic romances. Philip Henderson is almost certainly wrong in his contention that in *Incognita* there 'is a complete detachment from the Romantic attitude'.[50] Such a remark is almost certainly based on a misinterpretation of Congreve's comments in the preface.

'History' was a word which appeared almost as often as 'novel' on the title pages of prose fiction in the late seventeenth and in the eighteenth century. The term was meant to imply that the work was an 'authentic chronicle', as opposed to those bogus chronicles, the heroic romances. Very few indeed of the so-called 'histories' were any more authentic than the romances, and the word 'history' came to mean 'simply "narrative" whether true or false'.[51] By the time Henry Fielding came to write, the appearance of the word 'history' on the title page of a fictitious work 'implied a feigned biography'.[52] In some cases, however, 'novel' and 'history' appeared in the one title, such as *The History of the Loves of Lysander and Sabina: A Novel*, written in 1688. There was, in effect, little distinction between the two terms.

Mrs Aphra Behn's *Oroonoko*, published in 1688, was one of the first and best examples of a heroic romance in miniature. As Philip Henderson remarks: 'although there is in this novel [*Oroonoko*] a perceptible tightening up, a greater synthesis of time and event than in the heroic romances of her predecessors, yet the "royal slave" himself is of their school.'[53] The qualities of Oroonoko as ascribed to him by the author are very much those of the hero of heroic romance. He possesses:

> that real greatness of soul, those refined notions of true honour, that absolute generosity, and that softness that was capable of

the highest passions of love and gallantry, . . . the most illustrious could not have produced a braver man, both for greatness of courage and mind, a judgement more solid, a wit more quick, and a conversation more sweet and diverting . . . He had an extreme good and graceful mien, and all the civility of a well-bred great man.[54]

The physical appearance of Oroonoko, as described by the author, is no less heroic:

He was pretty tall, but of a shape the most exact that can be fancy'd: The most famous statuary cou'd not form the figure of a man more admirably turn'd from head to foot. His face was not of that brown rusty black which most of that nation are, but of perfect ebony or polished jett. His eyes were the most awful that cou'd be seen, and very piercing; the white of 'em being like snow, as were his teeth. His nose was rising and *Roman* instead of *African* and flat. His mouth the finest shaped that could be seen; far from those great turn'd lips which are so natural to the rest of the negroes. The whole proportion and air of his face was so nobly and exactly form'd, that bating his colour, there could be nothing in nature more beautiful, agreeable and handsome. There was no one grace wanting, that bears the standard of true beauty. (154)

It is not just the 'royal slave' alone that is of the school of the heroic romances: the work itself displays most of the qualities associated with the school. Imoinda, the heroine, is the most beautiful creature on earth, and when she meets Oroonoko they fall violently in love. In spite of the custom of the country, 'where men take to themselves as many wives as they can maintain; and where the only crime and sin with woman, is, to turn her off, to abandon her to want, shame and misery . . .' (156), Oroonoko, like the true hero of heroic romance, 'aim'd at nothing but honour' (156). The lovers are married almost immediately, but fate contrives to separate them almost as quickly. The old king, Oroonoko's grandfather, conceives a violent passion for Imoinda, and sends her the royal veil, to compel her to become his concubine. He is aware of the relationship between Oroonoko and Imoinda, but consoles himself with the thought that 'the obedience the people pay their king, was not at all inferior to what they pay their gods;

and what love would not oblige Imoinda to do, duty would compel her to' (158). In no sense, however, does the story develop the theme of love versus duty.

When Oroonoko learns of the fate of his loved one, he tries to commit suicide, initially, in the best tradition of frustrated lovers. Having recovered from the first shock of the news, he utters a monologue which is not at all unlike the typical monologue in heroic romance. (160) In typical romance fashion, Imoinda is presumed dead at one point in the story, and Oroonoko tries to kill himself in despair. His attempt, on this particular occasion, takes the form of a battle with an opposing army: 'being animated with despair', we are told, 'he fought as if he came on purpose to die' (176). Imoinda is not dead, but has been sold into slavery 'in a foreign country'. Soon afterwards, Oroonoko himself is seized by an English slave trader and sold into service with another Englishman named Trefry, in Surinam. As might be expected, Imoinda is already in the service of Mr Trefry. This incident is very reminiscent of the one in the *Aethiopica* where Chariclea, presumed dead, has become a slave of Melitta; Melitta then marries Theagenes and the lovers are thus reunited.[55] Nor is Imoinda less concerned than was Chariclea in the defence of her honour. Everyone on the estate 'loves' her, and Trefry her master is no exception. Trefry, indeed, admits to Oroonoko that having failed to seduce Imoinda he had considered making use of 'those advantages of strength and force' (188) nature had given him. But Imoinda's modesty and weeping had disarmed him on each occasion. The remainder of the work is quite different to anything in any previous romance, and suggests a basis in actual fact. Oroonoko feels compelled to execute his wife to preserve her from his enemies: he himself is then killed by slow torture. *Oroonoko* displays a further subtle yet significant variation on the general pattern of heroic and, indeed, Greek romance – a variation which was to suggest the new pattern for romance. In *Oroonoko* Mrs Behn makes an obvious attempt to emphasise the character and personality of the hero, rather than the action. Though the work does contain the basic action of romance – love, separation, abduction, attempts at rape, and battles – it is the character of the hero and heroine that is important rather than any action in the work. Nor can this concern with character at the expense of action be attributed to the shortening and 'tightening up' of the heroic romance, since few of Mrs Behn's contemporaries showed similar concern with character.

The example she gave began to bear fruit quite early in the eighteenth century and culminated in *Pamela* and *Clarissa*.

PASSIONATE ROMANCE

By the early years of the eighteenth century, a sufficient number of short romances, which were broadly similar in kind, had been written, so as to justify a new 'label'. These are usually called 'romances of passion' or 'amatory novellas', today. The authors themselves avoided the word 'romance', particularly since the eighteenth century regarded 'romance' as synonymous with 'delusion', a picture of the world as it is not, a 'product of an extravagant imagination'.[56] The term 'novel', too, was being used less often, authors preferring the word 'history', with its implication of truth to human nature and moral reality rather than to literal realism.

In spite of all the protestations of their authors, however, the romances of passion which eventually replaced heroic romances, were simply modifications of the situations, themes, and style of the heroic romances. Not that this modification was an improvement; it was, rather, what John Richetti calls 'a simplification or vulgarization'[57] of the heroic romance. Richetti goes on to claim that the 'great majority of the amorous novellas written in English before 1740 merely condensed the excesses of the heroic romance, substituted a debased and inflated but simplified heroic rant for the involved *préciosité* of the romances, and used that style to deliver stories of some external complication, but of extreme moral and emotional simplicity.'[58]

There are, of course, several distinctions to be made between heroic and so-called passionate romance, as the following resumé of a typical romance of passion will illustrate. The heroine initially falls in love, at first sight, with a handsome rake, and immediately loses interest in all else, and, in particular, loses interest in the reputable suitors presented by her parents. She usually begins to correspond with her rake, and eventually elopes with him. After very many 'passionate' scenes, the rake either rapes or seduces the heroine, who is almost invariably pregnant as a result. The moment the rape or seduction has been accomplished the rake loses all interest in the girl, whom he abandons. She suffers one misfortune after another (which are dwelt on at length), and becomes, at last, painfully aware of her folly: her endless self-recriminations serve, supposedly, as a warning to other young women, but are, in reality, simply an attempt to justify whatever prurience might have appeared in the work.

The first notable feature of the romance of passion is that it, too, like the heroic romance, portrays a conflict between love and duty. But this time duty invariably loses the battle. Love is portrayed as an overpowering, uncontrollable passion which all the duty in the world cannot check. The reasons for this seemingly sudden turnabout are not too difficult to discover. Licentiousness and indecency in fiction had been fostered as early as 1660 by the French *chroniques scandaleuses*, short, lurid accounts of illicit love affairs and other indiscretions amongst the nobility of the day. The popularity of these reports was as great in England as it was in France, and English imitators soon flourished, Mrs Behn being one of the first. It soon became apparent to the professional writers of fiction and their publishers, that lubricity in fiction would be a much better seller than chastity, and they quickly made the necessary adjustments. Concomitantly, they developed a justification for their lubricity, claiming an ulterior moral purpose for gross licentiousness. Passionate romance was one of the fictional vehicles for the dissemination of this licentiousness. But despite the change in emphasis, the authors still relied heavily on the heroic romance conventions for their stock materials and narrative techniques. The amorous oriental despots, lascivious sea captains, pirates – all make a reappearance on the new stage. The languishing beauty of the heroic romance takes on a different role in the romance of passion, but is, essentially, the sister of her 'heroic' counterpart. As Charlotte Morgan observes, the heroine in heroic romance 'does little, but being sensitive to a degree, suffers much and enjoys nothing more than describing her every emotion. A drop in the social scale, and we have the . . . tearful heroines of the eighteenth century.'[59] The 'heroic' heroes of seventeenth-century romance become – with a similar drop in the social scale – 'insipid parlor heroes'.[60] The style of the romances of passion, vulgarised through it may be, is undoubtedly in the tradition of the heroic romance also, and is most obvious in stock scenes such as the 'warm' ones so beloved of the authors and readers of the eighteenth century.

The popularity of early eighteenth-century fiction was naturally due to more than a mere portrayal of lubricity. It was also a 'fantasy machine' which presented an opportunity for the middle and lower classes to 'participate vicariously in an erotically exciting and glittering fantasy world'[61] of the aristocracy. The romances of passion also reflected the 'well known eighteenth-century preoccupation'[62] with the myth of the destruction of female innocence by a representative of the aristocratic world of male corruption. Richetti demonstrates how the romances of passion 'in spite of their stylized and extravagant characters and situations, are firmly rooted in certain basic if distorted economic realities . . . the persecuted maiden's story is an oblique comment on the absolute economic dependence of eighteenth-century women'.[63]

One of the earliest and best of the romances of the eighteenth century was *Lindamira*, published in 1702. Chronologically, and otherwise, *Lindamira* can be regarded as a 'half-way house' between the heroic romance of the seventeenth, and the realistic novel of the eighteenth century. Benjamin Boyce is of the opinion that one would be disinclined to believe that the 'foreign art' of Madeleine de Scudéry had fostered the fiction of Defoe, Richardson and Fielding, without *Lindamira* 'to show how the thing could happen'.[64] He also describes *Lindamira* as a 'remarkable demonstration of how something of situation, motivation, and sentiment could be abstracted from the now rather demodé French heroic romance and adapted to English middle-class life'.[65] Boyce is careful, however, to emphasise that *Lindamira* is not simply an heroic romance in miniature, but, rather, an attractive modification of the worst aspects of the French fictions. The story tells, in epistolary form, of the love of Lindamira and Cleomidon and of the numerous obstacles which prevent their marrying. The major obstacle is an economic one: Cleomidon is not very well off, and his rich uncle will only settle his vast estate on him if he marries the wealthy Cleodora. Lindamira refuses to marry her lover and thus deprive him of his fortune: Cleomidon has, thus, little option but to marry Cleodora. Lindamira and Cleomidon are eventually rescued from their abject misery, when Cleodora dies in childbirth, years later. But other problems arise and have to be overcome before the lovers can marry. John Richetti regards *Lindamira* as a precursor of the romance of passion. He describes *Lindamira* as an 'ideologically simple fable of virtue and constancy rewarded', and explains that it is 'their simplicities, further simplified and rendered in bright lascivious colours that are the main feature of the really popular amatory novella'.[66]

The amatory romance's most successful exponents were Mrs

Mary de la Riviere Manley, and Mrs Eliza Haywood. Although Mrs Manley had been writing for quite some time, it was *The Secret History of Queen Zarah and the Zarazians* which brought her fame when it was published in 1705. This 'Secret History' was a long tale of illicit passion and intrigue amongst the aristocracy of the day, and was an attempt by Mrs Manley to discredit the whig politicians (1705 was an election year), and in particular the Duchess of Marlborough. The continued popularity of *Queen Zarah*, long after the Duchess of Marlborough and her clique were forgotten, shows that the work's attraction for the reading public of the day in no way depended on the political allusions, though these were, obviously, an added bonus. In this work of 'casual adultery and sexual intrigue',[67] Zarah is, at first, the typical innocent female abroad. But she soon becomes quite the reverse: she is shown, later, as Richetti demonstrates,[68] to have given over the virtues of the heroic female, i.e. true, selfless, love, innocence and passivity before passion, and adopted instead the male role of aggression, involving, as it usually does, ambition and self-aggrandisement.

Even more popular than *Queen Zarah* was Mrs Manley's next work of prose fiction, *Secret Memoirs and Manners of Several Persons of Quality of Both Sexes, from the New Atalantis, an Island in the Mediterranean*, published in 1709. Astraea returns to Atalantis (England) to see if men and manners have improved any. She meets Virtue and Lady Intelligence, and tours the island with them. Lady Intelligence narrates various scandals, and the trio meet others who tell their own tales of woe and scandal. The work is, as one might expect, a rather jumbled hotchpotch, containing scandalous anecdotes as well as short romances of passion. One of the short romances, the one concerning the Duke and Charlot, bears most of the hallmarks of the type. The Duke is an attractive rake who becomes the guardian of a young girl, Charlot, when a friend of his dies. After some time, the Duke falls madly in love with his ward, and, despite frantic attempts to rid himself of her hold on him, he fails. At length, he determines to enjoy Charlot, having decided that he has:

> strugled [sic] more than sufficient, Virtue ought to be satisfied with the terrible Conflict he had suffered! but Love was become Master and 'twas time for her to abscond. After he had settled his Thoughts, he grew more calm and quiet; nothing shou'd now disturb him, but the manner how to corrupt her. (i,61)

Charlot is innocence personified, having, indeed, been thus moulded by her would-be seducer, who painstakingly sets about the preparations for her undoing. Books and poetry are his first weapons, which have the desired effect; these he follows with a rumour that he has married another. When Charlot retires to the Duke's villa, grief-stricken at the news, he follows in order to rape her. The scene is typical of almost every rape described in eighteenth-century literature. The heroine is in her night clothes, and is 'uncovered in a melancholy, careless Posture' (i,71), when the Duke enters. He assaults her immediately, and the actual rape – as all early eighteenth-century ones – is described in the most euphemistic terms imaginable. In spite of the rape, Charlot's love for her ravisher is greater than ever, and she remains uncorrupted. Perhaps the most significant passage in this story, and, indeed, in the whole work, comes when Charlot tries to convey the extent and quality of her love to a widowed Countess. The Countess is at a loss to understand this type of love; she would often tell Charlot:

> that no Lady ever suffer'd herself to be truly touch'd, but from that moment she was blinded and undone. The first thing a Woman ought to consult was her Interest, and Establishment in the World; that Love shou'd only be a handle towards it; when she left the Pursuit of that to give up herself to her Pleasures, Contempt and Sorrow were sure to be her Companions. No Lover was yet ever known so ardent, but time abated of his Transport; no Beauty so ravishing, but that her Sweetness wou'd cloy; nor did Men any longer endeavour to please, when nothing was wanting to their Wishes: Love, the most generous and yet the most mercenary of all the Passions, does not care what he lavishes, provided there be something still in view to repay his Expence; but that once over, the Lover possess'd of whatever his Mistress can bestow, he hangs his Head, the *Cupid* drops his Wings, and seldom feels their native Energy return, but to carry him to new Conquests. (i,73,74)

This statement by the Countess, which requires little commentary, epitomises, on the one hand, the philosophy of the worldly-wise female, and, on the other, the inevitable consequences of allowing oneself to be 'truly touched'. With some qualification, it can be argued that the statement demonstrates the general pattern of all romances of passion. And the one in question bears this out: the Duke soon becomes tired of Charlot, abandons her, and marries the worldly-wise Countess. Charlot ends her days in the mandatory 'horror, Sorrow, and Repentance', (i,83) and eventually dies 'a true Landmark, to warn all believing Virgins from Shipwracking their Honour upon (that dangerous Coast of Rocks) the Vows and Pretended Passion of Mankind'. (i,83)

Even more popular than Mrs Manley – with whom she is invariably linked as one of the numerous 'women scribblers' of the age – was Mrs Eliza Haywood. Between the years 1720 and 1730 she wrote 38 works of fiction, and even had a collected edition of her works published in 1725. Her astonishing success was undoubtedly due to her ability to gauge the temper of her readers to perfection, and to give them what they wanted. For this reason, the attitudes of pre-Richardson readers can, perhaps, be more accurately gauged from the works of Mrs Haywood than from the works of her contemporaries. Mrs Haywood must have had some say, too, in the formation of this audience, and in the actual moulding of attitudes to, and expectations from fiction in the eighteenth century. That she was a follower of Mrs Manley is evident from Mrs Haywood's *Memoirs of a Certain Island adjacent to the Kingdom of Utopia* (1725), which follows the basic format of *The New Atalantis*. In *Memoirs of a Certain Island*, 'A Noble Youth' arrived in the island (England) adjacent to Utopia, where he meets the god, Cupid, who conducts him on a tour of the country. As in *The New Atalantis*, the emphasis in all the anecdotes and the romances of passion is on the complete absence of honour and virtue, and the dominance of lust and avarice. A résumé of two of the romances of passion, one from the first volume of *Memoirs of a Certain Island*, the other from the second, will serve to illustrate the general pattern of the stories in the work. The first romance concerns Mazonia, the Daughter of a Gentleman of a distinguished family, who has had a liberal education, and is possessed of a vast fortune. Her father arranges to have her married, when still quite young, to Count Marville, who treats her in the most abominable manner. There were several who rejoiced in the hope that Mazonia's:

> ill Usage at *Home*, might induce her to accept of better Entertainment *Abroad*; and grew bold enough to make Declarations to her, of a nature which, had the *Count* been less notorious in his Behaviour, they never wou'd have presum'd to have done: But

never were the Seeds of Virtue more deeply rooted, than in the
Heart of this abused Lady, and as she had been taught to
abhor Unchastity, as a Vice the most pernicious to a Woman's
Character, so she also found not in herself the least Propensity,
to wish it were not so. The falling Snow, or Air new rarefy'd by
Phoebus's Beams, is not more pure, more free from Stain than
was her spotless Mind; – she sinn'd not even in Thought that
way, – nor was her Soul less guarded against Anger and Revenge;
she endeavour'd, rather by Patience and Resignation to baffle
the Malice of her Fate, than by returning Infidelity for Infidelity,
deserve it – Thus for a long time did *she* continue an eminent
Example of suffering Virtue . . . . (i,158)

Eventually, the Count Riverius, 'one of the most loose and
debauch'd of all the young Noblemen about the court' (i,160), falls
madly in love with Mazonia and sets about winning her favour by
writing her letters 'expressing only the most pure Affection,
without the least mixture of loose Desire' (i,172). In spite of her
full knowledge of his libertinism, Mazonia decided that she could
'safely trust the Conversation of so disinterested a Tenderness,
and began to think it would be a prodigious Alleviation of her
Misfortunes to have such a friend to condole them, and advise her
what Method she should take to make them less' (i,160,161). Before
long, Mazonia has fallen in love with Riverius and spends much
time in his company, since she considered him 'a Lover not
dangerous to her Honour'. Not very long afterwards, a typical
'warm' scene occurs when Riverius comes upon Mazonia in her
garden, where she is described as follows:

She was fallen asleep, and the Heat of the Day having prevented
her from dressing, she was in a loose Dishabillé of green
Lutestring flower'd with Silver; which being as it were only
carelessly thrown over her Shoulders, and quite unfastened
before, discover'd Beauties 'till that ravishing moment he had
never seen but in Imagination: the whole Proportion of her fine-
turn'd Neck, and heaving Breasts, were now exposed to view,
excepting only where here and there an unty'd Lock of the most
lovely Hair in the world fell scattering down; and by seeming to
endeavour to hide some part of Beauty, disclos'd another by
showing itself. – Nor were her Legs and Feet with greater
Caution skreen'd, the Bank being rais'd a pretty height above

the Ground they hung over it, and her Petticoats being shorter than Ladies generally wear, except in an Undress, the happy Count had a full Opportunity of feasting his Eyes with the sight of those Charms so dear to a Lover's Fancy. (i,172)

The prospect before him is too much even for the Count, and he – untypically for the eighteenth-century libertine – falls 'amidst the Extasy of Pain and Pleasure quite motionless on her Breast' (i,173). Riverius' failure to take advantage of her situation and violate her honour merely impels Mazonia to love him all the more, and Riverius realises this. Within a few days he has rushed upon her 'in a Tempest of Desire' and triumphed 'over all the faint Efforts of her Virtue'. (i,176) Typical of many of the heroines of romances of passion, Mazonia, 'From the most strict reserve fell immediately into the other extreme of giving the most inordinate loose to Inclination; she despised the Censure of the World, would scarce suffer Riverius a moment from her Sight, shunn'd all other Society . . .' (i,176). Mazonia gives birth, first to a daughter, and, later, to son, by which time Riverius has grown tired of, and abandoned her. Her repentance for her sin takes a strange form: 'her Aversion ran to unpardonable Extremes; and the Punishments which ought to have been confined to the *guilty Causes* of her Shame, she extended to the *innocent Effects* – with the most unheard of and unnatural Barbarity, abhorring, and throwing out to Misery, those unhappy Infants, the Pledges of that Tenderness she one had for *Riverius.*' (i,181)

The first tale in the second volume concerns Gerion and Marilla. Once again it is the libertine male who falls in love first. Marilla – 'of a Birth equal to his own, a Fortune but little inferior to what he cou'd hope, a Reputation unsully'd, and a most excellent Beauty' (ii,7) – is quite indifferent to Gerion's advances. She is, nevertheless, won over, eventually, and falls violently in love with him. Gerion, for his part:

no sooner discover'd the advantage he had gain'd over her, than he changed the form of his Addresses, and as he had never presum'd in her days of indifference to think of her but with the utmost Honour, and plac'd his whole Felicity in the hope of attaining possession of her by lawful means; he now entertained wishes of a contrary nature, and resolving, if possible, to satiate his Passion with her, look abroad for a Wife among those more capable of gratifying those ambitious Views, which he began now to have a notion of. (ii,7)

Gerion tricks Marilla into going with him to visit a relation in the country. The relation is, in effect, a dependant of Gerion who has been instructed by him how to impersonate the 'Air of a Woman of Fashion' so as to deceive Marilla. The deception is a success, and Marilla is given a sleeping potion on the night of her arrival. Gerion, 'perpetrated his villainous intention, and she, unknowingly, unyielding, fell an innocent Sacrifice of Lust and Cruelty . . .' (ii,8). On discovering what has occurred, Marilla lapses into an 'extremity of Grief' (ii,8), and, because he fears the anger of her father, Gerion convinces Marilla that it was his passion and love for her which drove him to the rape. She not only pardons Gerion but permits him also:

> to renew those Raptures with her own Consent, which to know he had enjoy'd, had lately cost her so many Tears; and it was this criminal Condescension, this fond Infatuation, which . . . abandon'd her to all the Miseries which attend that Sex, when loose Desire gets the better of Virtue. (ii,9)

Marilla's father dies soon afterwards, and Gerion abandons her immediately. She does all in her power to win him back, even more so when she discovers herself to be pregnant. Eventually, 'the apprehensions of being exposed to the Censure of an unpitying World, joined to her Despair and disappointed Love, made her resolve to put a period to those Misfortunes which she could not remedy . . . in fine she swallowed Poison, and with herself destroy'd the innocent Effect of her too guilty flame' (ii,10).

Mrs Haywood's most popular work was *Love in Excess* (1719), which was, indeed, as W. H. McBurney demonstrates,[69] one of the three most popular works of fiction before *Pamela*. D'elmont, the male libertine of *Love in Excess*, has most of the attributes of his predecessors, but since he is to be converted in the end, is never made entirely vicious or aggressive in pursuit of his aims. D'elmont first plots against Amena. She is in love with him, but fearful of her honour because of his reputation. Although the relationship between D'elmont and Amena is the story of one near-seduction after another, no violation of Amena actually occurs, because she is sent to a convent by her father to escape the attentions of the libertine. D'elmont marries Aloisa for her wealth and is soon madly in love with another, this time Melliora. Melliora's father dies, and D'elmont, her lover-to-be, becomes her guardian. On his deathbed, Melliora's father emphasises to D'elmont that his daughter has been (like Charlot), raised in solitary innocence and purity. Melliora's love for her guardian is as sudden and as violent as his for her. A major conflict arises in the heart of D'elmont: he has never been a man of honour in love, but his conduct otherwise has always been above reproach. In the present situation his desire for the possession of Melliora is counteracted by 'too much Honour, too much Gratitude for the Memory of Monsieur Frankville [his friend]' (ii,9,10). In spite of all his pangs of conscience, Melliora is almost violated on several occasions, occasions very similar to those in the earlier part of the work. The Baron D'Espernay eventually convinces D'elmont that he is being far too scrupulous, and argues as follows:

My Lord, said he, you do not only Injure the Dignity of our Sex in General, but your own Merits in Particular, and perhaps even Melliora's secret Inclinations by this unavailing distant Carriage, and Causeless dispair [sic]. – Have you not confest that has she [sic] look'd on you with a Tenderness like that of Love, that she has Blushed at your sight, and trembled at your Touch? – What wou'd you more that she shou'd do, or what indeed can she do more, in Modesty, to prove her Heart is yours? A little Resolution on your side wou'd make her all yours – Women are taught by custom to deny what most they Covet, and to seem angry when they are best pleas'd; believe me D'elmont that the most rigid Virtue of 'em all, never yet hated a Man for those faults which Love occasions. (43)

Almost immediately D'elmont sets about planning the rape of Melliora. The heroine is asleep when D'elmont approaches. In her sleep, Melliora has 'thrust down the Bed-Cloths so far, that all the Beauties of her neck and Breast appeard'd to view' (ii,47). D'elmont hesitates, when, suddenly, still asleep, Melliora embraces him, and he is about to rape her when interrupted. Several other such scenes occur, but they all end in failure. The work concludes with the marriage of D'elmont and Melliora – Aloisa having been accidentally killed by her husband – rewarded, it would seem, by the author, for having preserved their chastity intact, in spite of the numerous attempts to violate it. Just before the end of *Love in Excess*, as D'elmont and Melliora are about to be married, D'elmont's page, Fidelio, is found dying. The page is, in fact, a girl called Violetta, in love with D'elmont, whom she has served for quite some time. She dies in D'elmont's arms, a victim of unrequited love; but before she breathes her last, she pictures the future, blissful married state for D'elmont and Melliora, Richetti, in what is perhaps one of his most perceptive insights, analyses the death of Violetta, and the impending marriage, and concludes as follows:

We have had, in effect, a double ending, a tragic apotheosis followed by a glorious conjugal consummation, the two kinds of beatitude recognized within the fable of persecuted innocence. Death and Marriage transport the worthy heroine to suitable heavens. Both bring release from the heroic tribulations of love, but both, of course, are beyond description . . . Having rewarded Melliora with marriage, she [Mrs Haywood] fears, perhaps, a let-down, and so Violetta is brought on stage to expire in happy tears. Her death is, in a sense, an orgasm, a suitably violent and spectacular end to the story. It is an orgasm we have been waiting for, the one we have approached so often throughout the story in the many near-consummations.[70]

Death is not the only prospect for the rejected heroine: retirement to a nunnery was a popular alternative, and in *The British Recluse: or, The Secret History of Cleomira, Suppos'd Dead* (1722), Mrs Haywood suggests a further possibility. In this story two young women, Cleomira and Belinda, discover that each has been violated and then abandoned by the same man, one whom each had thought to be the most honourable and faithful of lovers. The two ladies decide to leave the world of treachery and lust, and live in a pastoral retreat, where they live 'happily ever after'.

RELIGIOUS ROMANCE

Not all love fiction written prior to 1840 fits neatly into either of the two categories, 'heroic' or 'passionate' romance. The works of Mrs Jane Barker, and, in particular, those of Mrs Penelope Aubin, while combining many of the elements of both heroic and passion-

ate romance, add an additional, major element of sufficient importance to make a further category of romance relevant: the most
obvious title for this new category is 'religious romance'. John
Richetti prefers to describe these works as 'novels of pious pole-
mic'.[71] 'Mrs Aubin's novels', he remarks, later, 'were presented to
her public as an undisguised attempt to seduce them into virtue
through the familiar diversions of popular narrative'.[72] The passionate romance was a shortened, lubricious version of the heroic
romance, and, with the exclusion of lubricity from the works of
Mrs Aubin and Mrs Barker, the line of descent becomes more
clear. Religious romance is simply Greek, or heroic romance
Christianised, as well as shortened. Robert Boyle had, of course,
shown the way as early as 1687, with the publication of his heroic–
religious romance, *Theodora and Didymus*, a work which had
little to recommend it as entertainment. 'I esteem'd it a kind of
Profaneness to transform a piece of Martyrology into a Romance,'
Boyle wrote in the preface:[73] his aim, he continued, 'was to do
some good by rendering Vertue Amiable, and recommending Piety
to a sort of Readers, that are much more affected by shining
Examples, and pathetical Expressions, than by dry Precepts, and
grave Discourses.'[74] One can hardly regard the introduction of
religion into heroic romance and into the shorter romances of
the early eighteenth century as striking innovations when one
considers the predominance of the religious theme in Greek
romance: the only significant variation is the substitution of the
Christian for the pagan.

The extent to which religious romance has reverted to the
pattern of Greek and heroic romance should be obvious from an
examination of the type. To begin with, virtue is again restored to
the lofty eminence she had previously held. There is never a
conflict between love and duty here. The heroine always chooses
her lover correctly in the first instance: love and duty invariably
coincide, therefore. At the commencement of the typical religious
romance, the hero and heroine are actually married or tied to each
other by unbreakable vows. There follows almost immediately a
succession of misfortunes which (particularly in the case of Mrs
Aubin), take the hero and heroine halfway round the world. There
are the age-old, numerous attempts to rape the heroine, all of which
fail. Nor do the authors of religious romance take advantage of the
rape scenes to depict them erotically: all such scenes are perfectly
free from any kind of lubricity. Unlike the heroines of passionate

romance, those of the religious romance have nothing whatever
to fear from themselves – their virtue is utterly impervious. The
only way in which their honour can be violated is by brute force,
and they have complete faith in a just God who will preserve their
innocence untainted. Thus, a just God and a kindly Providence
have taken the place of malevolent, pagan Fortune. In religious
romance there is a continuous emphasis on both the possibility of
a faultless virtue and the vigilance of heaven to reward it. Marriage,
and an assurance of a heavenly reward are the prizes for the
virtuous, while the wicked not only lose battles, and fail in their
attempts at rape, they also face the interminable torments of the
damned, in hell, when they die.

In 1721, two of Mrs Aubin's works were published, *The Life of
Madam de Beaumont* and *The Strange Adventures of the Count de
Vinevil*. Mrs Aubin was not willing to lure readers into virtue by
any pretence that her romances are stories of passion: on the
contrary, each contains what might be described as an agressive
preface, in which she clearly states her aims. The preface to *The
Count de Vinevil*, for instance, states categorically that the story to
follow is not a romance of passion where innocence is violated,
rather is it a story:

> where Divine Providence manifests itself in every Transaction,
> where Vertue is ty'd with Misfortunes, and rewarded with
> Blessings: in fine, where Men behave themselves like Christians,
> and women are really vertuous, and such as we ought to
> imitate. (6)

Madam de Beaumont tells the stories of the heroine who gives the
work its title, her husband, and her daughter. When the novel
opens, Madam de Beaumont has been married for many years,
and has spent fourteen of those with her daughter, Belinda, in a
cave in Wales, away from her husband. He had gone to fight in
some war, and had sent her to England for safety. On her way to
England her ship was wrecked on the Welsh coast, and she is
presumed dead. A Welsh gentleman marries Belinda, having
proved himself a worthy suitor. This Mr Lluelling goes in search
of Belinda's father, and leaves his wife in the care of his nephew.
The nephew, a typical libertine from the pages of Mrs Haywood
or Mrs Manley, immediately declares his passion for Belinda and

threatens rape if she fails to succumb voluntarily. Her reply is indicative of the new breed of 'religious' heroine:

> By Heaven, I'll never give Consent, and if you force me like a Brute, what Satisfaction will you reap? I shall then hate and scorn you, loath your Embraces, and if I ever escape your hands again, sure Vengeance will o'ertake you; nay, you shall drag me sooner to my Grave, than to your Bed; I will resist to Death, and curse you with my last Breath: but if you spare me, my Prayers and Blessings shall attend you, nay, I will pity and forgive you. 'I'm deaf to all that you can plead against my Love, he cry'd, yield or I'll force you hence.' 'No, says she, I'll rather die; now, Villain, I will hate you: help and defend me Heaven.' (62)

This is the attitude of all the heroines of religious romance: for each of them there is a simple choice, death – which they will gladly endure as a kind of martyrdom – or dishonour. When all turns out well in the end, Mrs Aubin appends the following remarks, which demonstrate, not only a philosophy of life, but fiction too:

> Thus Providence does, with unexpected Accidents, try Men's Faith, frustrate their Designs, and lead them thro a Series of Misfortunes, to manifest its Power in their Deliverance; confounding the Atheist, and convincing the Libertine, that there is a just God, who rewards Virtue and does punish Vice: so wonderful are the ways of God, so boundless is his Power, that none ought to despair that believe in him. You see he can give Food upon the barren Mountain, and prevent the bold Ravisher from accomplishing his wicked Design: the virtuous Belinda was safe in the hands of a Man who was desperately in love with her, and whose desperate circumstances made him dare to do almost any thing, but Virtue was her Armour, and Providence her Defender: these Tryals did but improve her Vertues, and encrease her Faith. (142,143)

Mrs Jane Barker, a predecessor of Mrs Aubin's in the writing of religious romance, suggested what might be done in the new variety of fiction. Mrs Barker, while an innovator, is much less sure than Mrs Aubin in the handling of her material, and certainly less polemical. But Mrs Barker's heroines, contrary to contemporary trends, were paragons of virtue, and her works, in spite of numerous opportunities for eroticism, shunned it completely. Her works include *Loves Intrigues; or the History of Bosvil and Galesia* (1713); *Exilius; or, The Banish'd Roman* (1715); *A Patch-Work Screen for the Ladies; or Love and Virtue Recommended* (1723); and *The Lining for the Patch-Work Screen* (1726).

The works of Mrs Elizabeth Rowe were more polemical and less artistic than those of either Mrs Barker or Mrs Aubin. Yet Mrs Rowe's works were almost as popular as those of Mrs Aubin, with much less reason – or so it seems to the modern reader at any rate, who can account, to some extent at least, for the popularity of Aubin's works. Mrs Rowe's most popular work is accurately described as 'a deadening book, written in ecstatic and inflated prose and full of the most explicit and tedious moralizing about the pains of a life of sin and the comforts of living virtuously. Its situations and characters are mechanical and verbose, and strike any modern reader as almost comically unreal.'[75]

Mrs Rowe's most popular work was *Friendship in Death, in Twenty Letters from the Dead to the Living,* published in 1728. The twenty letters are written by souls newly arrived in heaven, to their friends in this world. As well as containing glowing descriptions of heavenly bliss, the letters contain plenty of advice and warnings with regard to conduct on earth – advice and warnings to be taken seriously if the recipients of the letters wish to join their friends in heavenly bliss. In 1728, also, Part I of Mrs Rowe's *Letters Moral and Entertaining* was published, with a second Part published in 1731, and a third in 1732. These letters are written by earthly instead of heavenly beings, and are intended as intimate exchanges between friends. The letters tell various stories, the stock themes of which have been abstracted by Charlotte Morgan.[76] A typical letter tells the tale of a young woman who, having retired to the country to recover from an unhappy passion, was led by solitary meditation 'to religion' and shortly afterwards marries a devout young man. Other letters tell of a pious country maid preferred by a wealthy lord to court beauties because of her 'virtue', while more detail the history of a rake who is led to repent by a pious woman, and is rewarded for his conversion by winning both her hand and her wealth. More letters deal with the story of a pious girl who falls into a decline on the death of her lover, and soon joins him in immortal bliss.

One of the more interesting of the tales in *Letters Moral and*

Entertaining tells the story of Rosalinda,[77] who runs away from home when forced by her father to marry a foreign gentleman, who had the added disadvantage of being a Catholic. Rosalinda becomes a servant in a country house, and shares in all the joys of the simple, pastoral life. She is not even tempted to return to the 'world' on learning that her father intends leaving all his wealth to a monastery.

It is to John Richetti one must turn again for a masterly account of how Mrs Rowe's fiction typified the general trend of English fiction in the early years of the eighteenth century:

Her crude and explicit exploitation of the clichés of the popular novellas and scandalous memoirs of the day is nothing less than a sign of the crucial transformation of fiction which takes place during the first four decades of the eighteenth century: the aimless if graceful literature of love which floods into England from France and Spain during the late seventeenth century and through the eighteenth century is subtly changed by the ideological climate, and in English Protestant hands responds to the pressure of the times to become fiction which is essentially a dramatization of the plight of an embattled and self-consciously 'virtuous' individual in a hostile and innately vicious world.[78]

4
Richardson and Romance

Very little has been written about the elements of romance in the novels of Samuel Richardson, and perhaps this is understandable since the majority of students of eighteenth-century fiction are more interested in what is new in his fiction than what is borrowed or adapted. There is also the prevalent tendency to regard the elements of romance in Richardson's fiction as lapses of one kind or another, occasions on which his artistic genius failed him and he was forced to resort to the standby of romance. William Sale, for example, talks of Richardson being 'reduced' to blending romantic material with the 'realism of Dutch genre painting'.[1] And Morris Golden writes of 'the distressing tendency'[2] of Richardson to exploit the effects of romance. It is precisely this attitude which has so adversely affected the study of English fiction in general. When 'realism' comes to be synonymous with all that is desirable in fiction, 'romance' becomes synonymous with all that is undesirable. To discuss and analyse the revolutionary use of realism in Richardson's fiction, to the complete exclusion of the romance elements, is to do the author an injustice. It is only when Richardson's adaptation and transformation of romance themes and conventions are fully understood and appreciated, that a true appreciation of the extent of his achievement can be gained.

To discuss Richardson and romance is not in any way to detract from his striking innovations in English fiction, rather to lead to a greater understanding of those innovations. Richardson himself claimed to have invented a 'new species of writing',[3] and while his claim is a valid one in some respects, one must continually stress that his fiction was also an example of 'mass art', though at a 'higher level of coherence and intensity'[4] than his now-forgotten contemporaries could muster. John Richetti does much in his work on early eighteenth-century fiction to redress the imbalance created by Ian Watt in *The Rise of the Novel*, where he discards almost all traces of a literary context. Richetti's thesis is that one cannot properly understand, say, Defoe or Richardson, unless one takes into account their participation in the early eighteenth-century milieu, and unless one appreciates also that their contemporary popularity was 'the result of their being able to use or exploit much more capably *the same raw materials* . . . [my italics] as their fellows Their great achievement as realistic artists,' Richetti continues, '. . is only part of the explanation of their great contemporary success'.

Richardson himself has little to say concerning romance in his voluminous writings about his fiction. What he does say is generally of a derogatory nature. One of his professed aims in writing *Pamela* for instance, was to decry 'such Novels and Romances as have a Tendency to inflame and corrupt' (SL,46,47). He also stated that *Pamela* was intended to 'turn young people into a course of reading different from the pomp and parade or romance writing . . .' (SL, 41). *Clarissa*, was not, he claimed, a 'mere Novel or Romance' (SL, 158). Indeed, Warburton's suggestion, in the preface to the third volume of the first edition of *Clarissa*, that Richardson was influenced by the French romancers, so upset him that he dropped the preface completely in the second, and later editions. He also made his position quite clear in a letter to Warburton:

> Then as to what you are pleased to hint, that I pursued in my former Piece [*Pamela*] the excellent Plan fallen upon lately by the French Writers, I would only observe that all that know me, know, that I am not acquainted in the least either with the French Language or Writers; And that it was Chance and not Skill or Learning that made me fall into this way of Scribbling. (SL,85,86)

Richardson's claims concerning his fiction, and the distinction he draws between his own and all other fiction need not be taken too seriously. Every writer of fiction for well over a century, whether in England or the Continent, had expressed similar views.

In one of his earliest comments on his art of fiction, Richardson makes an all-important admission, and one which implicitly suggests that he has followed the contemporary fashion and popularity of romance in *Pamela*. Doctor George Cheyne had written to Richardson, upbraiding him for his handling of some of the scenes in *Pamela*. 'You ought to avoid Fondling – and Gallantry', he wrote, 'Tender Expressions not becoming the Characters of Wisdom, Piety and conjugal Chastity especially in the Sex' (SL,46,n). In his reply to Dr Cheyne, Richardson showed what a well-defined conception

of his audience he possessed, and also revealed his designs upon
this audience:

> I am endeavouring to write a Story, which shall catch young
> and airy Minds, and when Passions run high in them, to show
> how they may be directed to laudable Meanings and Purposes
> in order to decry such Novels and Romances, as have a Tendency
> to inflame and corrupt: And if I were to be too spiritual, I doubt
> I should catch none but Grandmothers, for the Granddaughters
> would put my Girl indeed in better Company, such as that of
> the graver Writers, and *there* they would leave her; but would
> still pursue those Stories, that pleased their Imaginations without
> informing their Judgements. (SL,46,47)

It is difficult to exaggerate the implications and ramifications of
this statement.[6] The readers he wishes to 'catch' are the 'young
and airy ones', viz. the typical reader of conventional romance. To
lure such readers to his fiction, he realises he must at least adhere
to the conventional formula of romance. The major distinction
aimed at between *Pamela* and the conventional romance is that
when 'Passions run high' in the readers of *Pamela*, Richardson will
then direct them to 'laudable Meanings and Purposes': the high-
running passions of the romance of passion, on the other hand,
tend only to 'inflame and corrupt'. Richardson's aim is to please
the imaginations of his readers with a typical romance formula,
while, at the same time, 'informing their Judgements': passionate
romance does not do this, he claims. Richardson appreciates that
if he does not fashion his lures well, he will be neglected, and, in
the meantime, romances of passion will continue to be read: the
alternative is to use his readers' expectations and desires for his
own ends – to seem to give them what they want, but in, the
process, to reexamine the formula and draw new conclusions for
the captive audience.

It must, of course, be acknowledged that Richardson's insistence
that his work was written to inculcate the principles of virtue and
religion in his readers was not revolutionary, or even new. Every
writer of fiction, for over one hundred years before Richardson,
made a similar claim. And the typical reader was probably quite
as sceptical about Richardson's claims to show the way to virtue
as they were of all the previous claims. The difference in Richardson's case is that – at least as far as one can tell – he was sincere in

his intentions. And yet, ironically, he fell, unsuspectingly, into a
trap he had laid for himself, in *Pamela*; and his work, is, in almost
every sense of the word, just another variation of the romance of
passion. But his failure in *Pamela* led Richardson to revise his
techniques, and the result was *Clarissa*, one of the classics of
English fiction – a work which successfully adapts and transforms
the early eighteenth-century romance into something truly revolutionary.

There might seem to be an inherent contradiction between
Richardson's claim to have, on the one hand, initiated a new species
of writing, and, on the other, to have implicitly acknowledged that
he was following a conventional formula for fiction. But there is
no contradiction. The modern student typically assumes that when
Richardson speaks of his 'new species of writing' that *he* was
aware – as the student obviously is – of the striking innovations in
Pamela and *Clarissa*. It is perhaps not too great an exaggeration to
state that Richardson was utterly unaware of the true extent of his
own originality. It is obvious from the context in which it occurs
that Richardson intends *Pamela* to be a new species of writing
because of its 'easy and natural manner' of composition (SL,41)
as opposed to the 'pomp and parade' of romance-writing. He may
also have intended 'newness' to indicate the new direction in
which the passions would be guided in *Pamela*.

PAMELA AS ROMANCE

A typical eighteenth-century reader would – without looking even
further than the title – have presumed that *Pamela* was a romance
of one kind or another. With very few exceptions, the heroines of
all romances for hundreds of years, had names which ended with
the letter 'a' – names such as Clelia, Cleopatra, Parthenissa,
Lindamira, Melliora, Lucinda, Cleomira. Even the subtitle of
Richardson's first work of fiction would have recalled previous
romances of passion. *The Surprize: or Constanty Rewarded* was
published in 1724, and *Vertue Rewarded; or, The Irish Princess* was
published as early as 1693. Even a superficial acquaintance with
the subject matter of *Pamela* would have confirmed the view of
readers that it was a conventional romance. It deals – as do
numerous other works – with the well-known preoccupation of
the age, the attempts at the destruction of female innocence by a

representative of the aristocratic world of male corruption. Indeed, *Pamela* illustrates perfectly John Richetti's 'two basic conflicts', dramatised so often in the romances of the early eighteenth century, i.e. 'latent social antagonism – the values of corrupt aristocracy condemned by a sobriety and rectitude implicitly classless – and sexual antagonism – helpless and virtuous females destroyed by a malign masculine ethos.'[7]

Of course Pamela is not 'destroyed', and the failure to destroy her is one indication of the peculiar combination of elements which the novel contains – a combination fashioned partly from passionate, partly from heroic and/or religious romance. The hero and heroine are a good illustration of this combination of elements. Mr B. *is* the typical libertine of passionate romance, and, what is more, actually regards himself as just such a typical libertine. His big mistake is to regard Pamela as his opposite number in a romance of passion, believing she is a typical 'virtuous' heroine, half-willing, half-afraid of seduction, but finally, and inevitably, to be won over. Pamela, unfortunately for Mr B., is a heroine who, unaccountably, has found herself starring in the wrong production. And it is this 'miscasting' which gives the work an added touch of originality. Mr B. decides that Pamela's refusal to comply with his demands is owing to her having read the wrong romances. Early in the novel he writes as follows to Pamela's father:

> I never knew so much romantic invention as she is mistress of. In short, the girl's head is turned by romances, and such idle stuff, to which she has given herself up, ever since her kind lady's death. And she assumes airs, as if she was a mirror of perfection, and every body had a design upon her.[8]

The 'mirrors of perfection' Mr B. writes about were the heroines of heroic or religious, rather than passionate romance. Mr B. has, in fact, isolated the difficulty which has plagued readers of *Pamela* for over two hundred years, when he speaks of her assuming airs, and her presumption that everybody has a design on her. He also highlights a major distinction between Pamela and a true heroine of religious or heroic romance. It is true to say that even the heroines of religious and heroic romances were constantly 'pursued' by every male who appeared on the scene. But to suggest that any of them was aware of her charms and their effects on males, would not only be inaccurate, but contrary to the canons of romance. Yet this is a charge laid against Pamela, and with great justification. Later, Mr B. suggests that when Pamela is eventually raped or seduced, she will consciously follow the pattern established by the heroines of romance, by echoing 'to the woods and groves her piteous lamentations for the loss of her fantastical innocence', because she is a 'romantic idiot' (i,141). In the same vein, Mr B. can only retort 'Romantic girl!' when Pamela says, 'my honesty is dearer to me than my life' (i,213). Mr B. is certainly accurate if he meant to imply that Pamela was simply another in a very long line of girls from heroic, religious, indeed even Greek romance, who were willing to die rather than be violated. But Mr B.'s remark also implies that Pamela is simply adopting a pose she has read about so often in these particular romances, and that it is merely a pose. He is amused, also, to find, on reading her letters, that the relationship between them has been given 'a pretty air of romance' (i,205).

In spite of his opinion of romances, Mr B. does implicitly acknowledge, on one occasion, that his own intrigues savour of romance. Soon after Pamela has been hurried off to Mrs Jewkes, her father comes to see her at Mr B.'s home. Mr B. tries to fob Andrews off by claiming that his daughter is in London, living in the home of a bishop, as servant to his wife. Andrews wishes to know the name of the bishop so that he may go visit his daughter. 'Why Goodman Andrews,' replies Mr B., 'I think thou hast read romances as well as thy daughter: thy head is turned with them. May I not have my word taken?' (i,80). Mr B. implies, here, that Andrews, from his reading of romances, thinks that, in accordance with romantic intrigue, Pamela might not be at the home of a bishop. But Pamela *is not* at the home of a bishop, and Mr B. thereby convicts himself of romantic intrigue. The significant point here, however, is that the intrigue is that of passionate rather than heroic romance, and, as stated above, Mr B. regards himself as a hero of passionate romance.

The basic plot-situation of *Pamela* is that of passionate romance. Charlot of *The New Atalantis* and Melliora of *Exilius* are, for example, both left orphans on the death of their fathers, and consigned to the care of their fathers' best friends. This 'friend' falls in love with his ward and does all in his power to seduce or rape her. The variation in *Pamela* is obvious: here, her 'mother' in the person of Lady B., dies, and Pamela is left in the power of Mr B. Lady B.'s dying words to her son 'remember my poor Pamela' (i,1), confirm

her role as 'mother' and also Pamela's role as 'ward' of Mr B. Mr
B. falls in love with Pamela, and, like her predecessors, Charlot
and Melliora, Pamela falls in love with her 'guardian'. And the
remainder of the novel follows the general pattern of the Charlot
and Melliora story. There are several attempts at raping Pamela,
all of which are foiled. But the eighteenth-century reader, conditioned by similar situations in numerous, previous works of fiction,
would presume it to be only a matter of time before Mr B. succeeded
in his designs.[9] With every failure in *Pamela* came heightened
tension at the prospect that next time the libertine would succeed.
And readers must have presumed, too, that violence was the only
way in which Mr B. could succeed, given Pamela's character and
the disparity in rank between them. Marriage would hardly have
seemed an alternative in such a situation. When all of Mr B.'s early
attempts fail, Richardson varies the situation, making Pamela the
typically helpless heroine of passionate[10] romance by sending her
to a country retreat. All seems lost for Pamela and her virtue, but
again she wins through. By having Pamela acknowledge her love
for, and to Mr B. (i,199), Richardson again plays heavily on the
expectations of his audience: such acknowledgements by the
heroine of passionate romance usually implied her inevitable ruin
after many triumphs. But in this case there is no such ruin, despite
all the conventional indications.

The worldly-wise duchess of *The New Atalantis* shows how much
she and Pamela, rather than Pamela and Charlot, have in common.
It is worth quoting again, part of the duchess's remarks to Charlot,
as a commentary, now on Pamela:

The first thing a Woman ought to consult was her Interest, and
Establishment in the World; that Love should only be a handle
towards it; when she left the Pursuit of that to give up herself to
her Pleasures, Contempt and Sorrow were sure to be her
Companions. No Lover was yet ever known so ardent, but time
abated of his Transport; no Beauty so ravishing, but that her
Sweetness would cloy; nor did Men any longer endeavour to
please, when nothing was wanting to their Wishes. Love, the
most generous, and yet the most mercenary of all the Passions,
does not care what he lavishes, provided there be something
still in view to repay his Expence; but that once over, the Lover
possess'd of whatever his Mistress can bestow, he hangs his
Head, the Cupid drops his Wings, and seldom feels their native

Energy return, but to carry him to new Conquests. (i,73,74)

By echoing the remarks of the duchess at several points in the novel, Pamela demonstrates that, while she may consider herself a heroine of heroic or religious romance, she has also read the romances of passion. In a conversation with Mrs Jervis early in the novel, she makes the following remarks about Mr B.:

He may condescend, perhaps, to think I may be good enough for his harlot; and those things don't disgrace men, that ruin poor women, as the world goes. And so, if I was wicked enough he would keep me till I was undone, and till his mind changed, for even wicked men, I have read, soon grow weary of wicked ness with the same person, and love variety. Then poor Pamela must be turned off and looked upon as a vile abandoned creature . . . (i,29).

Later, in reply to his suggestion that he might marry her if she were to live with him for a year, Pamela retorts: 'Little Sir, as know of the world, I am not to be caught by a bait so poorly covered as this' (i,168).

While Richardson may have avoided the erotic excesses of the passionate romances, there is no doubting the inherently prurient quality of much of *Pamela*. It was this quality in *Pamela* which Coleridge had in mind when he wrote of the 'hothouse' atmosphere of Richardson's fiction. It is notable that Richardson does not follow the erotic tradition created by his predecessors, but formulates a new one. We never find Pamela in *déshabille*, asleep, or in a daze 'with all her many charms exposed to view'. The majority of attempts on Pamela's virtue open with Mr B.'s taking her hand, followed by a kiss, a forcing her on to his knee, and a 'putting his hand' in her bosom. Every scene contains two or more of these ingredients. The two major, premeditated attempts to rape Pamela occur when she is in bed. In the first scene, Mr B. hides in the closet, dressed in a 'morning-gown'. Pamela writes: 'I pulled of my stays and my stockings, and all my clothes to an underpetticoat (i,49). At this point Mr B. rushes out and takes her in his arms But Pamela faints, on finding 'his hand in my bosom', and is saved from rape by unconsciousness and the intervention of Mrs Jervis In the second scene, Mr B. impersonates a serving maid, Anne, who is to sleep with Pamela and Mrs Jewkes. This time, Pamela 'with my underclothes in my hand, all undressed' (i,177), as she says, passes by Mr B., who is sitting in a chair in the bedroom. When Mr B. gets into bed alongside Pamela, Mrs Jewkes holds one of her arms, he the other. When Mr B. puts his hand in Pamela's bosom, she again faints away, and is saved. Richardson may have avoided the erotic excesses of the passionate romances, but he leans heavily on his readers' expectations in order to make the most of the suggestive scenes he does depict: his method is quite different, but the result is almost identical. It must be remembered that there were no direct sexual descriptions in early eighteenth-century fiction: authors had to rely on implication and suggestion in order to achieve their erotic ends. Richardson, besides not having to describe any actual rape – just near-misses – adopts a new technique in *Pamela* of indirect sexuality: the numerous references to stockings, handkerchiefs, underpetticoats, and underclothing generally, is a notable feature of the work. Perhaps the prurience of *Pamela* is best exhibited in a reading of *Shamela*: an academic treatise on the subject could hardly expect to match Fielding's unerring eye.

PAMELA AS RELIGIOUS ROMANCE

The religious romances of the early eighteenth century are clear and explicit 'embodiments of an ideological pattern of beleaguered and necessarily "helpless" virtue in an vicious and aggressive world'.[11] By this reckoning, *Pamela* is certainly a religious romance, though the epithet 'helpless' does, perhaps, need some qualification. Pamela herself certainly seems to follow in the footsteps of her Christian sisters who never had to fear anything from themselves, since there was simply no chink in the armour of their virtue or duty. It is, in fact, the very inviolability of Pamela's virtue which leads Mr B. to taunt her with modelling herself naively on the heroines of religious and heroic romance. But the text of *Pamela*, and Richardson's letters, demonstrate the author's own attitude. Richardson claimed *Pamela* was written to serve the 'cause of Virtue and Religion' (SL,52,53). He stressed, too, that this heroine was 'pious and Virtuous' (SL,48), indeed objected to by some as being 'too pious' (SL,48). 'But Pamela's Gratitude and Thankfulness to the Supreme Being', Richardson wrote to Ralph Allen, 'I have on all such Occasions, as my Judgement wou'd enable me to think proper, kept up: And it was my Intention to avoid Affectation on this Head' (SL,51). Richardson certainly executed his intention to the full. The 'Supreme Being' is ever-present in the letters of Pamela, and most particularly does she link Him with her virtue. And, if example were needed, her father provides it in one of his few letters in the work. Speaking of the preservation of his daughter's virtue, he writes: 'no less depends upon it than my child's everlasting happiness in this world and the next . . .' (i,9) Pamela's own letters are no less religious in tone:

> Angels and saints, and all the host of heaven defend me! And may I never survive one moment, that fatal one in which I forfeit my innocence. (i,20)

> He [Mr B.] is and will be wicked, and designs me a victim to his lawless attempts, if the God in whom I trust, and to whom I hourly pray, prevent it not. (i,104)

> Save, then, my innocence, good Heaven! and preserve my mind spotless: and happy shall I be to lay down my worthless life, and see an end to all my troubles and anxieties. (i,137)

> Oh God! my God! this *time* this *one time*! deliver me from this distress! or strike me dead this moment. (i,178,179)

> Oh, how I blessed God, and, I hope, ever shall, for all his gracious favours to his unworthy handmaid. (i,241)

One other interesting aspect of Pamela's statements, above, is that she invariably views death as the alternative to, or consequence of dishonour. This is another aspect of the personality of the heroine of religious romance, though it is a moot point whether or not Pamela convinces us, as do her predecessors, that she will 'either die or survive with [her] genuine honour intact'.[12]

It is important, also, to demonstrate the way in which *Pamela* deviates from the pattern of the typical religious romance. As with all the writers of romance, religious and otherwise, Richardson claimed in his preface to *Pamela* that his aim was to 'inculcate Religion and Morality'.[13] But the writers of religious romance not only made such claims, their works confirmed the justice of them, and they steadfastly refused to provide any erotic bonuses for their readers. In passionate romance the eroticism could hardly be called a bonus, since it was a major ingredient in a successful popular art form, and the talk of virtue and morality in prefaces, mere cant. Richardson, of course, does provide erotic bonuses, and no amount of prefatory material, or religious cant in the text can make them otherwise. It is also true to say that Pamela – unlike the heroine of religious romance – is always aware of her charms, both physical and mental, and their power to extract a 'settlement' in her favour : never was heroine so worldly-wise and cunning – quite the reverse of the true 'innocent' of religious romance.

It is, perhaps, appropriate at this point to look in more detail at a work alluded to, briefly, above – *Vertue Rewarded; or, The Irish Princess*,[14] published in 1693. If Samuel Richardson based *Pamela* on a specific, earlier work, it seems more than likely that *The Irish Princess* is that work. Even if one cannot accept *The Irish Princess* as a source for *Pamela*, the many resemblances between the two works emphatically confirm Richardson's debt to the antecedent romances.

The story of *The Irish Princess* is set in Ireland immediately after the battle of the Boyne (1690) between King William, and King James. Serving in the victorious army of King William is an anonymous Prince of S——g, who, immediately after the battle, sets off with his command to Limerick. When he comes to the town of Clonmel, in County Tipperary, the Prince decides to rest there and await the arrival of King William and his forces. While in Clonmel, the Prince meets and falls in love with a native of the town, a beautiful gentlewoman called Marinda. He is 'resolved some way or other . . . to enjoy her' (22), but despite all his efforts, he is unsuccessful because of Marinda's spirited resistance. Ultimately, he offers marriage, and Marinda thus becomes the Irish princess. *The Irish Princess* has a good deal to recommend it on purely artistic grounds, and hardly deserves the total neglect to which it has been subjected ever since. This neglect seems particularly surprising in the light of the title of the novel, which is identical to the subtitle of *Pamela*. This coincidence, one imagines, should surely have led some curious critic to investigate the relationship between the two works long before the latter half of the twentieth century: yet no one ever has, to my knowledge. The reason for this neglect lies, almost certainly, in Richardson's own deliberate efforts to divert attention away from influences on his fiction, and a simultaneous emphasis on its originality. But even a cursory glance at *Pamela* and *The Irish Princess* reveals obvious similarities between the two works.

For a start, the basic pattern of both *Pamela* and *The Irish Princess* appears to be that of the passionate romance, but with a very significant difference in each case. When faced with aggressive and prolonged attacks on her virtue, the typical heroine of passionate romance, as we have already noted, almost invariably succumbs to the male, eventually. This capitulation occurs despite the female's strong-willed, seemingly inflexible resistance. It is against such a background as this, that one can appreciate the particular fascination of *Pamela* and, no doubt, *The Irish Princess*, also, for an eighteenth-century audience. At every stage, almost, of each novel, the contemporary reader must have expected the inevitable rape or seduction of Pamela and Marinda. The more this rape or seduction was postponed, the *more* inevitable it must have seemed next time. But the difference in each of these two cases is that, in spite of all the aggressive as well as benign attempts to overcome the resistance of both Marinda and Pamela, neither loses her honour. In each novel there is also a variation on the pattern of religious romance. Instead of being married to another, or tied to another by binding vows, both Marinda and Pamela feel she has a grave obligation to herself to preserve her virtue untainted. Both heroines are even prepared to die if that is the alternative to losing their virtue. Pamela declares that she has 'always been taught to value honesty above . . . life' (i,19), and that she will 'die a thousand deaths rather than be dishonest any way' (i,4). And, later, she writes to Mr B.: 'Were my *life* in question instead of my *honesty*, I would not wish to involve you or any body in the least difficulty for so worthless a poor creature . . . . Save, then, my innocence, good Heaven! and preserve my mind spotless: and happy shall I be to lay down my worthless life, and see an end to all my troubles and anxieties' (i,137). It is also in a letter, that Marinda, in *The Irish Princess*, states her case explicitly to the Prince, asking him to pardon her rashness towards him since it was 'in defence (of that which I prefer before all things) my Vertue' (160), she says. Earlier, when the Prince had saved Marinda from almost certain death at the hands of bandits, she exclaimed: 'go, leave me to be a prey to them whom thou has hunted away, for I had rather dye here, bemoaning this poor Gentleman who fell in the defence of my Honour, than take refuge with you, who whilst you defend it from others, endeavour to prey upon it your self' (150).

One of the great conflicts in much of eighteenth-century fiction, in particular in passionate romances, as we have seen, is the conflict in the breast of the heroine between love and duty. The heroine fully appreciates the obligations she owes to her parents in not eloping with, marrying, or, indeed, even consorting in any way with her rakish manfriend. In almost every case, however, the force of love proves much too strong for duty, which is swept aside. A conflict between love and duty is an important feature of both *Pamela* and *The Irish Princess*, but the variation is again distinctive. In each case, the heroine is in love with her would-be ravisher, and this sets up an obvious conflict between her love for him, and her duty to herself and her virtue, rather than to her parents. In this conflict, both Pamela and Marinda discover that they harbour within themselves powerful forces which take the side of love, and would overcome duty and give up the citadel of virtue in the cause of love. Pamela, because she believes she has given too obvious an indication of her feelings to Mr B., declares her readiness to 'bite my forward tongue (or rather to beat my more forward heart that dictated to that machine), for what I have said' (i,194). Later, she talks of her willingness to break 'this wicked forward heart of mine' (i,199), which she described as 'treacherous' (i,221), and 'too partial in his [Mr B's] favour' (i,220). Likewise, in *The Irish Princess*, Marinda says: 'if my tell-tale Eyes, or my Countenance has betray'd me, I'll disfigure this Countenance, and tear out these Eyes, rather than they shall invite, or assist, any enterprize, to the prejudice of my Vertue' (55). Later, she admits to the Prince that although a 'Traitor within' (140) takes his part, she has no intention of yielding to him.

While love versus duty is the typical conflict in the breast of the eighteenth-century fictional heroine, a corresponding conflict is taking place in the typical hero, i.e. that between love and ambition and/or interest. The conflict arises when, as is usual, the villain/hero falls in love with a girl who is his inferior in birth and wealth. It is not, therefore, consistent with either his interest or his ambition that he should engage in a marital alliance with such an individual, and thus love, and interest/ambition invariably come into conflict. This is precisely what happens in both *Pamela* and *The Irish Princess*; indeed the similarities between the two works are particularly marked in this area. In *Pamela*, the conflict, though fairly explicit throughout the whole work, is commented upon specifically only once, and then only when Mr B. has actually decided to marry

Pamela. He says: 'I so much value a voluntary love in the person I would wish for my wife, that I would have even prudence and interest hardly named in comparison with it; and can you [Pamela] return me sincerely the honest compliment I now make you? – In the *choice* I have made, it is impossible I should have any view to my interest. Love, *true* love, is the *only* motive by which I am induced' (i,241). In *The Irish Princess*, on the other hand, the reader's attention is specifically directed to the conflict on a number of occasions. In the introduction to the story, the author claims that his (her?) tale will show love, 'triumphant at once over two of these his greatest Enemies, the Noise of War and the Vanity of Ambition' (3). In the story itself, Marinda impersonates a fortune-teller and says to her lover, the Prince: 'I fancy your Highness has fallen in love with someone below you, and that your Love and Ambition are at variance'. (114) 'You guess as right', replies the Prince, 'as if you had seen my Heart; and if you can tell me how I shall succeed in my Love, I'll make that, or my Ambition conform itself to the other' (114). Later, the author describes how the Prince, 'was so equally divided betwixt Love and Interest, that they governed his breast by turns, sometimes one having the better, and sometimes the other' (141). Finally, when the Prince, like Mr B., decides that he will marry his loved one, he says: 'I will no longer indulge this vain Ambition, or let it cross my Love' (161). In each story, therefore, love has had an important victory over interest/ambition.

A good deal of attention in both *Pamela* and *The Irish Princess* is also devoted to the disparity in rank between the hero and heroine. This inequality is underlined in the early stages of both novels to suggest, it seems, the improbability of marriage between the hero and heroine,[15] or at least to give some idea of the obstacles in the way of such a marriage. When the Prince's friend and 'gentleman of horse', Celadon, is puzzled by a major alteration in humour which he perceives in his master, he says to him: 'By your words, Sir, I should guess . . . you are in Love, but the consideration of the place where we are corrects that thought, since in this Island there is scarce one worthy your high Affections' (20). When the Prince admits to the violence of his love for Marinda, and considers the possibility of living with her for many years, Celadon retorts: 'why sure . . . your Highness does not design any more than a Jest in't; for though her Person deserves a higher station in the World, yet, since fortune has given her neither Quality nor Riches suitable to it, you are not so prodigal a Lover as *Mark Anthony* was, to quit your Principality, and your Honour besides, for a Mistress' (21). If, as Celadon argues, it would be unbecoming for the Prince even to keep Marinda as his mistress, marriage to her seems out of the question. The scene, in the opening pages of *Pamela*, is set in much the same way. Mr B., we are told, 'may expect one of the best ladies in the land' (i.7), yet he loves his servant, Pamela, 'better than all the ladies in the land' (i.29). It is unfortunate, we are told, that Pamela is 'so much beneath' (i.30) Mr B.; that if 'he knew a lady of birth, just such another as yourself [Pamela], in person and mind, and he would marry her tomorrow' (i.34). The heroines, too, are well aware of their situation and its consequences. Marinda says: 'Nor am I so conceited, as to aim at Marriage [to the Prince]; for what private Gentlewoman could nourish such vain hopes as those of being raised to a Princess? 'Tis more than a bare prodigy, for Earthquakes, Inundations, and those wonders of Nature do sometimes happen; but that a Prince should marry a private Maid, is such a wonder, as I never found mentioned in all the Chronicles I have read' (122,123). Later, she writes to the Prince: 'your Highness's condescension must not make me forget, that you are a Prince, and that my highest deserts rise no higher than to be the Humblest of your Servants' (160). Pamela, too, is continually preoccupied with Mr B.'s 'high degree and my low degree' (i.29), with 'the distance between him [Mr B.] and me' (i.71). As in the case of Marinda, marriage to the man she loves seems beyond the wildest dreams of Pamela. When Mrs Jervis suggests that Mr B. might marry her, Pamela replies: 'No, no . . . that cannot be. I neither desire nor expect it. His condition don't permit me to have such a thought' (i.118,119). The remainder of the novel contains numerous references to this disparity in rank. When Mr B., for instance, offers the possibility of marriage to Pamela, if she lives with him, as his mistress, for a year, Pamela replies: 'I have not once dared to look so high as to such a proposal. . . . Your honour, well I know, would not let you stoop to so mean and unworthy a slave as the poor Pamela' (i,167). Later, she describes his regard for her as one 'unworthy your condition' (i,189), and, when he eventually hints at marriage, Pamela declares she has 'not the presumption to hope such an honour' (i.193).

The hero in each tale is equally preoccupied with the question of rank, and the inequality which exists between him and the woman he loves. Marriage is, of course, the complicating factor:

each hero would be only too happy to indulge in a sexual liaison, however lengthy, with his loved one, as long as marriage were not in question. Mr B. describes his passion as having made him 'stoop to a meanness' (i,143), and he says to Pamela: 'Consider the pride of my condition. I cannot endure the thought of marriage, even with a person of equal or superior degree to myself . . . how then, with the distance between us in the world's judgement, can I think of making you my wife' (i,188). The Prince is even more eloquent on the same topic. Like Mr B., he talks of his 'mean passion' (118, 134), and instead of 'stooping' he describes himself as having 'to cringe to one that was beneath him, and submit himself to one, who could not pretend to a higher Match, than one of his Dependants' (134). Earlier in the story, when the possibility of his marrying Marinda is put to the Prince, he replies as follows: 'Marriage! . . . why did not I confess to you, that she was a private Gentlewoman, one beneath me? I wonder you should ask such a question . . . . If . . . I can enjoy her on any terms, but those of Marriage, I shall think myself very happy; if not, my Love has so wholly blinded me as to make me forget my Interest and my Honour' (116).

Once marriage has eventually been offered by the male, all the female's problems are over. The male, however, given his previous opposition to marriage, has to make certain psychological adjustments. Each has to arrive at the conclusion that he could not, after all, have possibly married a better woman, and that her qualities and natural breeding are far superior to those of any lady in the land. A good deal of *Pamela* is given over to a proof of the heroine's ladylike qualities *after* Mr B. has proposed marriage, and after the marriage itself. Mr B. now thinks Pamela 'would grace a prince' (l.231) and that 'no lady in the kingdom can outdo her or better support the condition to which she will be raised' (l.232). The Prince, too, reassures himself in the following words: 'You deserve all things, Divine Marinda . . . what Title is too High, or Estate too Magnificent to admit you for a Partner? I will no more indulge this vain Ambition or let it cross my Love: tell me *Celadon*, (said he) does not *Marinda*, with her natural Beauty look finer than our Proudest Court Ladies, tho' decked with all their Gaudy Costly Dresses? Yet that lovely Body is but the Shell of a more glorious Inhabitant' (161).

In both *The Irish Princess* and *Pamela*, the pattern of courtship by the male is very similar. Each involuntarily falls in love with the heroine and then makes valiant efforts to rid himself of his 'mean' passion. Mrs Jervis is the first to tell us of Mr B.'s attempt to overcome his love for Pamela: 'and it is my opinion he finds he can't; and that vexes his proud heart' (1.29), she says. Richardson himself intervenes to tell us that Mr B. had 'in vain tried to conquer his passion' (1.76), for Pamela. Mr B frequently alludes to his struggle also. 'In vain, my Pamela, do I struggle against my affection for you' (1.222), he writes. And much earlier he had exclaimed: 'I, in spite of my heart, and all the pride of it, cannot but love you . . .I love you to extravagance' (1.69). Equally, in *The Irish Princess*, the Prince realises, too late, that he has been irrevocably hooked by love. The author tells us that the Prince 'had no power to over-awe or check his Love, or Relations to controul [sic] it' (43). Later, the Prince describes his love for Marinda as 'one so violent, and yet so unreasonable, that I am unable to curb it, nor have I any hopes of success, if I let it go on' (113). Yet, he resolves to 'shake off the mean Passion; but all his endeavours were vain; the more he tried it, the more sensible he grew, how unable he was to perform it' (118). The only antidote for the violence of Mr B.'s and the Prince's passion is to 'enjoy' the heroine. 'I will have her' (1.46), Mr B. says to Mrs Jervis: and to Pamela herself, he later says: 'I must have you' (1.188). The Prince, too, 'some way or other is resolved to enjoy' Marinda (21), and 'cannot endure the thoughts of losing her' (118). Nor is the anguish of the male, in his inability to enjoy the female, a mental one only: both heroes are actually in danger of death in their respective stories, and the possibility of losing the female forever is given as a major contributory factor. Mr B. becomes 'very ill indeed' (1.226), when Pamela leaves him, yet recovers immediately she returns. On her return to him, at his request, Mr B. says to Pamela: 'Life is not life without you! Had you refused me, and I had hardly hopes you would oblige me, I should have had a severe fit of it, I believe' (1.227). Celadon, in *The Irish Princess*,[16] accuses Marinda of endangering the life of the Prince by her cruelty, i.e. by her refusal to have anything further to do with him. He prevails upon Marinda to write to the Prince, and then uses her letter to 'cure his Body, by this sovereign Ballsom which he brought for his mind' (159). The balsam works, eventually, and the Prince, like Mr B., is restored to health. In each story, therefore, the love of the hero is so violent that it causes severe mental and physical distress, bringing him, we are led to believe, close to death. The heroine in each story, however, refuses to provide the necessary relief by being enjoyed unlawfully, and the dilemma is only resolved when Mr B. and the Prince agree to pay the ultimate price – marriage – as a cure for their ailment.

The deceptions practiced by Mr B. and the Prince in order to beguile Pamela and Marinda are of a kind also. Mr B. pretends he's going to marry someone other than Pamela; later, he has plans for a bogus marriage ceremony with Pamela. He hides in a closet, disguises himself, pretends he is gone on a journey to Stamford, all with the intention of effecting the rape of Pamela. In *The Irish Princess*, the Prince's first strategem is reminiscent of Mr B.'s pretended journey to Stamford. He organizes a ball, and hopes to lure Marinda to it by pretending that he himself has gone to Dublin. He rides out of Clonmel, but returns secretly in time for the ball. The remaining deceptions in the story are carried out on the Prince's behalf by Celadon – disguise, a pretence that the Prince will marry Marinda, then a pretence that he is already married.

In several other details, also, there is an obvious similarity between *Pamela* and *The Irish Princess*. Both heroines are concerned, for example, that the acknowledgement of their love for the hero will lead to inevitable ruin;[17] both attempt to escape from their lovers and almost die in the process;[18] each story concerns itself a good deal with 'terms' either honourable or dishonourable;[19] and each heroine assumes that if she accedes to dishonourable terms she will be abandoned as soon as her lover grows tired of her;[20] the dream of Marinda in *The Irish Princess*,[21] as well as recalling the dream of Pamela,[22] is strikingly similar to two of the attempts at rape in *Pamela*;[23] the heroes, too, as well as being anonymous, share a preoccupation about rivals for the love of their sweethearts.[24] One detail which deserves particular attention is the ending of *The Irish Princess* and the corresponding event in *Pamela*, i.e. her marriage to Mr B. Marinda is described as having 'received the reward of her invincible Vertue, in Loving and being Beloved, and in having gained a Prince, who raised her Quality as high (in comparison of what she was before) as a Woman's Ambition could desire' (184).[25] Pamela, for her part, thanks Providence, 'which has, through so many intricate mazes, made me tread the path of innocence, and so amply rewarded me for what it has enabled me to do.' (1.241,242). Another feature of *Pamela* which is particularly interesting, though one would hesitate to place too much emphasis on it, is the use of the words 'prince', and 'princess' in the story. Early in the novel, Pamela, in objecting to the liberties Mr B. has taken with her, exlaims: 'Yet, Sir, I will be bold to say, I am honest, though poor: and if you was a prince, I would not be otherwise' (1.12). Later, she claims that her soul, if not her body, 'is of equal importance with the soul of a princess . . .' (1.137). Mr B. takes up the refrain when he says to Pamela, after he has proposed to her: 'You would grace a prince, my fair one'. (231)

Mark Kinkead-Weekes in his preface to the Everyman Library edition of *Pamela*, refers to what he sees as a serious failure in the novel:

> The most central [failure] . . . concerns not Pamela but B. Once one has learned to read with the sensitivity to implications that Richardson demands, it becomes clear that after markedly crude beginnings B. does become a complex character in the grip of acute conflict. But if Pamela and B. are both on the stage, and we are required to understand and judge them both in their opposition, the fact remains that we live always in her mind and never in his because the novel is told from a single point of view. Not only is it fatally easy to miss the exact fluctuations of B's conflict through superficial reading, but we inhabit so continuously a mind in which he appears simply as a 'black-hearted wretch' that we tend to oversimplify him too. (It is always a danger in point-of-view writing that we are tempted to adopt the viewpoint of one character instead of holding them all against our own greater knowledge.) At important points we need the same direct experience of B's heart and mind that we have of Pamela's; but the single focus cannot provide this. The result is disastrous when we come to B's reformation.[26]

A notable feature of *The Irish Princess* is that in spite of its being written from the point of view of a single character – the Prince – the author cleverly seeks to avoid the dangers associated with this technique. At important points we *do* have direct experience of Marinda's heart, in spite of the single focus. On two vital occasions,[27] the Prince overhears conversations between Marinda and her confidant, Diana. Later, he agrees to allow Celadon to impersonate a fortune-teller in a successful attempt to induce Marinda to reveal her inmost thoughts.[28] Celadon is important in another way, too. He is courting Diana, Marinda's confidant, and uses his position continually to gain additional information as to the state of Marinda's heart. In spite of the novel's single point-of-view narration, therefore, the author has managed to convey a 'double vision'. The narrative technique of *Pamela* is, however, very similar to that of *The Irish Princess* in one way. A feature of *Pamela* is Mr B.'s continual awareness of the state of Pamela's feelings towards him, because of his access to her 'heart' in the varous ways described. In both stories, the heroine is unaware, for quite some time, of the extent of her lover's knowledge. After Mr B.'s proposal of marriage, Pamela agrees to let him have any letters he may not have already seen. This is, interestingly, paralleled in *The Irish Princess* by Marinda's having Diana 'acquaint the Prince with all she knew of her [Marinda's] thoughts, without disguising anything' (177).

There appears to be little similarity between the characters of Marinda and Pamela, yet they are quite alike in one way, i.e. in the way each is mesmerised by the man who is out to 'enjoy' her in whatever way possible. Marinda freely admits to being captivated by the Prince and his charms; Pamela never does, at least not until her marital prospects are almost assured. Each tries to escape from her lover, but it is more than physical bondage that is involved, as each learns. Each story, then, features a peculiar combination of attraction and repulsion. One major difference between the two stories lies in the area of sexuality. The Prince never actually attempts either to seduce or rape Marinda, though it appears he would attempt either in his effort to enjoy her. Marinda, for her part, is certainly apprehensive of such a possibility, and her confidant, Diana, warns her explicitly as follows: 'Have a care *Marinda* . . . that you do not engage too far with one who is so much above you; 'tis not safe Intriguing with Persons of his Quality; Inferiour Lovers may be jested with as long as we please, and thrown off at will, but such as he seldom leave us without carrying away our Vertue, or at least our Reputation: And you will too late curse your own Charms when they have exposed you to be ruined (like a young Conjurer) by raising a Spirit which you are not able to lay' (54, 55). *Pamela*, on the other hand, is a typical novel of procrastinated rape or seduction, with a continual emphasis on the prurient.

Having considered in some detail the resemblances between *Pamela* and *The Irish Princess*, one basic issue still remains to be explored, viz. whether or not Richardson ever actually read *The*

Irish Princess. I hope I have already given a strong indication that he did, but there is also further evidence to be examined. The repetition of the title of the 1693 work in the subtitle of *Pamela* deserves some attention, for instance. While this repetition might obviously be ascribed to simple coincidence, it is worth noting that no other work of fiction prior to 1740, so far as I am aware, contained 'vertue rewarded' in its title or subtitle. Another fact merits notice, also, though, perhaps, at the risk of seeming too obvious, i.e. that Richardson *could* have read *The Irish Princess*, given that it was published in 1693. Richardson's most recent biographers, Eaves and Kimpel, point out that he was 'inclined to deny'[29] that he had ever read other works of fiction. They are sceptical of Richardson's claim, however, and explain it as follows: 'We suspect that he did like the idea of being first in the field and did not want anyone to think him indebted to the French or anyone else.[30] In spite of his being inclined to deny having read fiction, Richardson became a printer in the first place because he thought it a profession which would gratify his 'Thirst after Reading'.[31] More interesting still, are the following remarks by Richardson in a letter of 1753: 'As a bashful and not forward Boy, I was an early Favourite with all the young Women of Taste and Reading in the Neighbourhood. Half a Dozen of them when met to work with their Needles, used, when they got a Book they liked, and thought I should, to borrow me to read to them.'[32] It is obviously not inconceivable that *The Irish Princess* was one of the books Richardson was asked to read to the needleworkers. The title, *Vertue Rewarded*, certainly seems to suggest a book which might appeal to young ladies of 'taste and reading': equally, it would appear not to be one which would offend the susceptibilities of a young boy – even a young Richardson.

One final problem remains to be addressed, i.e. Richardson's claim that *Pamela* was actually based on a true story told to him by a gentleman with whom he was 'intimately acquainted'.[33] Intriguingly, the anonymous author of *The Irish Princess* makes an identical claim as follows, in his 'Preface to the Ill-Natured Reader': 'know, that the main Story is true, I heard of a Gentleman who was acquainted with the Irish Princess, and knew all the Intrigue, and having from him so faithful a relation of it, I make the scene the very same where it was transacted, the time the same, going on all the way with the Truth, as far as conveniency would permit; I only added some few Circumstances, and interlined it with two or three other Stories for variety sake' (no pagination). One would hesitate to attach any significance to this claim, it is so typical of writers of fiction at that time. Yet Samuel Richardson's claim has never been doubted. Perhaps this is because his relation of the original Pamela story[34] bears the stamp of a true tale. Yet, a significant discrepancy remains. In one of his letters[35] Richardson claims that he heard the story around 1716, and, in another,[36] that he heard it in 1725. One other piece of this jigsaw is, perhaps, contained in this well-known passage from one of Richardson's letters: 'I recollect that I was early noted for having Invention. I was not fond of Play as other Boys: my Schoolfellows used to call me *Serious* and *Gravity*: and five of them particularly delighted to single me out, either for a Walk, or at their Father's Houses or at mine, to tell them Stories, as they phrased it. Some I told them from my Reading as true; others from my Head as mere Invention'.[37] It is not, surely, inconceivable, that *Pamela* was written from Richardson's 'reading as true', while *Clarissa*, on the other hand, was written from his 'Head as mere Invention'. Perhaps the most plausible explanation for the genesis of *Pamela* may be that it is a unique amalgam, formed from a synthesis of the true story Richardson once heard and a not dissimilar fictitious story, *The Irish Princess*, which he had once read. Most important of all, perhaps, *The Irish Princess* provided the general narrative technique and framework for *Pamela*. In this context, it is intriguing to note Eaves and Kimpel speculating on the various causes 'for the collapse of *Pamela* about half way through part one'.[38] In the light of my remarks so far, one obvious reason for this so-called collapse proffers itself immediately. *The Irish Princess* ends almost immediately after the Prince's offer of marriage. Could one not reasonably argue that it is when Mr B. offers marriage that *Pamela* starts to collapse, i.e. after the model has ceased to provide guidance?

One hopes that on the basis of both internal and external evidence, *The Irish Princess* has been shown to be a credible source for *Pamela*. It can be stated, with little qualification, that there is no other work of English fiction quite like either in the fictionally-fertile half century 1690–1740. Given that it was published forty-seven years before *Pamela*, *The Irish Princess* is, in its own way, as exceptional a work as Richardson's. It appeared long before the vogue of either passionate or religious romance, yet *The Irish Princess* appears to be a fascinating synthesis created from both forms, but without the sensuality of one or the sermonising of the other. *Pamela* is a later synthesis of the passionate and religious romance, and while Richardson avoids the excesses of each, he is obviously guilty of the lesser charge of gratuitously highlighting both sex and sermon.

In spite of the amazing superiority of *Pamela* to anything written within the hundred years prior to 1740, and in spite of its striking realism, there is little doubt but that Richardson failed in his aims. That *Pamela* could so easily be turned into a *Shamela* is one indication of this failure. In *Shamela*, Fielding keeps close to the original incidents in *Pamela*, but interprets them quite differently. Shamela feigns virtue because Booby's inexperience convinces her that it will serve her better. She writes to her mother: 'I thought once of making a little fortune by my person. I now intend to make a great one by my vartue.'[39] Ian Watt makes the point that Fielding, in *Shamela*, 'unerringly selects the most dubious aspects of *Pamela* and drives home its crucial moral and psychological ambiguities'.[40] Fielding was one of a minority of readers who recognised that, far from inculcating the principles of religion and morality, *Pamela* simply inculcated the principle of 'be good, it will *pay* you in the end', or the principle of the 'cash-value of chastity'. Maynard Mack puts the matter another way when he states that Richardson's Pamela, 'intended as a model woman, was in many respects simply a pioneer capitalist, a middleclass entrepreneur of virtue, who looked on her virtue not as a condition of spirit, but as a commodity to be vended for the purpose of getting on.'[41]

In spite of all the above, however, there is no valid reason to doubt the sincerity of Richardson in *Pamela*. In this regard, a limited comparison can be made between Richardson's first novel and *Paradise Lost*. In each case the author's intentions were far removed from his eventual achievements, and in each case the dichotomy can be laid at the door of inexperience – inexperience, that is, in the handling of narrative and its peculiar techniques. Richardson presumed, for instance, that he could lure an audience to *Pamela* with a suggestion of passionate romance, while throwing in some traces of lubricity for good measure. What he hoped to do was to transform the basic pattern of passionate romance into a religious one: it was in this attempt that he failed to achieve complete success. Pamela, instead of being an innocent abroad, as Richardson clearly intended her to be, becomes, on a close reading of the text, a shrewd minx, determined to make the best deal she can by 'virtue'. On such a reading, all her talk of God, virtue and poverty is reduced to mere cant.

Richardson, by default, indicates that he was less than pleased with his accomplishment in *Pamela*: after 1742, he seldom adverted to his first work, apart from short references. There is a similar, implicit acknowledgement in Part II of *Pamela*, where Richardson, in relating the events of Pamela's married life, greatly changes his technique. Allowing for the fact that a change was needed anyway for the new state in which Pamela finds herself, it is obvious that there is no over-emphasis on religion and virtue, and certainly no prurience. More significantly, perhaps, is the implication, in the continuation of the novel, that Pamela's virtue has not in fact been rewarded at all. Many are the trials and tribulations of the Pamela married to a rake who has not fully reformed. Richardson had certainly revised his concept of virtue rewarded.

Clarissa shows just how far short of his ideals Richardson fell in *Pamela*. He wrote *Clarissa* with the same objectives in mind as in *Pamela*, but this time he not only avoided the pitfalls, and, covering somewhat similar ground, created one of the greatest of all works of fiction. *Pamela* may have been, in some senses, a failure, but it certainly taught Richardson all he needed to know about the art of fiction.

CLARISSA AS ROMANCE

Volume I of *Clarissa* was published in December 1747. *Pamela* was, perhaps, Richardson's greatest advance publicity for this, his second work of fiction. And there was little to prevent readers from presuming that *Clarissa* was to be simply another *Pamela*. The name Clarissa followed in the tradition of the heroines of romance for hundreds of years: Miss Rawlins presumes, indeed, that the name is a 'feigned or love name',[42] and at another point Lovelace himself substitutes the name Clarissa for the original in lines by Otway:

> Clarissa! Oh there's music in the name,
> That, soft'ning me to infant tenderness
> Makes my heart spring like the first leaps of life!   (i,47)

The very length of the novel would inevitably lead an eighteenth-

century reader to associate it with the *romans à longue haleine*; and
the basic situation of the work as advertised in the preface to the
first volume, would inevitably suggest a typical romance of passion
to the same reader. Two of the aims of the work as outlined in the
advertisement are:

> To caution Parents against the *undue* Exertion of their natural
> Authority over their Children, in the great Article of Marriage:
>   And Children against preferring a Man of Pleasure to a man
> of Probity, upon that dangerous, but too commonly received
> Notion, *That a reformed rake makes the best Husband.*[43]

There is little doubt that Richardson actually encouraged his
readers to view *Clarissa* as a conventional romance: his disclaimers
he kept for his private correspondence. What other reason could
Richardson possibly have for suggesting that the work was intended as a caution to children against preferring a man of pleasure
to a man or probity? This was a common caution, advanced by
most writers of passionate romance as the 'moral of the story'.
Richardson suggests in his preface that Clarissa preferred Lovelace,
a man of pleasure, to Solmes, a man of probity, and married
Lovelace on the presumption that a reformed rake makes the best
husband, a maxim she discovers to be untrue, too late, to save her
from the miseries of such a marriage. This is obviously a gross
misinterpretation of *Clarissa*, not to say a naïve one; but Richardson's purpose is clear. His private disclaimers are quite as clear:
the work, he says, has appeared 'in the humble guise of a *Novel*
only by way of Accommodation to the Manners and Taste of an
Age overwhelmed with a Torrent of Luxury, and abandoned to
Sound and senselessness' (SL,117). He insists that *Clarissa* is not
'a mere novel or romance' (SL,141,158), and dropped Warburton's
preface, as we saw, for its suggestion that he was influenced by
the French romancers. The reason for Richardson's encouragement
of readers to regard *Clarissa* as a typical romance is obvious: as
with *Pamela*, he wished to catch 'young and airy minds' and felt
this was the best way to do it. Having 'caught' his readers, his aim
was akin to that attributed to Mrs Rowe by John Richetti: 'You
have read this story many times before in the course of being
merely amused, she says to her reader, now here is what it really
means to you.'[44] There is, of course, a world of difference between
the effects achieved by Mrs Rowe and those achieved by Richardson

in *Clarissa*. Having encouraged his readers to regard *Clarissa* as a conventional romance, Richardson then went on to manipulate those conventions and the expectations of readers for his own ends. He adopted romance conventions and subsequently undermined and reexamined them to achieve striking and significant new effects. *Clarissa* thus becomes, in a sense, a critical analysis of the conventions of romance, and also, perhaps, of conventions of the age. This policy, of, on the one hand, encouraging people to regard *Clarissa* as a romance, and, on the other, refusing to conform to the conventions of romance, posed some problems for Richardson with his admirers. All readers of *Clarissa* believed that the heroine's virtue must be rewarded in the best (and conventional) way – as they saw it – by marriage to Lovelace. Nor had they any reason to doubt Richardson's compliance with convention, since they had *Pamela* as evidence. When news leaked out, in advance, of Richardson's true intentions with regard to *Clarissa*, he was deluged with pleas for a change in the plot, all to no avail. Among those who pleaded with him were such notables as Fielding, Cibber, Lyttleton, and Thomson (SL,99). It is difficult to account for Richardson's disappointment at the reception which the death of Clarissa was accorded, in view of the preconceived notions his readers held. 'I find', he wrote to Aaron Hill, 'by many Letters sent me, and by many Opinions given me, that some of the greater Vulgar, as well as the less, had rather it had had what they call, an Happy Ending' (SL,87). Significantly, in this same letter Richardson expresses his fear that his failure to accommodate his reader's expectations would affect the sales of *Clarissa*.

The relationship between Richardson and his readers during the composition of *Clarissa* is worthy of a separate study. While there is no doubt that he basked in the admiration of so many flatterers, there is no doubt, either, that Richardson's correspondence served a very functional purpose, helping to prevent *him* from miswriting, his *audience* from misreading *Clarissa*. Richardson only published one volume of *Clarissa* in 1748 with the specific intention of testing public reaction, and intended to 'continue it, or discontinue it, or abridge it, according to the Reception it met with' (SL,77). His requests for advice during the composition of his second novel were not simply solicitations for compliments but a means of ascertaining how the work was being read. With these details in his possession, he was able to avert any possibility of anyone making a *Shamela* of *Clarissa*. He was also, on the other hand, able to guide his readers through *Clarissa* and head off any misreadings of the work which became apparent. Richardson found the majority of his readers less than competent to appreciate his art, 'But a great deal in charity to them, I attribute to their inattention', he wrote, and continued:

> Ye World is not enough used to his way of writing, to the moment. It knows not that in the minutiae lie often the unfoldings of the Story, as well as of the heart; judges of an action undecided, as if it were absolutely decided. (SL,289).

CLARISSA AS PASSIONATE ROMANCE

Reduced to its bare outlines, *Clarissa* bears a striking resemblance to the romances of passion – elopement, rape/seduction, and desertion. But this resemblance was intended by Richardson, who wished his readers to presume that *Clarissa* was a conventional romance of passion. Once readers had adopted their conventional attitudes, Richardson was perfectly placed to undermine all their presumptions and to show them the complete insufficiency of their evaluation – at least as far as *his* work is concerned.

The major episodes of *Clarissa*, as well as many of the characters and ideas, are to be found in the romances of passion of the early eighteenth century. A few examples will suffice to demonstrate the validity of this assertion. *Idalia* (1723), by Mrs Haywood, is, in its opening scenes, very reminiscent of *Clarissa*. Idalia is prevented from seeing or communicating with a known libertine, Florez, but she manages to correspond secretly with him. Without really intending to, she becomes involved in an affair with Florez, and doesn't care for the man. Idalia is eventually lured by Florez to his house, where she is deflowered. After many adventures, she ends her life in a nunnery. In *The British Recluse* (1722), Cleomira corresponds secretly with Lysander, a libertine with whom she has fallen in love. She is tricked into leaving her home, having been convinced that her mother is simply being capricious in objecting to her lover. Lysander soon ruins and abandons Cleomira: he refuses to return to her, in spite of her threats of suicide. Belinda, the second heroine of *The British Recluse*, has a similar tale to tell. Her father has chosen Worthy, a fine, upright man as her future husband, but Belinda falls violently in love with Sir Thomas

Courtal, a known rake, as his name would seem to imply. She agrees to meet Courtal secretly, and is about to be seduced by him when rescued by Worthy. Courtal and Lysander are discovered to be one and the same man, and Belinda and Cleomira retire to the country, abandoning the world which has been so cruel to them.

Memoirs of a Certain Island (1725), by Mrs Haywood, can be regarded as a succession of passionate romances. One of the more interesting of these as far as *Clarissa* is concerned, is the story of Marilla in Volume 2. Gerion, a noble, wealthy lord falls in love with Marilla, and she with him, eventually. The moment he discovers that she has fallen in love with him, Gerion:

> chang'd the form of his Addresses, and as he had never presum'd in her days of indifference to think of her but with the utmost Honour, and plac'd his whole Felicity in the hope of obtaining the possession of her by lawful means; he now entertained wishes of a contrary nature, and resolving, if possible, to satiate his Passion with her, look abroad for a Wife among those more capable of gratifying those ambitious Views, which he begun now to have a notion of. (ii,7)

Gerion, prosecuting his intention, first tricks Marilla into accompanying him to the house of a relation. The owner of the house to which Marilla is brought, is no relation, but a woman dependent on Gerion, who, 'to gain his Favour, would scruple nothing' (ii,7). This woman, having been instructed by Gerion 'in what manner she shou'd act, she personated the Air of a Woman of Fashion so well, that the unhappy Marilla . . . had not the least doubt that she was any other than the Person she represented' (ii,7,8). That night, Marilla is given a sleeping potion[45] which soon renders her unconscious: 'in this helpless Condition was she undress'd and put into a Bed, where he [Gerion] perpetrated his villainous intention, and she unkowingly, unyielding, fell an innocent Sacrifice of Lust and Cruelty . . .' (ii,8). Marilla's reaction on awaking and discovering what has taken place, is what one might expect. Gerion does all in his power to excuse the rape, and he eventually convinces Marilla of his sincerity: 'His counterfeit Softness prevailed so far on her, as to make her not only pardon him, but permit him also to renew those Raptures with her own Consent, which to know he had enjoy'd, had lately cost her so many tears' (ii,9). Gerion soon abandons Marilla who is now pregnant, and no amount of entreaties on her part can make him return. The 'Censure of an unpitying World', despair and disappointed love combine to make Marilla take her own life. Cupid, as commentator, rounds off the story as follows:

> The unborn Infant owed its death to her who ought to have given it Birth, doubly a Murd'ress of herself and Child! She sunk, unhoping Mercy, and despising Judgement. – Thus loaded with the most unnatural Crime Humanity can commit, the eternal Judges doom'd her to wander a long race of Years, shut out from Commerce and Society, thro' the wild Regions of the trackless Air, whence she at distance views the blissful Realms where happy Spirits dwell, but without hope of ever entring there – Condemn'd to Misery even by her own *Conscience*! that unceasing, that most cruel Monitor! her former fatal Softness, Horror now turns to Fury, and by despair, and the dire Sense of ever-during Woe provok'd, now like the Fiends, can find no *Ease* but in inflicting *Pain* (ii,10).

It is on Gerion the weight of all her vengeance falls – she haunts him every night making 'this Life a Hell' (ii,10), for him, and giving him 'a sample horrible to Thought, of that which is hereafter decreed for Crimes like his' (ii,10). Nor are Gerion's days much better: he has married a woman of a 'Spirit so untam'd, a Temper so morose, as renders it uneasy even to be of her acquaintance, but to live with her a perfect Hell' (ii,10). Gerion is condemned to know 'no ease in Life; and when the dreadful Day of dissolution comes, to prove at full the Torments he has had a taste of here' (ii,11).

The similarity between incidents and situations in these tales and in *Clarissa* are obvious enough. One feature of *Clarissa* which deserves mention, is the appearance, in the text itself, of summaries of what are obviously romances of passion. Two of these tales can be considered relevant in some ways to the main plot. The two in question, those dealing with the stories of Polly Horton and Sally Martin, come at the end of *Clarissa*, and are part of the conclusion 'supposed to be written by Mr Belford', in which Richardson 'summarily' relates 'the fortunes of those other principals in the story, who survived Mr Lovelace' (iv,532). Polly and Sally could hardly be accounted 'principals' in the story, but useful moral lessons can be drawn from their histories. The two girls, as well as playing minor roles in the plot of *Clarissa*, are also linked, like Belinda and Cleomira in *The British Recluse*, by having been ruined and then abandoned by the same man – Lovelace. It is Lovelace himself who gives summaries of four stories in the course of the work, to illustrate what he calls 'the workings and ways of passionate and offended women'. Three of the tales deal with the typical conflict in passionate romance between parents and children. Miss Dorrington 'ran away with her father's groom, because he would not let her have a half-pay officer with whom (her passions all up) she fell in love at first sight . . .' (iii,494). Miss Savage married her mother's coachman when prevented from marrying 'a remote cousin of unequal fortune', (iii,494), whom she fell in love with in a week. Sally Anderson, on 'being checked by her uncle for encouraging an address beneath her', eloped with a shoemaker's apprentice whom she had never seen before. No doubt, at this stage of the work – Clarissa having 'eloped' and having been raped by Lovelace – Richardson wishes to highlight the differences between Clarissa and other 'heroines' who *seem* so much like her.

An intriguing aspect of *Clarissa* is the way in which all the characters, with the exception of Clarissa herself, and perhaps Anna Howe, presume that they are witnessing, or are involved in, a passionate romance. Lovelace, for instance, regards himself as the rakish hero, and regards Clarissa as the 'virtuous' heroine of a passionate romance. And Clarissa's family, including Colonel Morden, regard themselves as powerless witnesses to the inevitable unfolding of a romance of passion. Mrs Howe, too, is of the same opinion. Lovelace is more than qualified to hold the title of hero of passionate romance. He is descended from a long line of libertines, who are invariably whited sepulchres. Richetti's comments on the arch-libertine, D'elmont (*Love in Excess*), are equally applicable to Lovelace. D'elmont is a 'combination of the scintillating hero and the aggressive *libertin*-seducer. . . . A traditional figure, the heretic of love's deity like Chaucer's Troilus, he rejects love in language which resembles the cant phrases of freethinking and religious infidelity in their tough-minded materialism'.[46] The following is Morden's description of Lovelace, to Lovelace, and we have no reason to doubt the accuracy of the picture:

you are a gallant gentleman, graceful in your person, easy and genteel in your deportment, and in your family, fortunes, and

expectations, happy as a man can wish to be. Then the knowledge
I had of you in Italy (although, give me leave to say, your
conduct there was not wholly unexceptionable) convinces me that
you are brave: and few gentlemen come up to you in wit and
vivacity. Your education has given you great advantages: your
manners are engaging, and you have travelled; and I know, if
you'll excuse me, you make better observations than you are
governed by. (iv,219)

His picture of Lovelace is borne out by information discovered
by an agent of the Harlowes (i,17), and by Mrs Fortescue (i,49).
Anna Howe (i,297), and Clarissa herself (i,197ff.) arrive at similar
conclusions. Lovelace attributes his libertinism to having been
jilted in his youth by a girl he had loved. Her infidelity he 'vowed
to revenge upon as many of the sex' (i,145), as came into his
power. Like all libertines 'newelty [sic] . . . was everything with
him' (i,17), and he has the inevitable 'unhappy kind of prejudice
to marriage' (i,180). His actions in the course of the novel speak
for themselves, and categorise him as a true libertine.

Lovelace, as libertine, shares many of the qualities of Mr B. of
Pamela, and the obvious similarity between the two characters is a
good foundation on which to base a judgement of Richardson's
developing art as novelist. Lovelace is in no doubt about his role
in life: like Mr B., he sees himself as both libertine and hero of a
passionate romance. 'But was ever hero in romance . . . called
upon to harder trials?' (i,149), he exclaims, when he considers his
own position *vis-à-vis* Solmes and the Harlowes. When Lovelace
has raped Clarissa, Belford suggests that he marry her. Lovelace
is astounded at the very suggestion of such a course of action, and
retorts: 'Were I to take thy stupid advice, and marry what a figure
should I make in rakish annals!' (ii,250) Marriage is simply not in
Lovelace's concept of passionate romance. He is even taken aback
at the vehement indignation which all his actions eventually arouse,
and can only ask what all the fuss is about: 'after all', he says,
'what have I done more than prosecute the maxims by which thou
and I and every rake are governed . . .' (iii,316). Most ironic of all,
perhaps, is Lovelace's comparison of himself with Aeneas. And
the drift of his argument is clear – that Aeneas was the first, and
perhaps greatest rake and hero of a romance of passion. Did he
not in fact ruin Dido and then abandon her, is Lovelace's suggestion. 'Yet this fellow is, at every word, the *pious* Aeneas with the

immortal bard who celebrates him' (iv,30). Lovelace, on further reckoning, thinks himself a much better and righteous man than Aeneas, so 'why then should it not be the *pious* Lovelace, as well as the *pious* Aeneas?' (iv,31)

Lovelace's major error in *Clarissa* is the same error which Mr B. made in *Pamela*, though with much less grievous consequences, there. Lovelace insists on viewing Clarissa as his opposite number in a romance of passion. His attitude has evolved from his primary, deep-seated belief that all women are vulnerable to violent passion and that they all find the handsome libertine irresistible. 'And indeed,' he writes to Belford, 'what occasion has a man to be a hypocrite, who has hitherto found his views upon the sex better answered for being known as a rake? Why even my beloved here denied not to correspond with me, though her friends had taught her to think me a libertine' (ii,18). This latter remark is an important one, pointing as it does, to a very significant fact, viz. that Clarissa gave Lovelace all the signs of being a *willing* heroine of a passionate romance. She did, after all, correspond secretly with him – the commencement of the downfall of so many heroines in romances of passion;[47] and she did – at least as far as Lovelace is concerned – elope with him. 'May not then the success of him who could carry her thus far', he writes to Belford, 'be allowed to be an encouragement for him to try to carry her further?' (ii,39,40) After this encouragement, as he sees it, Lovelace presumes he is entitled to proceed to the next stage in a typical romance of passion – rape or seduction. And he is upset when his presumption does not coincide with the presumption of Clarissa. When his first attempt on Clarissa is less than successful, he is forced to revise his attitude towards the heroine. 'How was I to know', he asks Belford, 'that a but blossoming beauty, who could carry on a private correspondence, and run such risks with a notorious wild fellow, was not prompted by inclination . . . ?' (ii,39,40). Lovelace is perturbed when Clarissa, having followed the conventional pattern for a heroine of passionate romance, fails to play the role to the end, by succumbing to his attempts at seduction. He presumes immediately that she is adopting a pose, and he, in turn, adopts the attitude of Mr B. towards Pamela, in similar situations. Lovelace presumes that Clarissa's pose is the result of reading too many romances of the wrong type – either heroic or religious. He gives ample evidence of his views on the matter. When Captain Tomlinson fears that something amiss may happen to Clarissa through his means, and tells Lovelace so, Lovelace retorts angrily:

> Nothing can happen amiss, thou sorrowful dog! What *can* happen amiss? Are we to form our opinion of things by the romantic notions of a girl who supposes *that* to be the greatest which is the slightest of evils? (iii,130)

After the rape of Clarissa, Lovelace can fob off her very real grief as simply further romancing; as he says to Belford: 'when all's done, Miss Clarissa Harlowe has but run the fate of a thousand others of her sex – only that they did not set such a romantic value upon what they call their *honour*; that's all' (iii,176).

Having disposed of the incongruity of Clarissa's failure to play the role he has assigned her, Lovelace continues to view the whole situation from his accustomed angle. He knows, for instance, exactly what will happen when Clarissa is once violated. One of 'our libertine maxims', he tells Belford, is, *'if once subdued . . . always subdued'* (ii,41). And the 'libertine maxim' is certainly accurate as far as the passionate romances are concerned. Almost the only exceptions to the maxim, indeed, are Charlot in the *New Atalantis*, and Belinda and Cleomira in *The British Recluse*. We've already seen one example in *Memoirs of a Certain Island*, where Marilla, having been raped in her sleep by Gerion, subsequently allows him to 'renew those raptures'. In the same work Mazonia is described in the following terms:

> never were the Seeds of Virtue more deeply rooted, than in the Heart of this . . . Lady, and as she had been taught to abhor Unchastity, as a Vice the most pernicious to a Woman's Character, so she also found not in herself the least propensity, to wish it were not so. The falling Snow, or Air new rarefy'd by Phoebus's Beams, is not more pure, more free from Stain than was her spotless Mind; – she sinn'd not even in Thought that way . . . (i,59)

But even the most virtuous Mazonia is eventually vanquished, seduced by Count Riverius, and, 'From the most strict Reserve, she fell immediately into the other Extreme of giving the most inordinate Loose to Inclination' (i,176). Lovelace goes on to detail his plans – inevitable, almost, as he sees them – for Clarissa once he has 'subdued' her: she is to live with him as his mistress. 'Will she not refuse?' he has Belford remark, and answers confidently: 'No, No, Jack! Circumstanced and situated as we are, I am not afraid of that' (ii,41). In similar circumstances and situations, the heroines of passionate romance never refused such an offer, so why should Clarissa? Lovelace's argument runs. As he demonstrates in the following passage, Lovelace also intends to play the typical trump card of the libertine – the 'inevitable' love of the heroine for the rake – to his own advantage:

> If she be a *woman* and *love* me, I shall surely catch her once tripping; for love was ever a traitor to its harbourer. And love *within* and I *without*, she will be more than woman, as the poet says, or I less than man, if I succeed not. (ii,41)

That love is ever a traitor to its harbourer, is perhaps the libertine maxim illustrated best of all in the romances of passion. Rape or seduction was taken for granted by readers, on the revelation of her love by the heroine to the rake. And *Clarissa* follows this pattern, with a slight variation. When Lovelace is taken seriously ill – or so it seems – Clarissa shows genuine concern for him, which he takes as a sure sign of love. 'I have gained my end', he writes triumphantly to Belford, 'I see the dear soul loves me' (ii,436). With this final piece of the preliminaries in place, Lovelace feels little compunction about the subsequent rape, which he attempts almost immediately. The 'slight variation' on the pattern is that Clarissa is *not* in love with Lovelace.[48] She does admit that his illness has 'taught me more than I knew myself', but later suggests she would be guilty of a punishable fault *'were I to love* [my italics] this man of errors' (ii,438).

The 'fire scene' gives Lovelace his first real opportunity to seduce or rape Clarissa. The scene, which brings heroine and villain into each other's arms, both in a state of undress, is perfectly typical of hundreds of similar scenes from passionate romances, but again with the important variation that Clarissa is fully sincere in her determination not to be seduced or taken by force. The whole scene is a 'warm' one: Clarissa is described by Lovelace as having 'nothing on but an under-petticoat, her lovely bosom half-open . . . how her sweet bosom, as I clasped her to mine, heaved and panted! I could even distinguish her dear heart flutter, flutter, flutter again mine . . . I lifted her to her bed . . . she rose from me, giving the whole of her admirable shape, her fine-turned limbs' (ii,501,502). Clarissa, for her part, far from being the heroine of a passionate romance – in spite of finding herself playing a major role in a 'warm' scene – is one of the few girls who have obviously read passionate romances and taken heed of the warnings and examples offered. When Lovelace vows to marry her the following morning, Clarissa takes this as an indication that he is about to 'proceed to the last extremity' (ii,502) – as well she might, with the examples of the passionate romance heroines as her guide.[49] Clarissa takes the only course open to her to try to prove the sincerity of her feelings: 'give me but the means' she cries, 'and I will instantly convince you that my honour is dearer to me than my life!' (ii,504). This, unfortunately, was the pose adopted by all the half-willing, half-afraid heroines of passionate romance, and Lovelace is hardly convinced – not, at least, until she attempts to put her words into action by stabbing herself with scissors.

At the end of the 'fire scene' Lovelace, as one might expect, is forced to reconsider his impression of Clarissa as a passionate romance heroine. Never before has he failed to take advantage of such an opportunity as provided by the fire scene. 'But why?', he asks Belford, and answers his own question: '*Because I never before encountered a resistance so much in earnest*: a resistance, in short, so *irresistible*' (ii,507). Before the actual rape, later, Lovelace again admits that he has never before met with 'so sincere, so unquestionable a repugnance' (iii,193) to his plans as he has met with from Clarissa. Lovelace continues in his plan, in spite of his discovery that Clarissa is not a typical heroine of passionate romance. While he still wishes to gain revenge on the Harlowe family, and is also worried about his reputation as a rake if he fails to take advantage of Clarissa, Lovelace's intention of carrying out his plan is still sanctioned by a convention of passionate romance – that marriage repairs all injuries. This atonement for past injuries was invariably accepted as valid by the characters in passionate romance, not least the violated heroine, and also, one may conjecture, by the vast majority of readers. This was a convention to which Richardson was utterly opposed, and his opposition is embodied in *Clarissa* and expressly stated in the postscript to the 1751 edition of the novel.[50] On two occasions prior to the rape of Clarissa, Lovelace states his position: 'I have no patience,' he says to Belford, 'with the pretty fools, who use . . . strong words, to describe a transitory

evil; an evil which a mere church form makes none!' (iii,177) Just
before the actual rape, he communicates to Belford his intention
of using force to achieve his ends, and adds: 'Can she resent the
last outrage more than she resented a fainter effort? And if her
resentments run ever so high, cannot I repair by matrimony?'
(iii,190) After the rape itself, Lovelace does not, ever, specifically
ask Clarissa to marry him: he is probably still worried about his
image as rake if he seem to be too concerned about her violation;
and he would have lost his opportunity for gaining revenge on
the Harlowes. He still regards marriage as the greatest reparation
he can make to Clarissa, a fact which is obvious from many of his
statements such as the one which follows:

> Will not the generality of the world acquit me if I *do* marry? And
> what is that injury which a *church rite* will at any time repair? *Is*
> *not the catastrophe of every story that ends in wedlock accounted happy,*
> be the difficulties in the progress to it ever so great? (iii,280,281)

Lovelace continues in his misapprehension that he is playing
out a conventional romance in which marriage is both a reparation
to Clarissa, and a punishment to himself – the only punishment
he has to fear, he feels. 'But after all, it would be very whimsical
would it not', he writes to Belford, 'if all my plots and contrivances
should end in wedlock? What a punishment would this come out
to be, upon myself too, that all this while I have been plundering
my own treasure' (ii,212). The truth about Clarissa dawns slowly
on Lovelace, and he is, at last, forced to admit that 'she gives the lie
to all our rakish maxims' (iii,261). One 'rakish maxim' upon which
Lovelace had based so many of his hopes, 'once subdued, always
subdued', he has now to admit is 'an egregious falsehood' (iii,261).
Lovelace plays *his* role as libertine in a passionate romance out to
the very end, in spite of his discovery of the truth about Clarissa
and his perseverance in the role involves a massive irony. He
attempts to exonerate himself from blame in the Clarissa affair, by
resorting to just those arguments which the libertines of passionate
romance resorted in an attempt to justify their abandonment of
the violated, and usually pregnant heroine.[51] But the irony in
Richardson's work is that rather than abandon Clarissa, he is willing
to make reparation after a fashion. When this is unacceptable, and
it is *he* who is abandoned, the exoneration commences. And his
excuses are certainly sanctioned by libertine tradition, and seen

quite plausible to him, therefore. He says he had never claimed to be other than a rake, indeed presented himself as such, because being known as one rendered him irresistible, he felt, to all women. Yet, he argues, Clarissa, 'denied not to correspond with me though her friends had taught her to think me a libertine' (ii,18). Later, he wonders 'what a devil had she to do, to let her fancy run a gadding after a rake? one whom she *knew* to be a rake?' (iii,316) 'And, after all,' he adds, 'what have I done more than prosecute the maxims by which . . . every rake . . . is governed?' (iii,316) The important distinguishing feature of the case – and one for which Lovelace makes no allowance whatever – is that the girl on whom he prosecuted his 'rakish maxims' is not the typical 'half-willing, half-afraid' female. It is the ambivalence of Clarissa's feelings towards Lovelace, so different from the love portrayed in the typical romance of passion, which makes her so incomprehensible to her family and to Lovelace: and, might one add, to the majority of readers also?

Almost from the very beginning of the novel, Clarissa's own family view her as a heroine from passionate romance, and all subsequent incidents as logical developments. 'All that has happened to the unhappy body you mention is what we foretold and expected' (iii,511), Arabella Harlowe writes to Anna Howe. It could be argued, of course, that, in the case of the Harlowes, they are simply using a ploy to disguise their true motives for persecuting Clarissa. And the ploy is an excellent one, insofar as Clarissa does seem to be a typical romance heroine. Her family can thus persecute her under the pretence of preventing her from adopting the disastrous course of so many of her sister-heroines. So when Solmes seems to be losing interest in Clarissa as a result of her treatment of him, James Harlowe pleads thus with him: 'For all our family's sake, and for *her* sake too, if you love her, persist! Let us save her, if possible, from ruining herself' (i,382). Anthony Harlowe, too, shows he is aware of the conventions of passionate romance when he writes to Clarissa: 'I know that you may love him [Solmes] if you will. I had a good mind to bid you hate him; then, perhaps, you would like him the better: for I have always found a most horrid romantic perverseness in your sex. To *do* and to *love* what you should not, is meat, drink, and vesture to you all' (i,161). Even her mother – the Harlowe least involved in the persecution of Clarissa – falls into the selfsame error of presuming her daughter to be a heroine of passionate romance. Mrs Harlowe refuses to believe that Clarissa has not rejected Solmes in favour of a libertine, in spite of her protestations. 'And let me tell you, ungrateful girl', Mrs Harlowe says, '. . . that it is evident to me that nothing but a love unworthy of your prudence can make a creature late so dutiful, now so sturdy' (i,103). And when Clarissa fulfils the expectations of all the Harlowes, her mother asks:

> Would anybody ever have believed that such a young creature as this, who had by her advice saved even her over-lively friend from marrying a fop and a libertine, would herself have gone off with one of the vilest and most notorious of libertines? (ii,290).

And when Clarissa is eventually raped and seemingly abandoned, her uncle, John Harlowe, can only speak of the 'fruits of preferring a rake and a libertine to a man of morals' (iv,100), while her sister writes of the 'miserable hand' Clarissa has made, of her 'romantic and giddy expedition' (iv,56). Anna Howe's mother, as an outsider, views Clarissa's story as typical of passionate romance. She implies that Clarissa's is 'no more than a passion begun in folly or thoughtlessness, and carried on from a spirit of perverseness and opposition' (i,294). Much later, Mrs Howe writes to Clarissa: 'you seem to be sensible enough of your errors now. So are all giddy[52] girls, when it is too late' (iii,323).

Clarissa consistently refuses to accept the general view of herself as the heroine of a passionate romance. At the end, she is primarily concerned with a self-acquittal but also nourishes some hope that her letters, as well as those of Lovelace, will combine to acquit her, in the eyes of the world also, of the charge of being a 'giddy' girl of passionate romance. Clarissa is, on the other hand, sufficiently circumspect to appreciate that without her letters and those of Lovelace all the circumstantial evidence convicts her of being a giddy girl of passionate romance. She acknowledges that to show preference for the rake Lovelace over Solmes would have 'the giddy appearance, disgraceful to our sex' (i,200): even her corresponding with Lovelace has, she allows, a 'giddy appearance' (i,85). And when she has been made a virtual prisoner in her own home, she objects to her mother that she is confined, 'as if, like the giddiest of creatures, I would run away with this man Lovelace and disgrace my whole family' (i,80). Such a thought is obviously furthest from Clarissa's mind at this point, yet she proves herself he giddiest of creatures' – at least in the eyes of the world – and isgraces her family, by 'running off' with Lovelace. Anna Howe, ecause she's the character, other than Clarissa herself, in posses- ion of most of the true facts of the heroine's situation, shares 'larissa's view of herself. Anna thus becomes a major source of omfort to the heroine in her affliction, when she confirms that 'larissa is not a conventional giddy girl. Anna continually distin- uishes between Clarissa's situation and that of seemingly similar nes where, 'giddy creatures . . . who . . . without half your rovocations and inducements, and without any regard to de- orum, leap walls, drop from windows, and steal away from their arents' house to the seducer's bed in the same day' (ii,280). 'larissa is peculiarly naïve, however, in believing that her departure rom home would be the last evil she would be involved in. Any eader of Mrs Manley or Mrs Haywood must have known how nevitable was the consequent rape or seduction. And Clarissa also as evidence of her own to suggest otherwise. She is taken aback t Lovelace's presumption that she is his, even before she has greed, finally, to go away with him. Her remarks to Anna Howe n the subject are significant: 'How one step brings on another vith this encroaching sex! How soon may a young creature, who ives a man the least encouragement, be carried beyond her ntentions, and out of her own power!' (i,437).

Although Clarissa lives through adventures which are almost dentical to those of hundreds of heroines of romances of passion, he moral judgements applicable to them are completely irrelevant 1 the case of Richardson's heroine. After having deliberately ashioned *Clarissa* in accordance with the external features of assionate romance, Richardson goes on to insist that there is, in ffect, no comparison at all between Clarissa and her predecessors. Richardson's achievement is such, therefore, that it is possible to nalyse almost every character and event in *Clarissa* to illustrate ow unconventional they are, in spite of appearances to the ontrary. Solmes, for instance, is hardly typical of the honourable, pright, if somewhat anaemic young men that parents convention- lly choose for their children in the romances of passion. He is gly, bordering almost on the grotesque, illiterate and crude: his onsummate greed and his inhuman attitude to his own relations omplete our picture of him. Neither can Clarissa's corresponding vith Lovelace be regarded as typical, since her mother, apprehen- ive 'of the consequences of the indignities offered to Mr Lovelace' (i,20), implies that Clarissa should correspond with him if it shoul 'prevent an impending mischief on *one* side' (i,20). Clarissa is thu almost forced by circumstances to correspond with Lovelace, i order, initially, to safeguard her own family: the letters themselve are never those of a lovesick, giddy girl. Neither can her elopemen be regarded as a conventional one, since she has no intentio whatever of going away with Lovelace, when he tricks her int doing so. All the characters in the book who are unaware of th actual facts, automatically presume that Clarissa, once she had lei her father's house, had become Lovelace's mistress. Nothing coul be further from the truth: Clarissa devotes all her energies on leaving home, to gaining independence from Lovelace an attempting to conciliate her family. And what seems to be a typica abandonment of the violated heroine by the satiated rake is, ii effect, quite the reverse – the abandonment of the rake by th heroine. The ambivalent feelings of Clarissa towards Lovelace hav already been discussed: this ambivalence places Clarissa completel apart from the giddy-girl tradition of passionate romance. Th gross outline of *Clarissa* is, therefore, a deceptive guide to the mora issues involved. But Richardson's construction did deceive, in spit of all his precautions and warnings. Even Aaron Hill, for example described by Richardson as a 'clear Discerner' (SL,82), completel misinterpreted at least one major incident in *Clarissa*, which h calls '*a rash Elopment with a Man*', voluntarily, '*running away fror her Father's House, with a worse man than Solmes of her own choosing* (SL,82). Richardson is understandably distressed that he is s 'unfortunate . . . to be so ill-understood' (SL,82). Hill, like so man others, had seen simply a conventional elopement, not a uniqu variation. Richardson must have known the risk he ran, of gros misinterpretation, by using a seemingly conventional romance c passion plot as a means of critically examining the very convention of romance. It takes but a few pages to trace the conventiona downfall of the likes of Polly Horton and Sally Martin, but almos a million words to demonstrate how unconventional was th downfall of Clarissa Harlowe.

CLARISSA AS RELIGIOUS ROMANCE

'Religion never was at so low an Ebb as at present', Richardso wrote to Lady Bradshaigh in 1748, 'And if my Work *Clarissa* mus be supposed of the Novel kind, I was willing to try if a Religious Novel would do good' (SL,92). In the postcript to the 1751 edition of *Clarissa*, Richardson went even further, and claimed that his purpose was nothing less than the revival of Christianity. He first describes in greater detail the 'low ebb' of religion:

It will be seen by this time that the author had a great end in view [in *Clarissa*]. He has lived to see scepticism and infidelity openly avowed, and even endeavoured to be propagated from the press: the great doctrines of the gospel brought into question: those of self-denial and mortification blotted out of the catalogue of Christian virtues: and a taste even to wantonness for out-door pleasure and luxury, to the general exclusion of domestic as well as public virtue. . . . In this general depravity, when even the pulpit has lost great part of its weight, and the clergy are considered a body of interested men, the author thought he should be able to answer it to his own heart, be the success what it would, if he threw in his mite towards introducing a reformation so much wanted. And he imagined, that in an age given up to diversion and entertainment, he could steal in, as may be said, and investigate the great doctrines of Christianity under the fashionable guise of an amusement; he should be most likely to serve his purpose . . . (iv,553).

Richardson was not the first to investigate the 'great doctrines of Christianity under the fashionable guise of an amusement', since Robert Boyle had attempted a similar feat in 1687, with *Theodora and Didymus*: Mrs Barker, Mrs Aubin, and Mrs Rowe followed Boyle's lead in the eighteenth century, and produced works closer in format to *Clarissa* than to *Theodora and Didymus*. Richardson was not content simply to adopt as his model the religious romances already in existence: instead, he transforms the pattern of religious romance, but in such a way as to fashion, in *Clarissa*, a critical analysis of all previous romances of religion.

Clarissa's story is, to a great extent, the story of the heroine's struggle with herself. Such a struggle is contrary to the very basis of religious romance, where there are no struggles except the purely physical one, when the heroine attempts to ward off one rapist after another. The conventional heroine of religious romance was fully self-confident, confident of retaining her virtue intact, and confident of her own unwavering goodness. In spite of all her assets, the religious heroine seldom had to rely on her own resources: providence was always at hand to forestall such possibilities as rape, and invariably rescued the heroine, miraculously, if need be. Providence is far from providing Clarissa with a deliverance, miraculous or otherwise, at any point in her many dilemmas. Indeed, one of the themes of the novel is Clarissa's gradual acceptance of the goodness of a providence she had come to doubt: 'for don't you see', she writes to Anna Howe, 'that we seem all to be *impelled* as it were, by a perverse fate which none of us is able to resist' (i,419). Later, she writes of the weight of the afflictions which God has placed upon her for reasons which she finds 'impenetrable' (iii,232). Even shortly before her death, Clarissa has reason to complain how hard it was that 'she should not be permitted to die in peace: that her lot was a severe one: that she began to be afraid she should not forbear repining, and to think her punishment greater than her fault (iv,176). *Clarissa* is thus the charting of progress towards total submission to the will of God and absolute faith in his providence. These are lessons to be learned by Clarissa, and are not, as in the case of the conventional heroine of religious romance, bestowed on her at birth. The story thus becomes, in one sense, the story of the *creation* of a truly religious heroine. it is worth noting Richardson's comment in his preface to *Clarissa*, that he refrained from making his heroine 'impeccable', because that 'must have left nothing for the divine grace and a purified state to do, and carried our idea of her from woman to angel' (i,xiv). Richardson is careful to point out, however, that Clarissa is 'perfect' – 'As far as is consistent with human frailty, and as far as she could be perfect, considering the people she had to deal with, and those with whom she was inseparably connected' (i,xiv).

John Richetti demonstrates that female innocence in the religious romance 'not only exists, but survives because there is male virtue extant to protect it, not just the sustaining masculine principle of Providence, but isolated and noteworthy paragons . . .'[53] Colonel Morden *seems* just such an isolated and noteworthy paragon, someone who will rescue Clarissa from the worst excesses of Lovelace. But Morden is no such paragon – indeed his moral standards are questionable – and he fails to rescue Clarissa. Nor does *Clarissa* open with a marriage, which is a feature of religious romance, and provides an unshakeable security for each of the lovers in their battles against evil forces. Clarissa has no such anchorage, nor does she love anyone, nor anyone her.

It is in her paragonhood that Clarissa most resembles the conventional heroines of religious romance. And yet it is, ironically, this same paragonhood which Richardson uses to highlight so effectively the major differences between his heroine and a conventional one. It is, for example, the perfection of Clarissa which creates all her problems. Initially, James and Arabella Harlowe become jealous of their sister because her perfection had led their grandfather to leave all his estate to her, instead of dividing it equally between his three grandchildren. But they have always been jealous of their exceptional sister, and have reason – in particular Arabella – to resent her even more when she succeeds with the aristocrat, Lovelace. Anna Howe becomes aware of the situation much more quickly than Clarissa, and writes:

It must be confessed, however, that this brother and sister of yours, judging as such narrow spirits will ever judge, have some reason for treating you as they do. It must have long been a mortification to them (set disappointed love on her side, and avarice on his, out of the question) to be so much eclipsed by a younger sister. Such a sun in a family, where there are none but faint twinklers, how could they bear it! Why, my dear, they must look upon you as a prodigy among them: and prodigies, you know, though they obtain our admiration, never attract our love. The distance between you and them is immense. Their eyes ache to look up at you. What shades does your full day of merit cast upon them. Can you wonder, then, that they should embrace the first opportunity that offered, to endeavour to bring you down to their level. (i,125)

Clarissa's virtue also, ironically, makes her vulnerable to attack, rather than preventing such an occurrence. Her previous obedience and strict filial devotion encourage the Harlowes in their belief that she will continue in such a course, in spite of any personal repugnance she might feel towards demands by her parents. Solmes, too, continues to press Clarissa, secure in the knowledge that once Clarissa has been forced to take vows of marriage, her 'virtue' will enforce their strict observation, and that she will make an excellent wife. 'Duty' is certainly one of the key words in *Clarissa* and almost deserves a separate study. As used in the work[54] it almost invariably refers to the duty owed by children to their parents, and inevitably recalls the love-versus-duty theme of the heroic and religious romances. In the religious romances the conflict between love and duty, while it did exist, followed an invariable pattern. No matter how overwhelming her love for the hero, the heroine's first allegiance was to filial duty, a fact she never ceased to emphasise. Luckily, the benevolance of providence brought about an ultimate reconciliation of love and duty, and the heroine was suitably rewarded for her obedience. Richardson introduces a significant variation on this conventional pattern. Instead of creating a conflict between love and duty, or dismissing the conflict entirely, Richardson brings one duty into a head-on collision with another. Clarissa does have very great obligations to her parents, and is keenly aware of these: but she appreciates that she has obligations to *herself* also, and the work analyses the conflict between these two equally powerful duties. Nor does Richardson provide an easy and painless resolution of the conflict, by rendering Lovelace acceptable, finally, to the Harlowes, as a husband for their daughter.

In fact the conflict is never quite resolved, because from the moment Clarissa is tricked into eloping with Lovelace, her freedom of negotiation with her parents is effectively wrested from her. She does remain true to herself, but in a manner not of her own choosing, and one with which she is gravely dissatisfied. From the time of her 'elopement' her energies are directed towards effecting a reconciliation with her family. The attitude of her family to Clarissa is conditioned not only by their past experience of her, but also by their notion of how a girl in her situation should behave. Their attitude towards Clarissa as a giddy girl of passionate romance has already been discussed: but prior to her going off with Lovelace they had – with the possible exception of James Harlowe – held a different view. This initial view regarded Clarissa as a conventional heroine of religious romance, torn between love and duty, a situation in which duty would inevitably prevail and she would marry the man of her parents' choice, going on to live happily ever after. All the advice that she receives from her elders emphasises the absolute quality of the duty she owes to her parents.

Great emphasis is placed, also, on the heroic quality of obedience a heroism which is proportionately greater in Clarissa's case if she marries Solmes, because of her utter aversion to him, and in consideration also of her rejection of such a match as one with

Lovelace. When Anna Howe tries to convince her own mother how odious a man Solmes is, as opposed to 'one of the finest figures of a man' (i,297) – Lovelace – Mrs Howe retorts that there would be 'the greater merit' in Clarissa's obedience on that account, and she continues later: 'let her [Clarissa] dislike one man and approve of another ever so much, it will be expected of a young lady of her unbounded generosity and greatness of mind, that she should *deny herself*, when she can oblige all her family by so doing'. (i,298) When Clarissa refuses to marry Solmes, her family fall into another error, generated again by conventional romance. If she refuses Solmes, they argue, it can only be because she is in love with Lovelace. Her family cannot conceive of such a possibility as that she is simply unwilling to marry Solmes because of her repugnance to him. When she offers to take a vow *not* to marry Lovelace, on being released from pressure to marry Solmes (i,87), her mother and James Harlowe presume this is a trick to gain time or find an opportunity to deceive them. What her family cannot understand is that Clarissa wishes to take a course unprovided for in either passionate or religious romance. But Clarissa's wishes are not granted: instead, in spite of her qualifications for the role of heroine of a religious romance, she is, ironically forced to play the part of a giddy girl from passionate romance, by 'eloping' with Lovelace. And when she has gone, her virtues are used as ammunition against her, and, ironically, again, place her beyond compassion. Having detailed all of Clarissa's superior qualities, at length, to Mrs Norton, Mrs Harlowe continues:

> Her fault was a fault of premeditation, of cunning, of contrivance. She has deceived everybody's expectations. Her whole sex, as well as the family she sprung from, is disgraced by it. . . . Oh this naughty, naughty girl, who *knew* so well what she did, and who could look so far into consequences, that we thought she would have died rather than have done as she has done! Her known character for prudence leaves her absolutely without excuse. How then can I offer to plead for her, if, through motherly indulgence, I would forgive her myself? (ii,289,290)

Clarissa is a study of an exemplary heroine in a quite unexemplary world. Instead of being surrounded by noble companions, as is her due, she is, instead, placed at the centre of a petty, middle-class milieu, which indulges in tyranny, avarice and jealousy. Literally and metaphorically she is isolated – without even a loyal maidservant – and is forced to rely completely on her own resources. Because of this, the story of Clarissa immediately calls to mind the story of Samson as portrayed by Milton in *Samson Agonistes*. A reading of John Dussinger's article, 'Conscience and the Pattern of Christian Perfection in *Clarissa*',[55] confirms that there is more than a superficial resemblance between the two works – although Dussinger never mentions *Samson Agonistes*, and, in fact singles out *Paradise Lost*, rather, for comparison with *Clarissa*. Milton, one recalls, was attracted to the Samson theme because it illustrated – among other things – man's complete reliance on his own resources for salvation, without the need for reliance on the redemption achieved by Christ in the New Testament. *Clarissa* offers a much simpler variation on a similar theme. It is ironic, though, to discover that Clarissa's sentiments 'derive ultimately from the Old Testament',[56] and even more ironic, perhaps, to find that the meditations in *Clarissa* are literal extracts from The Book of Job, and that the *Meditations* privately printed by Richardson, 'are designed to follow the spiritual pattern of Job, moving from deep despair and grief under Clarissa's afflictions, to resignation and patience, and, finally, to joyful praises and thanksgiving for the lesson of confidence. . . .'[57] The relationship between *Samson Agonistes* and the Book of Job is too well known to bear restatement here. All through Dussinger's article one finds echoes of *Samson Agonistes*. He describes Clarissa's 'tragic flaw', for instance, as pride, which in turn, after the rape by Lovelace, turns almost to despair. Richardson, Dussinger writes, 'attempted to portray in *Clarissa* the nature of sin and guilt under the operations of conscience. . . .'[58] Dussinger later elaborates on what Richardson meant by 'conscience':

> Whether he calls it 'conscience' or 'feeling heart', Richardson implies throughout the novel that man has within him an intuitive judge to which one must answer for all his actions and that furthermore this inner voice is directly related to the Holy Spirit. Without proper deference to this internal monitor, man is lacking the practical means of regeneration and salvation.[59]

By this reckoning, Clarissa can certainly be regarded as a latter-day Samson.

But the *Samson Agonistes–Clarissa* analogy is not confined simply to the progression from pride, via despair, to salvation. Both works also share the problems involved in the concept of a Christian tragedy. The question has been asked time and time again whether Christian tragedy is possible at all, and arguments on the matter usually centre on the catastrophe. The only true catastrophe for the Christian is final damnation, such as occurs, say, in *Dr Faustus.* The ending of *Samson Agonistes,* on the other hand, seems the very antithesis of everything the word catastrophe stands for: 'it is directed wholly to reconciliation, to mitigating the sense of disaster: first on the human level, and, when that is completed, by invoking the overruling Power . . . *Samson Agonistes* thus becomes a tragic episode in a divine comedy'.[60]

Richardson regarded *Clarissa* as a 'dramatic narrative' (iv,554), and in, particular, as a 'Piece . . . of the Tragic Kind' (SL,99). And the following extract from a letter to Lady Bradshaigh demonstrates the specifically Christian quality of his tragedy.

> The Sale [of *Clarissa*] is pretty quick for an *imperfect* Work. Yet I know not whether it has not suffered much by the Catastrophe's being too much known and talked of. I intend another Sort of Happiness (founded on the Xn system) for my Heroine, than that which was to depend upon the Will and Pleasure, and uncertain Reformation and good Behaviour of a vile Libertine, to whom I could not think of giving a . . . Lady of such Excellence . . . And to rescue her from a Rake, and give a Triumph to her not only over him but over all her Oppressors, and the World besides, in a Triumphant Death (as Death must, at last, have been her Lot, had she been ever so prosperous) I thought as noble a View, as it was new. (SL.86,87)

This is little less than a confirmation that *Clarissa* is a divine comedy, a concept which found little favour with a reading public conditioned to accepting other forms of rewards in fiction. Richardson became aware of the groundswell of feeling against his anticipated conclusion to *Clarissa*; but in spite of this – and the knowledge that it would be financially inadvisable[61] – he persevered with his original plan. Richardson almost certainly revised later sections of *Clarissa* to try to make his intentions quite clear, and backed this up with page after page in his letters, defending the death of his heroine. Below, is one such defence from a letter to

Lady Bradshaigh, followed by a relevant quotation from the text of *Clarissa*.

> Who but the Persons concerned, should choose for themselves, what would make them happy? – If Clarissa think not an early Death an Evil, but on the contrary, after an exemplary Preparation, looks upon it as her consummating Passion, who shall grudge it her? – Who shall punish her with Life? (SL,95,96)

> What then, my dear and only friend, can I [Clarissa] wish for but death? And what, after all, *is* death? 'Tis but a cessation from mortal life: 'tis but the finishing of an appointed course: the refreshing inn after a fatiguing journey: the end of a life of cares and troubles; and, if happy, the beginning of a life of immortal happiness. (iii,521)

Richardson was not, of course, the first to regard death, in fiction, as the commencement of true happiness. All the writers of religious romances, and in particular Mrs Rowe, had adopted a similar attitude in their works. 'The joys of love', as John Richetti puts it, 'continually prefigure the joys of immortality',[62] in Mrs Rowe. What seems to have confused Richardson's audience – to put the matter, perhaps, over-simply – was Richardson's tagging a religious–romance ending on to what appeared to be a passionate romance. The readers of *Clarissa* felt they had a right to expect that their heroine be given some compensation *in this life*, as well as the next. Neither, I am sure, was their confusion made any clearer by the conventional punishments meted out to the villains of the work. And their punishment was, in all cases, death – with no explicit suggestion that any of them was going to Hell,[63] so where, the reader might well ask, lay the difference between the villains, and Clarissa, except that her happiness was assured? The ending of *Clarissa* would, one feels, have been much more acceptable had Richardson refrained from listing the villains and illustrating the operation of poetic justice in their cases, since poetic justice also demanded that Clarissa be rewarded in this life rather than the next.

It is a quite extraordinary achievement on the part of Richardson that the ending of *Clarissa*, which seems so unconventional, is, on closer examination, found to fit into the pattern of a typical romance. A fact of life which religious (and indeed passionate) romance emphasised again and again, for instance, is that the world cannot be changed: the only alternative for the wronged lover was escape. This escape from the world normally took one of two forms, either retirement to a convent as in the case of Idalia, and Amena (*Love in Excess*), or retirement to the country, the option taken by the two heroines of *The British Recluse*, Belinda and Cleomira. *Clarissa* offers a new variation on the retreat formula – retirement from the world to a heavenly home. But heaven offers more than a retreat; as the work draws to a close, more and more emphasis is placed on the 'marriage' between Clarissa and her Maker. '. . . I am upon a *better preparation* than for an earthly husband' (iv,2), Clarissa writes to Mrs Norton. More emphatic still, is the following extract from another letter to Mrs Norton, written by Clarissa just before her death:

> As for me, never bride was so ready as I am. My wedding garments are bought. And though not fine and gaudy to the sight, though not adorned with jewels and set off with gold and silver . . . yet will they be the easiest, the *happiest* suit that ever bridal maiden wore, for they are such as carry with them a security against all those anxieties, pains, and perturbations which sometimes succeed to the most promising outsettings (iv,303).

So, certainly in the author's view, *Clarissa* concludes, as do most romances, with the happiest of marriages, in which the happy-ever-after concept is not just a supposition, but a guaranteed fact. And as *Clarissa* draws to a close, it is obvious, also, that Richardson could well have added as a subtitle to *Clarissa*, the *Virtue Rewarded* subtitle of *Pamela*, and with much more justification. Richardson's own view was that heroism such as that exhibited by Clarissa 'could not be rewarded in this world' (SL,108), and the text continually stresses the magnificent reward she is about to be granted in her death. One of the psalms Clarissa chooses for her coffin[64] emphasises the reward she is to receive. 'O LOVELACE! LOVELACE!' writes Belford on learning of the rape of Clarissa, *'had I doubted it before, I should now be convinced that there must be a* WORLD AFTER THIS, *to do justice to injured merit . . .'* (iii,198). Anna Howe echoes these sentiments when she tells Clarissa, 'we must look to a WORLD BEYOND THIS for the reward of your sufferings!' (iii,375).

The aim of the foregoing analysis has not been to lessen the extent of the revolutionary impact which Richardson had on the English novel. This impact can be fully appreciated only when one realises to what extent *Pamela* and *Clarissa* are reworkings of models already in existence. And these reworkings were not simply the result of lapses in concentration or artistic failure on Richardson's part, as some critics have suggested: rather are they – and in particular *Clarissa* – a magnificent illustration of the rewards to be gained from a judicious combination of romance and realism. One of Richardson's innovations was not so much to introduce realism into fiction, as to fuse this realism with romance. After *Pamela* and *Clarissa*, the rules for romance have to be recast: the emphasis has shifted quite obviously from action to character. Put another way, one could say that *Pamela* and *Clarissa* are simply a reworking on a vast canvas of one of the major themes of ancient Greek romance – that of the virtuous heroine with her virginity in danger.

5
Henry Fielding's Comic Romances

RICHARDSON AND FIELDING: ROMANCE AND ANTI-ROMANCE?

It is one of the major ironies in the history of English fiction that Henry Fielding should have been almost driven into the writing of fiction by Samuel Richardson. It was the publication of *Pamela* and the public reaction to it which decided Fielding on composing a reply.[1] Fielding seems to have been one of just a few who did not join in the general furore which greeted the publication of Richardson's work. Fielding did *not* object to Pamela's character or to any of her actions in the work: indeed these could justifiably be claimed to have been drawn from the 'real life' which he himself was to set such store by, in his own fiction. What upset Fielding was that Richardson, instead of making *Pamela* 'an admirable and profound psychological study, pitilessly true, the penetrating portrait of a little eighteenth-century waiting-maid, rather mincing, cautiously romantic, and very skilled in making her virtue pay', had, 'under the pretence of giving us an edifying and moral novel . . . presented a salacious tale, the sole interest of which lies in discovering whether a ruffian will finally succeed in seducing a young woman . . . .'[2] Fielding saw only too clearly the inaccuracy of Richardson's claim that *Pamela* would inculcate 'Principles of Religion and Virtue': rather did he see that *Pamela* inculcated the principle of 'be good, because it will pay you in the end', or 'the cash-value of chastity'. His reply to *Pamela* was swift, savage and comprehensive. *Pamela* had appeared on 6 November, 1740; Fielding's parody, *Shamela*, was published on 4 April, 1741. The full title of *Shamela* adequately demonstrates the intentions of the author:

An Apology for the Life of Mrs. Shamela Andrews. In which the many notorious Falsehoods and Misrepresentations of a Book

197

called Pamela, Are exposed and refuted; and all the matchless Arts of that young Politician set in a true and just Light. Together with A full Account of all that passed between her and Parson Arthur Williams; whose character is represented in a manner something different from that which he bears in Pamela. The whole being exact Copies of authentick Papers delivered to the Editor. Necessary to be had in all Families. By Mr. Conny Keyber.[3]

Fielding's mimicry of *Pamela* in *Shamela* is 'complete and devastating. By changing the perspective of vision – by taking a hostile and sardonic view of Richardson's triumphant virgin, seeing her chastity . . . as artful rather than innocent – he has inverted, and subverted, Richardson's whole design.'[4] The real importance of *Shamela* lies, perhaps, in its introduction of Fielding to fiction, a form in which he was to excel later, beginning with *Joseph Andrews*, and concluding with *Amelia*. The controversy over the genesis of *Joseph Andrews* had never been adequately resolved, and, possibly, never will. One side of the argument is that Fielding intended *Joseph Andrews* as yet another parody of *Pamela*, but that, somehow, the novel got gloriously out of hand: the other side is that Fielding *never* intended *Joseph Andrews* as a parody of *Pamela*. The truth may well lie in a compromise between these two opposing attitudes. Martin Battestin is one of those who hold that the 'amusing parallel,'[5] between *Joseph Andrews* and *Pamela* has given rise to the 'inhibiting assumption'[6] that Fielding's work is another parody of Richardson's. 'Before we can understand what Fielding was about in this novel [*Joseph Andrews*] and what he achieved, this notion must be abandoned for good and all',[7] says Battestin. But a study of the arguments in support of his case, shows Battestin's position to be an extreme one, and one which can not be adequately supported by the text of *Joseph Andrews*. He first draws our attention[8] to Fielding's caveat in the preface of *Joseph Andrews* on the distinction between parody and satire – that parody may only be admitted in the diction, and must be excluded from the 'sentiments and characters'. Very little of what Fielding wrote in the preface to *Joseph Andrews* can be taken at its face value, and the text of the novel demonstrates exactly to what degree *Joseph Andrews* can be regarded as parody of *Pamela*. Battestin categorically denies that any parody was intended:

the most casual comparison of *Shamela* and the opening chapters of *Joseph Andrews*, where the recollection of *Pamela* is most vivid, should be proof enough that in the novel Fielding intended something much different – more ambitious, more his own – from what he attempted in his parody. With one or two deliberate exceptions, such as Joseph's two letters to his sister, there is no attempt to mimic the manner and style of Richardson's book.[9]

Before commencing any comparison between *Pamela* and *Joseph Andrews* it is important, first of all, to appreciate Fielding's concept of virtue. 'Against the . . . negative copybook morality of *Pamela*, stressing purity, discretion, propriety, and conquest of the passions', writes Homer Goldberg, Fielding 'espoused an impulsive virtue, stemming from benevolent feelings rather than Richardson's overestimated precepts, not solipsistically absorbed in its own preservation but actively promoting the good of others.'[10] There can be no doubt but that Joseph Andrews, in the opening chapters, demonstrates the same 'negative copybook morality' as his sister: there is, too, the same stress on purity, discretion, propriety, and conquest of the passions. But, as Fielding was well aware, it is one thing for a female to possess a negative copybook morality, quite another, altogether, for a male to be possessed of such. Fielding himself was obviously one who would agree wholeheartedly with Shakespeare's sentiment:

> . . . when a woman wooes, what woman's son
> will sourly leave her till she have prevail'd?[11]

For this reason, Fielding was able to add another dimension to his parody of *Pamela*, without the need to be over-explicit. It is extremely difficult to accept Battestin's view that no parody is intended, when, in the very first chapter of *Joseph Andrews*, Fielding states his intention unequivocally. Having spoken of *Pamela*, he then continues:

What the female readers are taught by the memoirs of Mrs Andrews is so well set forth in the excellent essays or letters prefixed to the second or subsequent editions of that work that it would be here a needless repitition. The authentic history with which I now present the public is an instance of the great good that book is likely to do, and of the prevalence of example which

I have just observed, since it will appear that it was by keeping the excellent pattern of his sister's virtues before his eyes that Mr Joseph Andrews was chiefly enabled to preserve his purity in the midst of such great temptations.[12]

Fielding's tongue-in-cheek attitude is obvious even to readers unaware of his authorship of *Shamela*, and of his general aversion for *Pamela*. He undoubtedly intends depicting Joseph as an utter prig. On Lady Booby's attempt at seducing him, Joseph writes to Pamela in the following terms:

O Pamela, my mistress is fallen in love with me – that is, what great folks call falling in love – she has a mind to ruin me; but I hope I shall have more resolution and more grace than to part with my virtue to any lady upon earth . . . I don't doubt, dear sister, but you will have grace to preserve your virtue against all trials; and I beg you earnestly to pray I may be enabled to preserve mine, for truly it is very severely attacked by more than one; but I hope I shall copy your example, and that of Joseph my namesake, and maintain my virtue against all tempt-ations. (42,43)

Joseph's copybook morality is emphasised even more in Lady Booby's second and final attempt on his virtue. In this scene, Joseph happens to say that he would never allow his passions to get the better of his virtue. Lady Booby is completely astounded at this statement, and, on recovering some composure, exclaims:

Your virtue! . . . I shall never survive it. Your virtue – intolerable confidence! . . . Did ever mortal hear of a man's virtue! Did ever the greatest, or the gravest, men pretend to any of this kind! Will magistrates who punish lewdness, or parsons who preach against it, make any scruple of committing it? And can a boy, a stripling, have the confidence to talk of his virtue? (38)

Joseph is quick to defend himself, but his defence is, to say the least, peculiar: it does not seem to be even virtue for virtue's sake he is interested in, so much as virtue for Pamela's sake. His reply to Lady Booby's attack is as follows:

Madam . . . that boy is the brother of Pamela, and would be ashamed that the chastity of his family, which is preserved in her, should be stained in him. If there are such men as your ladyship mentions, I am sorry for it, and I wish they had an opportunity for reading over those letters which my father hath sent to me of my sister Pamela's; nor do I doubt but that such an example would amend them. (38)

Battestin is obviously inaccurate, also, in his contention that, apart from Joseph's two letters to his sister, there is 'no attempt to mimic the manner and style of Richardson's book'.[13] In some of her first letters home, Pamela, in relating Mr B.'s initial manoeuvres, continually emphasises his attraction for her hand. As early as the first letter, for instance, we find her relating how 'he took me by the hand; yes he took my hand before them all' (1). And later, in the same letter, we hear how he again 'took her by the hand'. All through the work indeed, Mr B. almost invariably begins his attempts at seduction by taking Pamela's hand. And Pamela, for her part, is always aware of the significance attached to the taking of her hand. She tells how, at one point in the story, she began to tremble 'and the more when he took me by the hand, for no soul was near us' (11). In *Joseph Andrews*, Fielding's use of the same technique, and its implications for *Pamela*, are too obvious to ignore. Whenever Lady Booby stepped out of her coach, for instance, she would take Joseph 'by the hand and sometimes for fear of stumbling, press it very hard' (26). In the first bedroom scene, Lady Booby opens the action by 'accidentally' laying her hand on Joseph's, and in her second attempt at seducing him, again commences by 'laying her hand carelessly upon his' (37). Joseph, like Pamela, is aware of his hand being held, and its possible significance; he writes to his sister that Lady Booby 'naked in bed . . . held my hand' (30).

Pamela seldom talks of her virtue but as a priceless possession which is synonymous with 'rags and poverty'. 'I can be content with rags and poverty and bread and water', she writes, 'and embrace them rather than forget my good name, let who will be the tempter'. (4) 'I am honest, though poor', she tells Mr B. later, 'and if you were a prince, I would not be otherwise than honest' (12). Similarly, Joseph tells Pamela he hopes he will have 'more resolution and more grace than to part with my virtue to any lady upon earth' (43). Later, in a soliloquy, Joseph exclaims: 'O most adorable Pamela! most virtuous sister! whose example could alone enable me to withstand all the temptations of riches and beauty, and to preserve my virtue pure and chaste . . .' (52). Joseph has earlier suggested to Lady Booby that it is because he is poor that she expects his virtue to be 'subservient to her pleasures' (38).

Overt parody of *Pamela* ceases almost entirely in *Joseph Andrews* from Chapter XIII, Book I, onwards. Fanny Goodwill – who, it transpires later, is Pamela's sister – is obviously intended as a comment on the character of Pamela, but this is not parody. Fanny, it is emphasised, can neither read nor write – a striking contrast to the amazingly literate Pamela. Several attempts are made to rape Fanny, but instead of using these situations to her own advantage, she is much too frightened, and concerned to escape the ravisher. Nor could Fanny be called 'virtuous' in Richardson's sense of the word: her love for Joseph is such that she is willing to allow him to make love to her, and at one time gives 'a loose to her passion' (250) and initiates some love-play herself. Even the name Fanny is not in the romance tradition, and Fanny herself is described in quite 'unromantic' terms.[14]

Neither is parody the word to describe the final chapters of *Joseph Andrews*, where both Pamela and her new husband are introduced. Here, the subversion of Richardson's design in *Pamela* is taken a stage further by Fielding, but in a very subtle and effective manner. Booby is, initially, treated in a sympathetic manner by Fielding, but Pamela and Lady Booby soon force him to adopt a rather churlish attitude. It seems likely that Fielding intends to suggest that Booby is a weakling when dealing with women – a defect of which Pamela took full advantage to further her own ends. When Booby first arrives at Booby Hall, he is just in time to have Joseph and Fanny released from gaol. While this trio are on their way to Booby Hall, they happen to meet Parson Adams, whom Fanny describes as 'the best person living' (250). 'Is he?', says Booby, 'then I am resolved to have the best person living in my coach' (250). He takes the parson in – scruffy and bedraggled as he is – an obvious contrast with Lady Booby's earlier refusal to allow the parson in the same coach with her. Fielding's sympathetic treatment of Booby continues on his arrival at his aunt's residence. He tells Lady Booby that since he has married 'a virtuous and worthy woman', he is resolved to 'own her relations and show them all proper respect . . . . I shall think myself therefore infinitely obliged to all mine who will do the same' (250), he continues. Lady

Booby easily convinces her nephew of the inadvisability of allowing
Joseph to marry Fanny, since such an alliance would 'still enlarge
their relation to meanness and poverty' (258). When Booby next
meets Joseph, he demands that he have nothing more to do with
Fanny: 'if you have any value for my alliance or my friendship',
he tells Joseph, 'you will decline any thoughts of engaging farther
with a girl who is, as you are a relation of mine, so much beneath
you' (259). The irony of such a statement coming, as it does, from
Booby, of all people, is only too obvious. Pamela is quite equal to
her husband when she comes on the scene, and says:

> Brother . . . Mr Booby advises you as a friend; and no doubt my
> papa and mama will be of his opinion, and will have great reason
> to be angry with you for destroying what his goodness hath
> done and throwing down our family again after he hath raised
> it. It would become you better, brother, to pray for the assistance
> of grace against such a passion than to indulge it. (260)

Joseph makes the obvious reply to his sister: 'Sure, sister, you
are not in earnest; I am sure she is your equal at least' (260); to
which Pamela replies: 'She was my equal . . . but I am no longer
Pamela Andrews; I am now this gentleman's lady, and, as such,
am above her' (260).

All the textual evidence seems to suggest that Fielding intended
Joseph Andrews as a full-length parody of *Pamela*, following the
pattern of the opening chapters. 'The authentic history with which
I now present the public', Fielding wrote in the prefatory chapter
to the first book of *Joseph Andrews*, 'is an instance of the great good
that book [*Pamela*] is likely to do . . . .' (20). This is a grossly
misleading statement in the context of the whole work, but it does,
along with the textual evidence available, suggest what Fielding's
original plan had been. Joseph rejects Lady Booby's advances,
basically, it is implied, because of Pamela's example. Lady Booby
regards Joseph, with his talk of his virtue, as an insufferable prig,
an attitude shared by the reader, and one obviously intended by
the author. But when Joseph's love for, and betrothal to Fanny
Goodwill is revealed, later, our whole view of Joseph is transformed.
His treatment of Lady Booby becomes, in retrospect, more acceptable, and his love for Fanny becomes – both in Fielding's eyes and
the eyes of the reader – a perfectly valid reason for rejecting the
advances of a comely woman. But not only does Fielding not reveal

the existence of Fanny and the relationship between her and Joseph – he even has Joseph deny any interest in women. Lady Booby specifically asks Joseph if he is in love with some girl or other, to which he replies that 'all the women he had ever seen were equally indifferent to him' (28) – a remark utterly inexplicable in the light of later revelations. Another indication of Fielding's original plan for *Joseph Andrews* is the character of Lady Booby. She is called 'the heroine of our tale' (35), which seems more than likely at the time: yet she fades out of the story almost entirely, and reappears only in a minor role, at the end of the work.

On the assumption, then, that Fielding deviated from his original plan, why did he not revise the inconsistencies outlined above? Did he mistakenly overlook the inconsistencies, or did he – which is much more likely – realise that his short parody of *Pamela* would be rendered quite ineffective if, say, the true relationship between Fanny and Joseph were revealed too early? It is worth noting, also, that the title of the novel, containing, as it did, the name Andrews, would immediately suggest a relationship between *Pamela* and *Joseph Andrews*, a relationship which could only favour sales of Fielding's work. A revision of inconsistencies would have weakened this relationship, and suggested much too soon to readers that Joseph was not to be a 'male Pamela' after all.

Fielding's *Tom Jones* owes little or nothing to the influence of Richardson. One can say, however, that just as *Clarissa* consists largely in a realisation of possibilities which Richardson suggested to himself in the course of writing *Pamela*, so *Tom Jones* is a realisation of possibilities suggested in the writing of *Joseph Andrews*.

FIELDING'S THEORY OF FICTION

Henry Fielding's position as a writer of prose fiction in the eighteenth century, was almost identical to that of sophists such as Achilles Tatius or Heliodorus in ancient times. Prose fiction in ancient times simply did not constitute a legitimate form of literature and was utterly disregarded by the *literati*. Initially, this fiction was written by naïve, uneducated authors, but it soon attracted the attention of the sophists. For them, the typical romance in vogue at the time was a genre with which they were almost ashamed to be associated. But they appreciated just how popular the romance was, and that it would bring them readers, so they conformed to popular taste. The digressions in the sophistic romances, on philosophical or scientific topics, are really the *sine qua non* for the sophist. But the sophists did try to improve on the basics of Greek romance by the injection of a somewhat more respectable kind of subject matter, plus artistic display. These injections could be regarded as an attempt by the sophists at dignifying an illegitimate form of literature. And their association with Greek romance helped to draw the attention of the world of formal learning to the genre.

The English literary critic of the early eighteenth century also tended to regard prose fiction as an illegitimate form of literature. The first forty years of the century, in particular, were marked by a 'generally hostile attitude on the part of the critics, who were offended by the frivolity and immorality of much contemporary fiction'.[15] Prose fiction was, in effect, widely regarded as a typical example of the 'debased kind of writing by which the booksellers pandered to the reading public.'[16] Because of the low reputation of fiction, almost all writers tried to avoid the charges of frivolity and immorality by pretending not to be writing fiction at all. In such a situation, a theory of fiction was not likely to emerge, and, as far as most commentators were concerned, 'novel and romance remained on the outskirts of literature, to be treated perfunctorily, merely with reference to their obvious potential danger'.[17]

No radical change in attitudes to fiction had occurred by the time Henry Fielding decided to become a writer of fiction in 1741. He was, in effect, a modern sophist – not in the sense that fiction was to be solely a vehicle for the display of his sophistical wares – but rather in the sense that he was a well-educated man, unlike any of his more immediate predecessors in fiction. Despite the fact that it may have been financial need which drove Fielding to write fiction in the first place, he refused to become associated with the denizens of Grub Street: rather did he set about dignifying the genre with which he was to be associated. He began by trying to give a neo-classical legitimacy to his fiction, and followed this by emphasising the distinction between his work and heroic romance on the one hand, and the products of Grub Street on the other. Fielding was not being strikingly original in claiming to have founded a 'new province of writing'.[18] Even Richardson claimed to have initiated a 'new species of writing' (SL,41), and both he and Fielding were following a well-established tradition in doing so. Richardson and Fielding also condemned all previous fiction, Richardson objecting to it on purely moral, Fielding on artistic grounds. One of Richardson's aims in writing *Pamela*, it is worth recalling, was to decry 'such Novels and Romances as have a Tendency to inflame and corrupt' (SL,46,47): *Pamela* was also intended to 'turn young people into a course of reading different from the pomp and parade of romance writing . . . (SL,41). *Clarissa*, he was to claim, later, was not a 'mere Novel or Romance' (SL,158). In the preface to *Joseph Andrews*, Fielding asks the reader not to 'confound' his work with 'those voluminous works commonly called romances, namely *Clelia, Cleopatra, Astarea, Cassandra*, the *Grand Cyrus* . . .' (vi). And in *Tom Jones* he writes of 'those idle romances which are filled with monsters, the productions, not of nature, but of distempered brains . . .' (151). Fielding actually admits in *Tom Jones* that he would have been 'well enough contented' with the term romance, but for the 'universal contempt' which the world had cast on all historical writers who failed to draw their materials from records. 'And it is the apprehension of this contempt', he writes, 'that hath made us so cautiously avoid the term romance' (436).

Fielding seems to have felt that the classical heritage which he claimed for his fiction was insufficient to distinguish between his works and those of previous writers of fiction. At any rate, in two prefatory chapters of *Tom Jones*,[19] he suggests the qualifications necessary for the writing of works such as he is attempting, and points out some features which might help to distinguish his work from other fiction. The general opinion, Fielding argues, is that 'to the composition of novels and romances, nothing is necessary but paper, pens, and ink, with the manual capacity of using them' (436). The qualifications which he lists as necessary for the writing of his kind of fiction include: genius, a good share of learning, conversation, and a good heart, capable of feeling. And in case his work might be likened to the labour of other writers of fiction, Fielding claims to have 'taken every occasion of interspersing through the whole [of *Tom Jones*] sundry similes, descriptions, and other kind of poetical embellishments' (151). Even the introductory chapters to each book, Fielding says, can be regarded 'as a kind of mark or stamp, which may . . . enable a very indifferent reader to distinguish, what is true and genuine in this historic kind of writing, from what is fake and counterfeit' (435). These chapters, he argues later, are not only a distinguishing feature of his work, but secure him also, 'from the imitation of those who are utterly incapable of any degree of reflection, and whose learning is not equal to an essay' (435). Intriguingly, Fielding's introductory chapters, and his digressions generally, are fundamentally analogous to the philosophical and scientific digressions of the sophists in the Greek romances. And it was not that Fielding imitated the ancient practitioners, but rather that he and they were forced by circumstances to adopt a similar stance. In each case – that of Fielding and the typical sophist – fiction had come into the hands of authors trained in the intellectual or classical traditions. Aware of the apparent incongruity of their involvement in an illegitimate art form, they set about elevating it as far as possible: hence Fielding's list of 'qualifications' for the writer of fiction, and hence, too, his claim that the hack writer will be unable to imitate his introductory chapters.

Fielding's major claim to distinction for both *Joseph Andrews* and *Tom Jones* was that each was a 'comic epic poem in prose'. In this claim lies his main attempt to provide neo-classical legitimacy for an art form considered low by the *literati*. Fielding's adoption of comic epic as his model was an ingenious move. Homer had written a comic epic, and Aristotle had sanctioned the genre by adverting to it in the *Poetics*. But, fortunately for Fielding, Homer's comic epic, the *Margites*, was lost and never found, and Aristotle had very little of note to say about the comic epic. All he does say is that the *Margites* 'bears the same relation to Comedy that the *Iliad* and *Odyssey* do to Tragedy'.[20] There are further clues as to the nature of comic epic in Aristotle's later discussion of the distinctions between comedy and tragedy, but, generally speaking, the nature of comic epic was a matter for intelligent speculation only. Little or no attention was devoted to a critical examination of the comic epic down through the centuries: it was invariably overshadowed by the serious epic. Consequently, Henry Fielding had very little theoretical precedent or existing literary parallels on which to base 'rules' for a comic epic. But this vacuum suited him perfectly: he was able, on the one hand, to claim classical sanction for his novels; on the other, to write almost as he pleased.

And yet, for his theory of epic generally, as opposed to comic epic specifically, Fielding undoubtedly relied on the theories of the writers of seventeenth-century heroic romance in France. 'The appearance of the heroic romance in seventeenth-century France', writes Ioan Williams, 'accompanies the formulation of neo-classic doctrine and was the result of a serious attempt by writers of high standing to bring romance within the bounds of the neo-Aristotelean system of kinds'.[21] The French writers of romance saw, as Fielding was to, later, that an extended fictional narrative was the modern form most closely allied to the ancient epic. All the writers of heroic romance claimed to be attempting works modelled on the epics of either Homer or Virgil. Some, such as Madeleine de Scudéry, included amongst their ancient models not only Homer and Virgil, but also Achilles Tatius and Heliodorus. But since Achilles Tatius and Heliodorus were considered to be simply imitators of Homer, then they, too, were acceptable as models. It is quite inconceivable that Henry Fielding was unaware of the elaborate theory of prose fiction which the writers of heroic romance had delineated in the previous century. One could, in all probability, argue that the theories of the heroic romance writers and Fielding owed their similarity to a common origin, i.e. classical epic. If this is the case, then Fielding is remarkably like Mr Casaubon in *Middlemarch*, 'groping around in the woods with a pocket compass,' when others 'had made good roads'.[22] On the assumption that Fielding did plagiarise the prose-fiction theories of the French, his failure to acknowledge his debt is not difficult to explain. And the explanation has little to do with the common eighteenth-century practice of unacknowledged literary theft.[23] The true explanation undoubtedly involves the low reputation of heroic romance in the eighteenth century, in England,[24] and Fielding's strenuous attempts at drawing a sharp distinction between his works and heroic romances. It would have been out of the question for him to suggest that although he had based his theory of fiction on that of the seventeenth-century French writers, his works bore no relation to the heroic romances. Fielding appreciated only too well that complete dissociation from the French was the best course to adopt. It is not without irony that Fielding, in his attempts, in *Joseph Andrews*, to distinguish his work, as epic, from the heroic romances, actually qualifies all the French romances for inclusion in the epic category. The relevant extract from *Joseph Andrews* runs thus:

> And farther, as this [epic] poetry may be tragic or comic, I will not scruple to say it may be likewise either in verse or prose: for though it wants one particular which the critic enumerates in the constituent parts of an epic poem, namely, metre, yet, when

any kind of writing contains all its other parts, such as fable, action, characters, sentiments, and diction, and is deficient in metre only, it seems, I think, reasonable to refer it to the epic; at least, as no critic hath thought proper to range it under any other head or to assign it a particular name to itself. (5)

By this reckoning all the heroic romances qualify as epics also: they possess – like *Joseph Andrews* – all but one of the constituent parts of an epic poem. And the deficiency they share with *Joseph Andrews* is metre. The similarities between Fielding's theories of fiction and those of the writers of heroic romance are manifold: these include topics such as 'history' versus 'fiction', 'probability' in fiction, and the construction of a work of fiction. A. L. Cooke in an excellent article entitled 'Henry Fielding and the Writers of Heroic Romance',[25] more than adequately demonstrates the remarkable affinities between the theories of Fielding and those of his French counterparts. Cooke, in spite of the evidence he produces, thinks it 'more sensible as well as more charitable',[26] to presume that Fielding and the romance writers arrived at the same theories independently. Cooke thinks this is a sensible view because of Fielding's many references to Davier, Le Bossu, Aristotle, and Horace: but these references might well be regarded as an elaborate facade, and charity only would then remain.

JOSEPH ANDREWS AND *TOM JONES* AS COMIC ROMANCES

A reading of *Joseph Andrews* and *Tom Jones* shows that 'comic romance' rather than 'comic epic poem in prose' is the term Fielding favoured most in describing these two works. Indeed the preface to *Joseph Andrews* opens thus: 'As it is possible the mere English reader may have a different *idea of romance* [my italics] from the author of these little volumes . . .' (v). And, later in the same preface, Fielding shows that he regards the two terms as synonymous when he writes: 'Now, a comic romance is a comic epic poem in prose . . .' (vi). While controversy has centred on whether Fielding's works are best regarded as epics or romances, insufficient attention has been given to the word which both of Fielding's terms share – 'comic'. By describing his works as comic, Fielding knowingly placed them in a solid, classical tradition. Aristotle had treated briefly of comedy in the *Poetics*, stating:

> Poetry now diverged in two directions, according to the individual character of the writer. The graver spirits imitated noble actions, and the actions of good men. The more trivial sort imitated the actions of meaner persons . . . (iv,7) . . . Comedy is an imitation of characters of a lower type . . . (v,1).

Comedy thus became sanctioned as the literary genre which concerned itself with low or everyday subjects, and represented these in a suitably low style. Comedy, in classical times, was distinguished from tragedy not only because it dealt with the actions of 'mean' as opposed to 'noble' men but also because it dealt with contemporary actuality rather than past events or ancient legend – the conventional preserve of tragedy. Donald Fanger regards classical comedy as the basis of modern realism; he writes:

> Classical times, with the exception of Petronius' fragmentary *Satyricon*, have left us no body of realistic fiction, and yet the starting point of the evolution of realism must be sought in antiquity because classical poetics bequeathed to posterity something perhaps more important even than a body of work: a way of thinking about literary art, a hierarchy of forms, styles, and values. Epic and tragedy ranked at the top of the list, since both treated of the destinies of men on that borderline where human greatness and divinity confronted one another. For such subjects of basic human concern the grand style was prescribed, where the majesty of the action was matched by the beauty of words; where – as Sidney observed of all poetry – nothing is false because nothing is affirmed; and where the illusion produced was justified by its intensity and not at all by its referential precision. Toward the other end of the scale, comedy, a far less consequential literary genre, could concern itself with low (everyday) subjects and render them in the low (colloquial, referential, even scurrilous) style. The basic work of comedy was and is an irreverent look at what society agrees to regard as reality, the deflation of all kinds of idealistic pretensions by confronting them with all that our Anglo-American culture means by 'the facts of life'. Thus realism first evolved as a tendency of the comic, because only in this area could its own tendencies be

legitimized. For a long time it would not lose the marks of this inheritance; indeed, it can be argued that it never has.[27]

It was within this classical tradition of comedy that Fielding developed his realism, and it was this tradition also which enabled him to discard the pretence of literal authenticity which had hamstrung even Richardson. Fielding did, like Richardson, claim that his work was grounded in 'truth' and 'nature', but it was the classical rather than the popular concept of truth and nature which he espoused. In one of the prefatory chapters in *Joseph Andrews*, he states his case explicitly:

> I question not but several of my readers will know the lawyer in the stagecoach [in *Joseph Andrews*] the moment they hear his voice. It is likewise odds but the wit and the prude meet with some of their acquaintance, as well as all the rest of my characters. To prevent, therefore, any such malicious applications, I declare here once for all I describe not men but manners; not an individual, but a species. Perhaps it will be answered, Are not the characters then taken from life? To which I answer in the affirmative; nay, I believe I might aver that I have writ little more than I have seen. The lawyer is not only alive, but hath been so this four thousand years and I hope G—— will indulge his life many yet to come. He hath not indeed confined himself to one profession, one religion, or one country; but when the first mean selfish creature appeared on the human stage who made self the centre of the whole creation, would give himself no pain, would incur no danger, advance no money, to assist or preserve his fellow creatures, then was our lawyer born, and whilst such a person as I have described exists on earth, so long shall he remain upon it. It is therefore doing him little honour to imagine he endeavours to mimic some little obscure fellow, because he happens to resemble him in one particular feature, or perhaps in his profession, whereas his appearance in the world is calculated for much more general and noble purposes . . . . (162)

An analysis of the word 'romance' as contained in Fielding's term 'comic romance' is not a simple matter, mostly because of Fielding's own uncertain attitude towards the word. He would, as was noted previously, have been 'well enough contented' (*TJ*436) with the word romance, but for the 'apprehension of . . . contempt"

(*TJ*436) which this might draw upon his works. Nor was Fielding's apprehension unfounded. 'For the late seventeenth-century writer', says Arthur Johnston, 'it was axiomatic that romantic fabling was the product of an extravagant imagination. This extravagance manifested itself in improbable and impossible fictions . . . .'[28] More important, perhaps, in the present context, is Johnston's remark that it was 'the unrealistic quality of romances which impressed critics of the seventeenth and eighteenth centuries, and determined the usages of the epithet "romantic".'[29] In one way, Fielding, in the preface to *Joseph Andrews*, had drawn a very valid distinction between his romance and all previous ones, by noting that his was a 'comic', as distinct from a 'serious' or 'grave' romance. And he elaborated on this:

> Now, a comic romance . . . differs from the serious romance in its fable and action in this, that as in the one these are grave and solemn, so in the other they are light and ridiculous; it differs in its characters by introducing persons of inferior rank, and consequently of inferior manners, whereas the grave romance sets the highest before us; lastly, in its sentiments and diction, by preserving the ludicrous instead of the sublime. (vi)

But it is actually in Fielding's *combination* of the two words 'comic', and 'romance', that a major difficulty arises. If the term romance, as applied to fiction in the eighteenth century, suggested the unrealistic quality of that fiction, it seems utterly paradoxical to combine it with the word 'comic' which is practically synonymous with realism. And yet, ironically, these two words combined, do more to highlight the peculiar quality of Fielding's first two novels, than any other combination could, because *Joseph Andrews* and *Tom Jones* 'seem to deal with romance in two opposite ways, often managing a synthesis: they accept courtly love and much of its romantic sublimity, and they mock heroic adventure with the picaresque scuffling of low life'.[30] But the synthesis which Fielding achieved between the comic and the romantic in *Joseph Andrews* and *Tom Jones* was not a new or revolutionary development. Cervantes, for instance, had shown what might be done in this line with *Don Quixote*, and Maurice Johnson's comments in this regard are significant. He remarks that in reading *Don Quixote* we are 'first involved in burlesque, sharing Cervantes's critical amusement at preposterous chivalric romance, laughing at an archaic rhetorical style; and then as we watch, the mad burlesque is wonderfully metamorphosed into 'good' comic romance'.[31] It remained for the Frenchman, Paul Scarron, to exploit the full potentiality of the comic romance, some fifty years after the publication of *Don Quixote*. While we must acknowledge the very great direct influence of Cervantes on Fielding,[32] he undoubtedly inherited a deal of Cervantes through Scarron. Like Fielding, almost a century later, Scarron had gravitated to the comic romance via parody: two of his more famous works prior to *Le Roman Comique* were long burlesque poems, *Le Typhon*, and *Le Virgile Travesti*.

The numerous similarities between *Le Roman Comique*, and *Joseph Andrews* and *Tom Jones*[33] suggest that Scarron was, perhaps, the single most important influence on Fielding's fiction. It was from Scarron that Fielding borrowed the term 'comic romance', and, more important still, Scarron showed him how effectively comedy and romance might be synthesised. *Le Roman Comique* was published in 1651, and the title must have obviously implied that the work was to be a 'low' humorous version of the *romans heroiques* which were then at the height of their vogue. It would certainly be inaccurate, however, to regard *Le Roman Comique* simply as a parody of heroic romance; as Homer Goldberg remarks:

> Scarron made uncomplimentary references to the heroic romances, and parodies some of their epic mannerisms; but in transplanting the conventional plot motifs and narrative structure of this exalted genre to the *milieu declassé* of the provincial theater, he was not attempting to reduce it to absurdity. Instead, like Cervantes in his interpolations, he sought to create his own more realistic version of those 'aventures de princes' substituting for the 'héros imaginaire de l'antiquité qui sont quelquefois incommodes à force d'être trop honnêtes gens' a personable and unassuming young leading man.[34]

The story of Destiny – the unassuming young leading man – could hardly be more romantic. It began late one night when a gentleman usher named Gariquet came upon a young woman in childbirth. He delivers a son for the woman, who tells him that the child is illegitimate. She entrusts the boy to Gariquet and gives him a ring for a token. Eventually, the father of the child – the Count of Glaris – marries the young woman and they recover their son from Gariquet. But the boy foisted on the unsuspecting couple is the son of Gariquet – who sees the advantage to be gained in having one of his family inherit the lands and title of the Count of Glaris. Destiny, who is the true Earl of Glaris,[35] does possess some token, one which is to restore him eventually to his rightful position.

It is hardly an exaggeration to suggest that Fielding was indebted to Scarron for the plot of *Tom Jones*. Tom, like Destiny, is quasilegitimate, and his upbringing is quite similar. Destiny and the 'Earl', like Tom and Blifil, are educated together. 'The natural antipathy said to have been between Jacob and Esau in the very womb of their mother', says Destiny, 'was never greater than that which was between the young earl and me'.[36] Such, also, is the antipathy between Tom and Blifil. Destiny has a 'love problem' and Tom's we discover, is almost identical. Destiny's problem begins when he falls in love with the beautiful Leonora and courts her for some time. His 'noble mien' has led Leonora's mother to believe that Destiny is a young man of quality, but on discovering that he is a nobody, she turns him away. Destiny is keenly aware of the disparity in rank between Leonora and himself, and of the consequences of such a disparity. He can only wish:

> that Leonora were not the legitimate daughter of a person of quality, that the blemish of her birth might excuse the meanness of mine; but however I soon repented so criminal a thought, and wished her fortune answerable to her merit. This last thought cast me into despair; for as I loved her more than my life, I plainly foresaw that I could never be happy without enjoying her, nor enjoy her without making her unhappy. (i,81)

Tom Jones finds himself in an almost identical situation. He courts Sophia after a fashion, but when the relationship dawns on Western, Tom is rejected. Tom's thoughts are not unlike those of Destiny. He thinks of Sophia's nobility and his own meanness, and despairs of ever 'obtaining the consent of her father' (221) for such a match. Later, he contemplates eloping with Sophia, but comes to a conclusion like that of Destiny:

> Can I think of soliciting such a creature to consent to her own ruin? Shall I indulge any passion of mine at such a price?—Shall I lurk about this country like a thief, with such intentions? No, I disdain, I detest the thought. (30)

Fielding, in *Tom Jones*, does not try to emulate Scarron's heaping of intrigue upon intrigue in the story of Destiny and Leonora. Perhaps *Joseph Andrews* is closer to Scarron in this respect. Leonora, for instance, is not a 'straight' character like Sophia Western, since her origins, like Destiny's, are quite mysterious. When we meet them first in the work, Destiny and Leonora are travelling as brother and sister, and there seems little reason to doubt that evidence has been produced – as in *Joseph Andrews* – which suggests that they *are* brother and sister. By the time the story (as Scarron wrote it), had ended, they had not been released from this kinship. Fielding was not a mere plagiarist: he may have borrowed details from Scarron, but both authors were simply the inheritors of the romance tradition. Scarron may never have finished *Le Roman Comique*, but *Joseph Andrews* and *Tom Jones* show just how he would have terminated the story. The romantic structure in *Le Roman Comique*, *Joseph Andrews*, and *Tom Jones*, does sustain these stories, but the articulation of the romance is effected in comic terms. And it is the more obvious comic aspect of these works which tends to shade their romantic frameworks.

JOSEPH ANDREWS AND *TOM JONES* AS CONVENTIONAL ROMANCES

There is little to be said about *Joseph Andrews* as romance. And yet, paradoxically, Sheridan Baker is correct in suggesting that 'the framework of romance is more evident in *Joseph Andrews* than in *Tom Jones*': 'babies exchanged in the cradle, lovers taken as brother and sister, the gold amulet tried to Joseph's arm, the strawberry mark, the gentle lineage'.[37] The more obvious romantic framework of *Joseph Andrews* is due to Fielding's inexperience in the art of narrative. For this reason he felt obliged to follow the lines of the conventional pattern of romance. The pattern is obvious in other ways also: Joseph 'begins his high life downstairs, must adventure for a period separated from his loved one, has the mandatory white skin, and is an accomplished horseman'.[38]

As in so many other ways, *Tom Jones*, as romance, shows a remarkable development from *Joseph Andrews*. By 1748 Fielding felt sufficiently sure of his narrative ability to be able to dispense with some of the more obvious ingredients of romance which he had used in his first work of fiction: in *Tom Jones* there is no exchange of babies, no token, and no strawberry mark. But in almost all other respects, Fielding has elaborated on ingredients first presented in *Joseph Andrews*. Tom Jones is of obscure origins; he, too, must adventure for extended periods separated from his loved one. But the separation in *Tom Jones* is both literal and metaphorical. The disparity in rank between Tom and Sophia means that unless Tom is discovered to be a 'somebody' he must remain forever separated from his loved one. But all the clues are present in the novel to suggest the inherent nobility of Tom. He has no equal as a sportsman, is a magnificent horserider, boxing champion, and can even leap over 'five-barred gates' (148). He is also 'one of the handsomest young fellows in the world' (170), and his skin is 'the most [sic] whitest that ever was seen' (196). Tom's noble mien impresses all who meet him: even landladies are duped by his 'genteel appearance' (398), into giving him credit. Nor does he simply *look* noble, he has concomitant personal qualities, a 'natural, not artificial good breeding' (619), and an 'obliging, complaisant behaviour to all women in general' (163). Like all the heroes of traditional romance, Tom undertakes an odyssey. He must, like Odysseus, try to go 'home', and the road home becomes the road to the West Country, while Odysseus's 'battles and storms' become, in *Tom Jones*, the bouts of fisticuffs at various inns. Squire Western could, in turn, be regarded as the Polyphemus of *Tom Jones*, Molly Seagrim the Circe, Jenny Jones the Calypso. Most important of all, perhaps, Tom is, like Odysseus, schooled by his experiences into achieving a degree of maturity. Sophia Western makes it quite plain that without this maturity she would not marry Tom, in spite of his becoming a 'somebody'.

The final touch is added to the romance of *Tom Jones* by the marriage of Tom and Sophia. But this, it should be noted, is not the only marriage with which the book ends: Nightingale has married Nancy Millar, Parson Supple marries Jenny Jones, alias Mrs Waters, and Partridge marries Molly Seagrim. And they all, one presumes, lived happily ever after.

TOM JONES AS PASSIONATE ROMANCE

In 1925, Aurelien Digeon, in *The Novels of Fielding*, wrote: 'I look forward to the day when an authentic document will be discovered, proving that *Tom Jones* was really written to oppose *Clarissa*'.[39]

Digeon elaborated on this remark, later, as follows:

> It is probable that while he was writing *Tom Jones*, Fielding had
> only an indirect knowledge of *Clarissa*. He knew the subject and
> the main lines of the narrative, he condemned its tendencies
> and had nothing but antipathy for Richardson's point of view;
> and it seems probable that he decided to write a novel on an
> analogous theme with the object of drawing from it a different
> moral lesson, and one which he thought healthier. Then, when
> the first two books of *Clarissa* were published, he was moved to
> the heart, as no one could help being moved, by the pathetic
> grandeur and psychological realism of these portraits, and
> expressed his sincere admiration in two articles in the *Jacobite's
> Journal* . . . .[40]

Digeon was, in a sense, accurate in his assessment, but what he
did not appreciate was that *Tom Jones* was written, not to oppose
Clarissa in particular, but to oppose the romance of passion in
general. The reason for the distinct resemblance between *Tom Jones*
and *Clarissa* is simply that both Fielding and Richardson were
attempting to oppose the same popular literary form, i.e. the
romance of passion. Each author went about his task in his own
way, however, leading Digeon to assume that *Tom Jones* had
actually been influenced by *Clarissa*. The 'authentic document' to
which Digeon referred has, therefore, been in rather conspicuous
existence for quite a long time: because any one of the numerous
romances of passion written prior to 1740 can be considered such
a document.

It seems somewhat peculiar that so little attention has been paid
to the resemblance between *Tom Jones* and the romance of passion,
particularly since Fielding seems to have intended that contemporary readers would notice it. *Tom Jones*, for instance, contains within
it a few short romances of passion: these were obviously meant as
to prepare us for the new variation of the basic pattern in the main
plot. The most obvious example of a romance of passion in *Tom
Jones* is the Jack Nightingale/Nancy Millar story. Jack Nightingale,
a handsome young rake, having first promised to marry Nancy
Millar, then seduces her. When Nancy becomes pregnant, Jack
abandons her, whereupon she twice attempts to kill herself. She
also becomes subject to numerous 'fits'. Fielding's description of
Nightingale shows him to be a fairly typical rake: 'This Nightingale

. . . was in the ordinary transactions of life a man of strict honour, and what is more rare among gentlemen of the town, one of strict honesty too; yet in affairs of love he was somewhat loose in his morals . . . it is certain he had been guilty of some indefensible treachery to women, and had in a certain mystery, called making love, practised many deceits, which, if he had used in trade he would have been counted the greatest villain upon Earth. But . . . he was so far from being ashamed of his iniquities of this kind, that he gloried in them, and would often boast of his skill in gaining of women, and his triumphs over their hearts . . .' (669).

When Tom Jones takes it upon himself to upbraid Nightingale because of his behaviour, he replies with the typical arguments of the rake: 'Common sense', he says to Tom, 'warrants all you say; but yet you well know the opinion of the world is so contrary to it, that was I to marry a whore tho' my own, I should be ashamed of ever showing my face again' (680). Ironically, for a rake, Nightingale actually claims 'duty' to his father as an additional reason why he must break with Nancy Miller. Tom Jones eventually overcomes the objections of Nightingale and convinces him that he should marry Nancy. So the circuit of the conventional romance of passion is broken – broken by the intervention of another so-called rake, Tom Jones himself.

Another important romance of passion in *Tom Jones* actually involves Tom himself, and on this occasion the circuit is not broken. In this romance Tom 'seduces' Molly Seagrim, who becomes pregnant. Molly is then 'abandoned' by the rake/seducer Tom. These are the bare facts of the case, but Fielding has taken some care to protect the character of Tom at each stage of this escapade. Fielding suggests, for instance, that it was Molly who seduced Tom: 'In the conduct of this matter', he writes, '*Molly* so well played her part, that *Jones* attributed the conquest entirely to himself, and considered the young woman as one who had yielded to the violent attacks of his passion. He likewise imputed her yielding to the ungovernable force of her love towards him . . .' (170). Fielding, here, manages to have it both ways, i.e. to show that Molly is the seducer, but that, importantly, Tom believes himself to be the seducer. Tom cannot think of 'abandoning his *Molly*' (171), and when she becomes pregnant he imagines her in circumstances typical of the abandoned heroine of the romance of passion: 'He now saw her in all the most shocking postures of death; nay, he considered all the miseries of prostitution to which she would be liable, and of which he would be doubly the occasion; first by seducing, then by deserting her . . .' (208). However, because of his love for Sophia Western, Tom decides he must abandon Molly, no matter how distressed this must leave her. The only explanation he offers Molly for deserting her is that Mr Allworthy has forbidden him to see her again – 'duty' once more – and if his meeting her on this occasion is discovered, it would end in 'his ruin and consequently in hers' (214). Tom suggests that Molly find some other man to marry her and promises to help her financially as best he can. Molly's reply is typical of the protestations of the heroine of the romance of passion in the same circumstances: 'And is this your love for me, to forsake me in this manner, now you have ruined me? How often, when I have told you that all men are false and perjury alike, and grow tired of us as soon as ever they had their wicked wills of us, how often have you sworn you would never forsake me? And can you be such a perjury man after all? What signifies all the riches in the world to me without you, now you have gained my heart, so you have – you have—? Why do you mention another man to me? I can never love another man as long I live. All other men are nothing to me . . . . I shall always hate and despise the whole sex for your sake' (214, 215). Tom does abandon Molly, but here again his guilt is mitigated by Fielding in two ways. First, Mr Square is discovered in Molly's room, and then Tom is told that a man called Will Barnes had been the first seducer of Molly, and may just as likely be the father of Molly's child. Nevertheless, Tom had decided to abandon Molly before either of these discoveries, and it is still probable that he is the father of Molly's child.

One conclusion to be drawn from Tom Jones's involvement with Molly Seagrim is that he is undoubtedly a rake, a fact confirmed by his later relationship with Mrs Waters and Lady Bellaston. Fielding, however, having depicted Tom as a typical rake, then proceeds to show that there is more to the personality of a man than sexual immorality – that villainy, for instance, is not necessarily a concomitant attribute. In this context *Tom Jones* may be regarded as another stage in a campaign commenced earlier by Fielding in *Shamela* and *Joseph Andrews*. In these two early works Fielding had reacted to the very narrow interpretation of morality as embodied in Richardson's *Pamela*. As Homer Goldberg remarks, Fielding 'espoused an impulsive virtue stemming from benevolent feelings rather than overestimated precepts, not solipsistically absorbed in its own preservation but actively promoting the good of others'.[41] Tom Jones is the embodiment of this ideal of virtue. While Tom is grossly immoral, in the conventional, sexual sense of the word, he is, nevertheless, kind, generous, and just to a remarkable degree. These qualities are apparent even in his sexual exploits, which never have any significant element of injustice or exploitation in them. As Tom himself remarks to Jack Nightingale, 'I am no canting hypocrite, nor do I pretend to the gift of chastity more than my neighbours. I have been guilty with women, I own it; but am not conscious that I have ever injured any – nor would I, to procure pleasure to myself, be knowingly the cause of misery to any human being'. (668) The principle embodied in this remark has, however, been adequately demonstrated in the behaviour of Tom. In his relationship with Sophia Western, in particular, Fielding clearly exemplifies the theory that sexual looseness does not inevitably involve a general depravity. Tom loves Sophia violently, and has her completely in his power, such is her reciprocal love for him. In spite, however, of the overwhelming force of his sexuality, Tom refuses to complete the circuit, described so often in the passionate romance, by eloping with and seducing Sophia. He claims his love for her 'is not of that base kind which seeks its own satisfaction at the expense of what is most dear to its object' (632). 'I would sacrifice every thing', Tom continues, 'to the possession of my *Sophia*, but *Sophia* herself' (632). Indeed, Tom Jones's sense of justice is so well developed that it is with some difficulty that he is persuaded, later in the novel, to leave his position as *gigolo* to Lady Bellaston.

The main plot of *Tom Jones* – up to a certain point – is obviously based on the pattern of a typical romance of passion. Tom is the typical handsome rake, for example: He is 'one of the handsomest young fellows in the World' (175); he is also called a 'profligate and abandoned . . . libertine' (185), 'one of the wildest fellows in *England*' (273), 'so terrible a rake' (614) and a 'profligate' rake (484). Fielding, as narrator, describes Tom as having 'naturally violent animals spirits' (235). Sophia Western falls in love 'to distraction' (222), with this acknowledged rake. Sophia's father presents a respectable suitor for her – William Blifil – described by Allworthy as 'the worthiest and best of men' (799).[42] But the worthy, upstanding suitor is rejected by Sophia. This rejection does not come easily to Sophia because of the powerful emotional conflict

which has been aroused in her. And the conflict is the old
one between love and duty, which eventually becomes a major
ingredient in the novel. In Book IX, the conflict in Sophia's mind
is described explicitly as being between love and duty. The two
forces are strong and equally matched; though, as the following
extract shows, duty has, if anything, the upper hand:

> She [Sophia] reverenced her father so piously, and loved him
> so passionately, that she had scarce ever felt more pleasing
> sensations, than what arose from the share she frequently had
> of contributing to his amusement; and sometimes, perhaps, ot
> higher gratifications; for he never could contain the delight of
> hearing her commended, which he had the satisfaction of hearing
> almost every day of her life. The idea, therefore, of the immense
> happiness she should convey to her father by her consent to
> this match, made a strong impression on her mind. Again, the
> extreme piety of such an act of obedience, worked very forcibly,
> as she had a very deep sense of religion. Lastly, when she
> reflected how much she herself was to suffer, being indeed to
> become little less than a sacrifice, or a martyr, to filial love and
> duty, she felt an agreeable tickling in a certain little passion,
> which tho' it bears no immediate affinity to religion or virtue, is
> often so kind as to lend great assistance in executing the purposes
> of both (330,331).

Later, Sophia tells her father that she had 'almost worked up a
resolution to endure the most miserable of all lives to comply with
your inclination' (745). Squire Western, for his part, is quite clear
as to Sophia's duty to him as far as marriage is concerned: 'Did I
not beget her?' he says to Allworthy, 'But I believe you will allow
me to be her father, and if I be, am I not to govern my own child?
. . . And if I am to govern her in other matters surely I am to
govern her in this marriage which concerns her most' (785).
Similarly, Sophia's aunt expresses strong views on the duty her
niece owes to her family. 'So far, madam, from being concerned
alone', she says to Sophia, 'your concern is the last, or surely the
least important. It is the honour of your family which is concerned
in this alliance; you are only the instrument. . . . You ought to
have a greater regard for the honour of your family, than for your
own person . . .' (306).

The more Sophia objects to marrying Blifil, the more obdurate her father becomes. 'I am resolved upon the match', he tells her, 'and unless you consent to it, I will not give you a groat, not a single farthing; no tho' I saw you expiring with famine in the street, I would not relieve you with a morsel of bread'. (275) Eventually, Western resorts to imprisoning Sophia, having resolved to marry her off to Blifil the following morning. Under the circumstances, Sophia decides that 'rather than submit to be the wife of that contemptible wretch I would plunge a dagger into my heart' (320). The only other alternative to suicide available for Sophia is escape from the clutches of her father, and so, on the night before her proposed marriage to Blifil, she contrives to run away from home. This can hardly be called a typical elopement, but it does put Sophia in an extremely vulnerable position. Clarissa Harlowe's predicament was identical, the consequences disastrous for her. While being confined by her father, Sophia corresponds with the rake, Tom Jones, just as the giddy girls of passionate romance did.

There are, of course, many details in *Tom Jones* which continually recall the romances of passion. The more interesting of these are where Fielding amusingly parodies the originals. The description of Sophia, for instance,[43] is a send-up of all such descriptions in the passionate (and perhaps all) romances. And the many comments and soliloquies[44] of Tom Jones himself on his love for Sophia, are, in part at least, motivated by Fielding's penchant for parody.

This is about as far as a comparison between *Tom Jones* and the typical romance of passion can be sustained. Because, like Richardson in *Clarissa*, Fielding followed a particular fictional model only to deviate from it, in order to highlight the flaws in the moral framework of that model. It must be emphasised that the contemporary readers would have been much more familiar than a twentieth-century one with Fielding's models and consequently more alive to his attempts at recasting in *Tom Jones*.

While Fielding's following of a certain fictional model and his deviation from it in *Tom Jones* is of significance, it is by no means the ultimate comment on the novel. The failure of critics to notice the relationship between *Tom Jones* and earlier romances of passion is adequate testimony to that. And yet this failure is quite understandable: because once Fielding has used the romance of passion as the basis of the plot of *Tom Jones*, and has had his say about the questionable moral framework of the romance, the novel goes on to become a great, original work of fiction. This originality, has in turn, tended to obscure Fielding's indebtedness and his aim in the early part of the novel.

Since Henry Fielding is the last in a long line of authors whose works have been examined, it is interesting to indicate some features of Greek romance which recur in Fielding. Why these features recur, however, is another matter entirely.

Fortune plays a part in *Joseph Andrews*, as it did in Greek romance. But in *Tom Jones* Fortune becomes a character in its own right: it is attributed a significant role in the plot and is mentioned specifically almost fifty times. Nor is its function in *Tom Jones* unlike its function in Greek romance, if one makes allowance for the necessary modification in comic romance. The verbiage of Greek romance is obvious in Fielding too, but again with a significant modification – he burlesqued the epic similes of Homer, and the monologues of Heliodorus to death, almost. In Fielding, the interpolated story, so common in Greek romance, seems to have regained its respectability – in *Tom Jones*, at any rate. Fielding in *Tom Jones* ensures that his interpolations – like Homer's in the *Odyssey* are woven into the main plot or thematic structure of his work. The philosophical and scientific essays of the sophistic Greek romances recur in Fielding, and for not dissimilar reasons. Fielding's digressions are not confined entirely to his prefatory chapters: within the body of *Tom Jones*, for instance, there are numerous philosophical essays on topics such as true wisdom,[45] and suspicion.[46] Other features of ancient romance which are apparent in Fielding are the preoccupation with virtue, the use of letters, and the dramatic conception of the story. Mention has already been made of the separation of lovers, the many journeys, the discovery of the true birth – all of which are common to Fielding and the Greeks. Homer was the obvious writer of fiction with which to begin a discussion of novel and romance, Fielding a fitting one with which to end.

Appendixes

Appendix I

The narrative diagram of the first twelve books of the *Odyssey* opposite, and the list of retrospective narrations set out, below, are an attempt (a) to illustrate the extent of the retrospective narration within these twelve books, and (b) to demonstrate the *seemingly* haphazard chronology of events narrated.

The Roman numerals on the left of the list, below, correspond to those in the diagram, and are intended as a key to it. The Arabic numerals on the right are an attempt at placing the events narrated in chronological order. Thus, the number 14, for example, represents the earliest incident of which we learn – Odysseus as spy in Troy – and 0 represents the latest – the arrival of Odysseus on Scherie.

i	The murder of (a) Agamemnon	8
	(b) Aegisthus	6
ii	Odysseus cursed by Poseidon for blinding Polyphemus	3
iii	Antiphus' son killed by Polyphemus	4
iv	The weaving of Penelope's shroud	2
v	The sacking of Troy	12
vi	The dissension over homecoming	11
vii	Murder of (a) Agamemnon	8
	(b) Aegisthus	6
viii	The safe homecoming of Nestor	10
ix	The safe homecoming of Menelaus	5
x	Odysseus as spy in Troy	14
xi	The Wooden Horse	13
xii	Menelaus' story of his homecoming	7
xiii	The murder of Agamemnon	8
xiv	The death of Ajax	9
xv	Odysseus' relation of	
	(a) his sojourn with Calypso	1
	(b) his journey to Scherie	0
xvi	Odysseus' relation of his adventures from leaving Troy to arrival on Ogygia	10–1

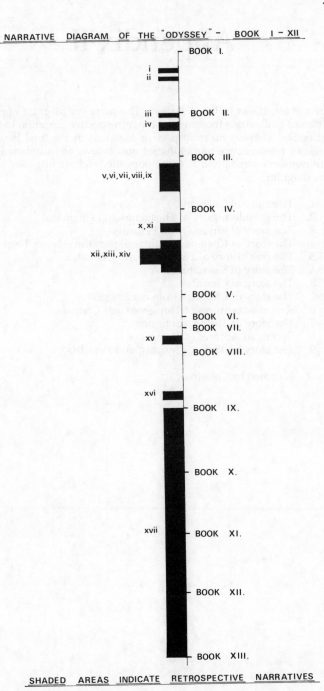

NARRATIVE DIAGRAM OF THE "ODYSSEY" - BOOK I - XII

BOOK I.

i
ii

BOOK II.

iii
iv

BOOK III.

v, vi, vii, viii, ix

BOOK IV.

x, xi

xii, xiii, xiv

BOOK V.
BOOK VI.
BOOK VII.
xv
BOOK VIII.

xvi
BOOK IX.

BOOK X.

xvii
BOOK XI.

BOOK XII.

BOOK XIII.

SHADED AREAS INDICATE RETROSPECTIVE NARRATIVES

Appendix II

There are ten books in the *Aethiopica*. The narrative diagram opposite is an attempt to illustrate the extent of the retrospective narration in the first eight books. There is no retrospective narration in the final two books. The list of retrospective narrations set out, below, are numbered 1 to 9. There numbers correspond to those opposite, and are intended as a key to the diagram.

1.	The story of Cnemon
2.	The pseudo-history of Theagenes and Chariclea
3.	The story of Thyamis and Petosiris
4.	The story of Cnemon, continued, plus the story of Thisbe
*5.	The *true* history of Theagenes and Chariclea
*5A.	The story of Sisimithres
*5B.	The story of Charicles
*5C.	The story of Chariclea from documents
6.	Recent adventures of Theagenes and Chariclea
7.	The story of Thisbe, continued
8.	Recent adventures of Theagenes
9.	The story of Arsace, Thyamis, and Petosiris

*	Narrated by Calasiris.

229

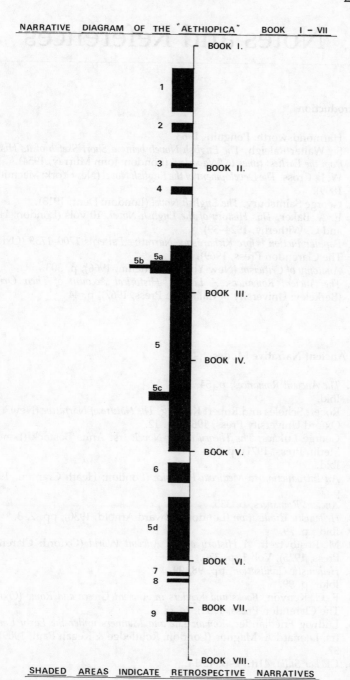

SHADED AREAS INDICATE RETROSPECTIVE NARRATIVES

Notes and References

Introduction

1. Harmondsworth: Penguin, 1963.
2. Sir Walter Raleigh, *The English Novel: being a Short Sketch of its History from the Earliest times to 'Waverley'* (London: John Murray, 1954).
3. W. L. Cross, *The Development of the English Novel* (New York: Macmillan, 1899).
4. George Saintsbury, *The English Novel* (London: Dent, 1913).
5. E. A. Baker, *This History of the English Novel*, 10 vols (London: H. F. and G. Witherby, 1924–39).
6. *Popular Fiction before Richardson: Narrative Patterns 1700–1739* (Oxford: The Clarendon Press, 1969), p. 2.
7. *Anatomy of Criticism* (New York: Atheneum, 1966), p. 303.
8. *The Ancient Romances: A Literary–Historical Account of Their Origins* (Berkeley: University of California Press, 1967), p. 44.

1. Ancient Narrative Modes

1. *The Ancient Romances*, p. 54.
2. Ibid.
3. Robert Scholes and Robert Kellogg, *The Nature of Narrative* (New York: Oxford University Press, 1966), p. 12.
4. George Lukács, *The Theory of the Novel*, trs. Anna Bostock (London: Merlin Press, 1971), p. 66.
5. Ibid.
6. *An Introduction to Medieval Romance* (London: Heath Cranton, 1930), p. 7.
7. *Ancient Romances*, p. 335.
8. *Hellenistic Civilisation* (London: Edward Arnold, 1930), pp. 2, 3.
9. Ibid., p. 79.
10. M. Rostovtzeff, *A History of the Ancient World* (Oxford: Clarendon Press, 1925), Vol. 1, p. 370.
11. *Hellenistic Civilisation*, pp. 98, 99.
12. Ibid., p. 99.
13. F. G. Kenyon, *Books and Readers in Ancient Greece and Rome* (Oxford: The Clarendon Press, 1932), p. 28.
15. Ludwig Friedlander, *Roman Life and Manners under the Early Empire*, trs. Leonard A. Magnus (London: Routledge & Kegan Paul, 1909), iii, 37.
16. Cf. *For Sulla*, 41ff., esp. 42.14.

17. Cf. *Natural History*, XXXV. II. 10, 11.
18. Cf. *Odes*, II, 20. 13–20; *Epodes* I. 20.13.
19. Cf. *Tristia (Laments from the Black Sea)*, IV, 9, 17ff.
20. Ibid., IV, 10, 115ff.; esp. 128.
21. iii, 36.
22. iii, 37.
23. *The Rise of the Novel*.
24. *Popular Fiction*, pp. 9, 10.
25. Cf. Perry, *Ancient Romances*, p. 119.
26. Cf. Perry, p. 169.
27. Robert Liddell, *A Treatise on the Novel* (London: Jonathan Cape, 1965), p. 18.
28. Ibid., pp. 17, 18.
29. *Ancient Romances*, pp. 56, 57.
30. Ibid.
31. Homer, *The Odyssey*, (Harmondsworth: Penguin, 1946), viii. All future references are to this edition.
32. *Ancient Romances*, pp. 50, 51.
33. Lucian, 'The True History', *Satirical Sketches*, trs. Paul Turner (Harmondsworth: Penguin, 1961), p. 250.
34. Ibid.
35. Richard Chase, *The American Novel and Its Tradition* (London: G. Bell, 1958), Introd. p. xi.
36. For a more detailed analysis see the unpublished dissertation (Stanford, 1971) by M. C. Davison, *The Metamorphoses of Odysseus*, p. 29ff.
37. Indeed much of what happens in Homer continually reminds one of Shakespeare: as in *Lear*, for example, Odysseus must be stripped naked – physically and mentally (deprived of *all* his men), before he can come home: the storm which besets Odysseus on leaving Ismarus reminds one, inevitably, of the storm on the heath in *Lear*, and indeed the details leading to the storms are not dissimilar.
38. The resemblance of Polyphemus to Caliban is obvious: both are of divine origin (Polyphemus is the son of Poseidon and Thoosa), and both are nearly human, but with the forms of monsters.
39. iv, 68.
40. Bk III, pp. 52, 54, 55.
41. Bk I, p. 23.
42. Bk XV, pp. 243, 244.
43. Bk XV, p. 248ff.
44. *Essays on the Greek Romances* (New York: Longmans Green, 1943), p. 58.
45. P. 350.
46. *Roman Life and Manners*, iii, 75.
47. Ibid., iii, 74.
48. P. 119.
49. Perry, p. 110.
50. Samuel Lee Wolff, *The Greek Romances in Elizabethan Prose Fiction* (New York: Columbia University Press, 1912), p. 128.
51. Ibid.

52. Perry, p. 112.
53. 'Fielding The Novelist', *The Times Literary Supplement*, 23 January, 1953, p. 56.
54. Perry, translated, p. 157.
55. Perry, pp. 157, 158.
56. Achilles Tatius, 'The Loves of Clitopho and Leucippe', *The Greek Romances of Helidorus, Longus, and Achilles Tatius*, trs. Rowland Smith (London: H. G. Bohn, 1855), i, 357ff. All future references are to this edition.
57. ii, 394ff.
58. iv, 421, 422.
59. iv, 418, 419.
60. iv, 420, 421.
61. iv, 435.
62. ii, 379.
63. i, 369.
64. Ibid.
65. i, 358ff.
66. iii, 396ff.
67. Cf. Donald B. Durham, 'Parody in Achilles Tatius', *Classical Philology* January 1983, Vol. XXXIII, 1–19.
68. Perry, p. 112.
69. *Ancient Romances*, p. 115.
70. Ibid.
71. It is very noticeable that Homer does not fall into a similar trap in the course of Odysseus' first-person narrative to the Phaeacians. At one point in his story Odysseus is careful to state: 'This part of the tale I had from the fair Calypso, who told me that she herself had heard it from Hermes the Messenger' (XII, 205).
72. *Greek Romances*, p. 119.
73. iv, 419.
74. Ibid.
75. ii, 389.
76. ii, 393.
77. v, 446.
78. v, 455ff.
79. vi, 465.
80. viii, 508.
81. ii, 378.
82. iv, 425; ii, 377.
83. Clitopho can even tell how the chest containing the sword happened to leave the ship.
84. ii, 411, 412.
85. vii, 479ff.; 496ff.
86. Heliodorus, *The Ethiopics; or, Adventures of Theagenes and Chariclea: The Greek Romances of Heliodorus, Longus and Achilles Tatius*, x, 260. All future references are to this edition.
87. It is tempting to view the Ethiopians' decision to do away with sacrificing human beings, as a triumph of reason and civilisation over

barbarism and the irrational, but it is difficult to sustain such a view. Theagenes and Chariclea are indeed responsible for the new, enlightened attitude among the Ethiopians: but then human sacrifices had always been made to Apollo, who had done precious little, it seems, to enlighten his people.

88. Fittingly, Apollo is a god with the gift of seeing the future.
89. vii, 172.
90. vii, 176.
91. *Essays*, p. 85.
92. ii, 37.
93. v, 109, et passim.
94. viii, 184.
95. Ibid.
96. x, 22.
97. Ibid.
98. x, 155, 156.
99. iii, 73ff.
100. v, 101ff.
101. vii, 155.
102. x, 229ff.
103. P. 188.
104. Pp. 140, 141.
105. Ibid.
106. Haight, *Essays*, p. 80.
107. i, 21.
108. The story of the Old Man of the Sea, within the story of Menelaus, *Odyssey*, Bk IV.
109. Cf. the narrative diagram in Appendix II for an illustration of what is involved.
110. Longus, *Daphnis and Chloe*, trs. Paul Turner (Harmondsworth: Penguin, 1968), p. 17. Hereafter all references are to this edition.
111. ii, 58, and iii, 88.
112. i, 22.
113. *Greek Romances*, p. 88.
114. *Ancient Romances*, p. 184.
115. Perry, p. 88.
116. P. 205.
117. Pp. 191, 192.
118. P. G. Walsh, *The Roman Novel* (Cambridge: Cambridge University Press, 1970), p. 72.
119. Tacitus, *Annales*, 16.18; quoted Perry, pp. 189, 190.
120. P. 205.
121. P. 88.
122. Cf. Petronius, *The Satyricon and the Fragments*, trs. John Sullivan (Harmondsworth: Penguin, 1965), fragments 1, and 4, p. 167. All future references are to this edition, except where stated otherwise.
123. Cf. H. D. Rankin, *Petronius the Artist: Essays on the Satyricon and its Author* (The Hague: Martinus Nijhoff, 1971), p. 58.
124. Cf. Rankin, p. 58.

125. This is the translation given by Jack Lindsay in his edition of Petronius (London: Elek, 1960), p. 60. Michael Heseltine's translation is 'robbers of romance' in his edition of Petronius (London: Heinemann, 1961), p. 23. Sullivan translates the phrase as 'unimaginably criminal', p. 37.
126. Petronius, p. 109; translated as 'fate' in this instance by Sullivan. The Latin word is *fortuna*.
127. Alexander A. Parker, *Literature and the Delinquent* (Edinburgh: Edinburgh University Press, 1967), p. 4.
128. *The Structure of the Novel* (London: Hogarth Press, 1928), p. 32.
129. *The Satyricon of Petronius: A Literary Study* (London: Faber and Faber, 1968), p. 97.
130. London: Heinemann, 1961, p. 297.
131. Petronius, p. 120ff.
132. Pp. 39, 48, 91, 104, 114, 117, 127.
133. Perry, p. 212.
134. Walsh, p. 114.
135. Apuleius, *The Golden Ass*, trs. William Adlington 1566, 1639 edition reprinted verbatim and literatim, 1946 (London: John Lehman), p. 68ff. All future references are to this edition, unless otherwise stated.
136. Walsh, p. 15.
137. *Ancient Romances*, p. 243.
138. Cf. *The Roman Novel*, pp. 150, 154, 158, 160ff. et passim.
139. Apuleius, *The Golden Ass: Being the Metamorphosis of Lucius Apuleius*, trs. W. Adlington, rev. S. Gaselee (London: Heinemann, 1947), p. 4.
140. *The Roman Novel*, p. 190.
141. Ibid.
142. P. 143.
143. Ibid.

2. Medieval Romance

1. Ernest A. Baker, 'Chrétien de Troyes', *The History of the English Novel* (London: Witherby, 1924), i, 111.
2. Ibid., i, 193.
3. Margaret Schlauch, *Antecedents of the English Novel 1400–1600* (London: Oxford University Press, 1963), p. 8.
4. Ibid., p. 4.
5. Ibid., p. 7.
6. Ibid., p. 57.
7. Ibid., p. 71.
8. Ibid., p. 23.
9. R. W. Southern, *The Making of the Middle Ages* (London: Hutchinson, 1953), p. 209.
10. Ibid., p. 212.
11. *The Medieval World: Europe 1100–1350*, trs. Janet Sondheimer (London: Weidenfeld & Nicolson, 1962), p. 1.

12. Ibid.
13. Johan Huizinga, *The Waning of the Middle Ages* (London: Edward Arnold, 1924), p. 271.
14. Ibid., pp. 271, 272.
15. Heer, p. 5.
16. Huizinga, *Middle Ages*, p. 56.
17. Ibid., p. 89.
18. Ibid., p. 96.
19. *An Introduction to Medieval Romance*, p. 81.
20. Scholes and Kellogg, *The Nature of Narrative*, pp. 248, 249.
21. *PMLA*, xxxviii (1923), p. 62.
22. London: Cambridge University Press, 1964, p. 211.
23. 'The Genesis of a Medieval Book', *Studies in Medieval and Renaissance Literature* (London: Cambridge University Press, 1966), p. 37.
24. *Enchanted Ground: The Study of Medieval Romance in the Eighteenth Century* (London: Athlone Press, 1964), p. 205.
25. P. 27ff.
26. 'The makers of the cheap booklets printed from worn-down type, which were hawked about by pedlars or chapmen, and hence called chapbooks, found in the heroes of medieval romance subjects to their liking, and retold some of their stories in the simplest prose and the barest outline. The unlettered who could read at all read chapbooks, and so did children of higher social station . . .' Gordon H. Gerould, *Patterns of English and American Fiction* (New York: Russell and Russell, 1966), pp. 18, 19.
27. Johnston, p. 9.
28. Ibid.
29. One must, of course, also ascertain what the relationship was between a medieval *Guy of Warwick* or *Valentine and Orson*, and the seventeenth-century version.
30. 'The Literary Influence of the Middle Ages', *The Cambridge History of English Literature* (Cambridge: Cambridge University Press, 1964), x, p. 217.

3. Pre-Eighteenth-Century Romance

1. It is of interest to note that Apuleius' *Golden Ass* had been translated into English in 1556.
2. *The Greek Romances in Elizabethan Prose Fiction*, p. 248ff.
3. Day Ten, Eighth Story.
4. P. 137.
5. *Idea and Act in Elizabethan Fiction* (Princeton: Princeton University Press, 1969), p. 121.
6. P. 358.
7. P. 309.
8. P. 309ff.
9. P. 355.
10. P. 338.

11. Pp. 365, 366.
12. P. 370ff.
13. P. 375.
14. Ibid.
15. Wolff, p. 457.
16. Davis, p. 163.
17. *Antecedents of the English Novel*, p. 175.
18. *Idea and Act in Elizabethan Fiction*, p. 158.
19. Charlotte E. Morgan, *The Rise of the Novel of Manners: A Study of English Prose Fiction between 1600 and 1740* (New York: Columbia University Press, 1911), p. 13.
20. *Shorter Novels of the Seventeenth Century*, ed. Philip Henderson (London: Everyman, 1967), Introd., p. vii.
21. *A History of the French Novel*, 2 vols (New York: Russell and Russell, 1917, 1919), i, 157.
22. Ibid., n.
23. Translated into English, 1607, as *The Pastorals of Julietta*, and in 1610 as *Honour's Academy*.
24. *The History of Fiction*, 3 vols (Edinburgh: 1816), iii, 230.
25. Ibid., iii, 230.
26. *The History of Fiction*, iii, 2.
27. *Ibrahim: or The Illustrious Bassa* (London: 1674), Preface, no pagination.
28. Ibid.
29. Ibid.
30. Ibid.
31. *The Rise of the Novel of Manners: A Study of English Prose Fictin Between 1600 and 1740* (New York: Columbia University Press, 1911), p. 31.
32. *History of the French Novel*, i, 176.
33. Ibid., i, 180, 181.
34. He has no need to ask her to swear; duty will compel her to keep her word.
35. *The Rise of the Novel of Manners*, p. 16.
36. iii, 30.
37. *Diary and Correspondence of Samuel Pepys*, deciphered by Rev. J. Smith. Third ed. (London: 1848, 1849), iv, 15.
38. Preface to *Theodora and Didymus*, reprinted in *Prefaces to Four Seventeenth-Century Romances*, ed. Charles Davis, Augustan Reprint Society no. 42 (Los Angeles, 1953), no pagination.
39. Roger Boyle, *Parthenissa*, (London, 1676), pt. 4, ii, 523.
40. Cf. *Novel and Romance*, Introduction, p. 3.
41. Morgan, *The Rise of the Novel of Manners*, pp. 1, 2.
42. Reprinted, Williams, p. 29.
43. *The Secret of Queen Zarah and the Zarazians* (London, 1705), Preface. Reprinted Williams, p. 30.
44. Ibid.
45. From a letter to Philip Stanhope, 1740–41?; reprinted, Williams, p. 100.
46. No. 26, Monday, 14 May 1787; reprinted, Williams, p. 341.
47. William Congreve, *Incognita and the Way of The World*, ed. A. N. Jeffares (London: Edward Arnold, 1966), pp. 32, 33.

48. *Ibrahim*, Preface, no pagination.
49. *Incognita*, Preface, p. 33.
50. *Shorter Novels of the Seventeenth Century*, ed. Philip Henderson (London: Dent, 1930), Introd., p. xiv.
51. Johnston, *Enchanted Ground*, p. 236.
52. Ibid.
53. Ibid., p. xiii.
54. Aphra Behn, *Oronooko*, in *Shorter Novels of the Seventeenth Century*, p. 153. Hereafter all references are to this edition. It is ironic that Oroonoko's tutor should be a Frenchman: no doubt this is the explanation for the hero's exhibition of all the accomplishments of the French and English courts.
55. It is interesting to note also that later in *Oroonoko* Imoinda again reminds one greatly of Chariclea, when she uses a bow and poisoned arrows 'which she managed with such dexterity that she wounded several . . .' (210).
56. Johnston, *Enchanted Ground*, p. 199.
57. *Popular Fiction Before Richardson*, p. 172.
58. Ibid., pp. 172, 173.
59. *The Rise of the Novel of Manners*, p. 31.
60. Ibid.
61. Richetti, p. 123.
62. Ibid., p. 125.
63. Ibid., pp. 149, 152.
64. *The Adventures of Lindamira, A Lady of Quality*, ed. Benjamin Boyce (Minneapolis: University of Minnesota Press, 1949), Introd., p. vi.
65. Boyce, pp. v, vi, 129.
66. Richetti, *Narrative Patterns*, p. 173.
67. Ibid., p. 129.
68. Ibid., p. 131.
69. 'Mrs Penelope Aubin and the Early English Novel', *HLQ*, xx (1957), p. 250.
70. Pp. 206, 207.
71. Ibid., p. 211.
72. Ibid., p. 216.
73. Reprinted in *Prefaces to Four Seventeenth Century Romances*, ed. Charles Davies (Los Angeles: Augustan Reprint Society, 1953), no. 42, no pagination.
74. Ibid.
75. Richetti, p. 245.
76. Cf. p. 94.
77. Cf. ii, 135ff. and iii, 211ff. of edition published Edinburgh, 1755.
78. P. 247.

4. Richardson and Romance

1. William M. Sale, Jr., 'From Pamela to Clarissa', *The Age of Johnson*, ed. F. W. Hilles (New Haven: Yale University Press, 1964), p. 132.

2. Morris Golden, *Richardson's Characters* (Ann Arbor: University of Michigan Press, 1963), p. 188.

3. *Selected Letters of Samuel Richardson*, ed. John Carroll (Oxford: The Clarendon Press, 1964), p. 41. Hereafter cited in the text as SL, followed by the page number(s).

4. Richetti, p. 5.

5. Ibid.

6. It is worth comparing Robert Boyle's justification of his style in *Theodora and Didymus* fifty-three years earlier. It is obvious that he, too, wrote with the intention of catching young and airy minds. '. . . I feared, that the Youthful Persons of Quality of both Sexes, that I was chiefly to regard', Boyle wrote, 'would scarce be sufficiently affected by unfortunate Vertue, if the interweaving of passages relating to Beauty and Love, did not help to make the Tragical story, Delightful, and the Excellent Sufferers Piety, Amiable.' (Augustan reprint, no. 42, no pagination)

7. P. 124.

8. Samuel Richardson, *Pamela*, Everyman's Library Edition, 2 vols (London: Dent, 1962), i, 77. All future references are to this edition.

9. Part of an advertisement for *Pamela* in the *Weekly Miscellany* for 11 October 1740, contained a letter to the author, and was later included by Richardson in the Introduction to *Pamela*, which was first published on 6 November 1740. In the letter mentioned, the writer says he has 'gone hand-in-hand, and sympathis'd with the pretty heroine in all her Sufferings, and been extremely anxious for her Safety, under the Apprehensions of the bad Consequences which, I expected, every Page, would ensue from the laudable Resistance she made'. (Reprinted, Williams, *Novel and Romance*, p. 96)

10. Cf. Melliora and D'elmont in *Love in Excess* and Charlot and the Duke in *The New Atalantis*, for variations on this isolation of the heroine.

11. Richetti, p. 18.

12. Ibid., p. 223.

13. Williams, *Novel and Romance*, p. 93.

14. Hereafter referred to as *The Irish Princess*: all references are to the 1693 edition.

15. Though one must admit that in each case the title of one narrative and the subtitle of the other, tends to give the game away.

16. P. 157.

17. *Pamela*, 1, 192, 199; *The Irish Princess*, 145.

18. *Pamela*, 1, 151; *The Irish Princess*, 123, 138ff.

19. *Pamela*, 1, 164ff.; *The Irish Princess*, 123, 138ff., 176.

20. *Pamela*, 1, 29; *The Irish Princess*, 50.

21. In her dream, Marinda imagines the Prince 'had hidden himself in my Bed-chamber, and, when I came in, started out upon me: He . . . catched me in his Arms, and told me I was his Prisoner, at which methought, I swooned away with a pleasing pain and at the fright of it I awaked' (53).

22. 1, 145, 146.

23. 1, 47ff. 1, 177ff.

24. *Pamela*, 1, 189ff. 1, 202ff.; *The Irish Princess*, 115, 154.

25. This latter phrase is very reminiscent of one used by Pamela when she hears of the bogus marriage Mr B. is about to offer her: 'Here should I have been deluded with the hopes of a happiness that my highest ambition could have aspired to!' (1, 199).
26. P. xi.
27. Pp. 49–55; 122, 123.
28. P. 129.
29. T. C. D. Eaves and B. D. Kimpel, *Samuel Richardson: A Biography* (Oxford: The Clarendon Press, 1971), p. 584.
30. Ibid.
31. *Selected Letters*, p. 229.
32. Ibid., p. 231.
33. Ibid., p. 39.
34. Ibid., pp. 39–42.
35. P. 39.
36. P. 232.
37. *Selected Letters*, p. 231.
38. *Samuel Richardson*, p. 110.
39. *Joseph Andrews and Shamela*, ed. Martin Battester (Lava: Methuen, 1965), p. 235.
40. Ian Watt, Introduction to *An Apology for the Life of Mrs Shamela Andrews* (Los Angeles, 1956). Reprinted *Fielding: A Collection of Critical Essays*, ed. Ronald Paulson (Englewood Cliffs: Prentice-Hall, 1962), p. 50.
41. Maynard Mack, Introduction to *Joseph Andrews* (New York, 1948), reprinted Paulson, pp. 52, 53.
42. Samuel Richardson, *Clarissa or, The History of a Young Lady*, Everyman's Library edition, 4 vols (London: Dent, 1962), iii, 61. All future references are to this edition.
43. Reprinted, Williams, p. 118.
44. Richetti, p. 251.
45. Mariana, in 'The Physicians Strategem' (one of the stories in *The Power of Love*) by Mrs Manley suffers a similar fate. The rapist is later murdered by Mariana's former lover.
46. Richetti, p. 184.
47. Clarissa herself acknowledges that her secret correspondence, against the wishes of her father, was the commencement of her downfall: cf. iii, 222.
48. Richardson wrote as follows in the Postscript to the 1751 edition: 'It was not intended that she [Clarissa] should be in love, but in liking only, if that expression may be admitted' (iv, 558).
49. Cf. *Memoirs of a Certain Island* (ii, 119), where Bellyna, objecting to her violation and subsequent abandonment by Ricardo, says to him: 'Did you not call all Heaven to witness that you were my Husband; that you would perform all the tender Offices of that Name; and that the Ceremony of the Church should authorize these Joys you then protested were in my power to give?' See, too, SL, 114, where Lady Bradshaigh wrote to Richardson saying that girls 'who are so weak as to be tempted by so old a Bait as a Promise of Marriage, deserve not that Justice'.
50. In the postscript Richardson writes: 'To have a Lovelace for a series

of years glory in his wickedness, and think that he had nothing to
do, but as an act of grace and favour to hold out his hand to receive
that of the best of women, whenever he pleased, and to have it
thought, that marriage would be a sufficient amends for all his
enormities to others, as well as to her; he [the author of *Clarissa*] could
not bear that' (iv, 553).

51. See *Exilius*, for instance, where the libertine Clodius happens to meet
   a girl he had once seduced and abandoned. He tells her explicitly that
   she 'was to accuse herself of her Ruin, forasmuch as she was not
   ignorant of the World. She knew the Town, and the Humour of the
   Times, and knew, that young Men would say and swear any Thing
   to gain their Ends on Girls, and then abandon them to Ruin and
   Despair; for, said he, that young Girl that will carry on secret Intrigues
   of Love without the Knowledge or Consent of her Parents deserves
   to be treated by her Gallant, as you have been by me; for how could
   you suppose I would make you a Lady, or a Wife, who could not
   keep yourself a vertuous Maid, nor a dutiful Daughter? No, no
   (continu'd he) those who bridle not their fond Desires with the Curb
   of Reason, or filial Duty, are only fit to be Wives to Monsters, or
   Mistresses to the least of Mankind. And such as will run to Balls,
   Theatres, and Treats with young Men of the Town, cannot expect the
   Vows we make, are made to be kept; but to become the broken Meat
   for lost Vertue to feed upon, and be the miserable Support of a ruin'd
   Reputation. Of all which you could not be ignorant, at least my
   Character was sufficiently known, to have inform'd you; therefore it
   is your self you are to reproach for all your Misfortunes' (ii, 76, 76).
52. It is worth noting that the heroine of romances of passion was
   frequently described as 'giddy'. The adjective is used very often by
   Richardson, and always with this connotation.
53. P. 226.
54. In the first volume alone, see pp. 37, 70, 71, 75, 76, 78, 96, 119, 128,
   179, 184, 297, 386, 416, 427, 458, et passim.
55. *PMLA*, LXXXI (June 1966), pp. 236–45.
56. Ibid., p. 238.
57. Ibid., p. 240.
58. Ibid., p. 240.
59. Ibid., p. 238.
60. A. S. P. Woodhouse, 'Tragic Effect in *Samson Agonistes*, *University of
   Toronto Quarterly* xxvii (1958/9). Reprinted *Twentieth Century Interpretations of Samson Agonistes*, ed. G. Crump (Englewood Cliffs: Prentice-
   Hall, 1968), p. 112.
61. His fears were well grounded, it seems: the later volumes of *Clarissa*
   did not sell as well as the initial ones. See SL, 86.
62. P. 157.
63. In a letter to Edward Moore, Richardson explains that Lovelace dies
   without ever acknowledging God's right to his soul or asking for
   mercy: 'What a Goddess does he make of the exalted Clarissa! –
   Yet how deplorably impious, hardly thinks of evoking the highest
   assistance and mercy!' (SL, 121) 'Have I not then,' Richardson con-

tinues later, 'given rather a dreadful than a hopeful Exit, with respect to Futurity, to the unhappy Lovelace!' (SL,122)
64. iv, 256.

5. Henry Fielding's Comic Romances

1. Martin C. Battestin, in his introduction to a combined edition of *Joseph Andrews* and *Shamela* (London: Methuen, 1965), argues as follows:
   Clearly there were ample reasons, more practical than moral and artistic indignation, that prompted Fielding's response to *Pamela*. A 'spoof' of Richardson's immensely popular book was sure to be financially rewarding, and Fielding desperately needed the money. But it would be a serious and rather cynical distortion to underestimate the importance of those other, less mercenary motives, which, after all, are the ones that chiefly matter to us as expressions of Fielding's art and his thought. (xx)
2. Aurelien Digeon, *The Novels of Fielding* (New York: Russell and Russell, 1925), p. 51.
3. Facsimile of title page of second edition, 1741. Reproduced, *Joseph Andrews and Shamela*, ed. Battestin, p. 299.
4. Battestin, Introd., p. xii.
5. Introd., p. xviii.
6. Ibid.
7. Ibid.
8. Ibid.
9. Ibid.
10. *The Art of Joseph Andrews* (Chicago: University of Chicago Press, 1969), p. 20.
11. Sonnet, xli.
12. *Joseph Andrews*, ed. Irvin Ehrenpreis (New York: New American Library, 1967), p. 20. All future textual references are to this edition.
13. P. xviii.
14. Cf. p. 132.
15. Ioan Williams, *Novel and Romance*, p. 1.
16. Ian Watt, *The Rise of the Novel*, p. 56.
17. Ioan Williams, *Novel and Romance*, p. 7.
18. *Tom Jones*, ed. R. P. C. Mutter (Harmondsworth: Penguin, 1966), p. 88. All future references are to this edition.
19. Books IV and IX.
20. *The Poetics*, iv, 9.
21. *Novel and Romance*, p. 3.
22. Bk ii., Chapt. 21.
23. Fielding refers, facetiously, to literary theft in the introductory chapter to Bk XII, p. 551ff., *Tom Jones*.
24. Cf. Johnston, *Enchanted Ground*, p. 199.
25. *PMLA*, LXII (December 1947), 984–94.
26. Ibid., p. 993.

27. *Dostoevsky and Romantic Realism: A Study of Dostoevsky in relation to Balzac, Dickens, and Gogol* (London: OUP, 1965), p. 4.
28. *Enchanted Ground*, p. 199.
29. Ibid. p. 202.
30. Sheridan Baker, 'Henry Fielding's Comic Romances', *Papers of the Michigan Academy of Science, Arts, and Letters*, XLV (1960), p. 416.
31. Maurice Johnson, *Fielding's Art of Fiction* (Philadelphia: University of Pennsylvania Press, 1965), p. 47.
32. Cf. my unpublished dissertation *Some Literary Influences on the Novels of Henry Fielding* (University College Galway, 1968), p. 96ff.
33. Ibid., p. 109ff.
34. *The Art of Joseph Andrews*, p. 45.
35. Scarron never completed *Le Roman Comique*, but the statements here are almost certainly accurate, bearing in mind the evidence available in the extant work.
36. Paul Scarron, *The Comical Romance, and Other Tales*, trs Tom Brown, John Savage, and others, 2 vols (London: Lawrence and Bullen, 1892), i, 70. All future references are to this edition.
37. 'Henry Fielding's Comic Romances', *Papers of the Michigan Academy of Science, Arts and Letters*, XLV (1960), pp. 415, 416.
38. Ibid.
39. *The Novels of Fielding*, p. 132.
40. P. 139.
41. *The Art of Joseph Andrews* (Chicago: University of Chicago Press, 1969), p. 20.
42. Blifil the 'worthiest and best of men', is intended by Fielding as the antithesis of Tom Jones. In sexual terms he is quite beyond reproach, at least to the extent that he has never, at least to our knowledge, committed a sexually immoral act. But in the more general sense of the term, Blifil is grossly immoral. Fielding is asking the reader to choose between the 'immorality' of a Tom Jones, and the 'morality' of a Blifil.
43. Pp. 155, 156.
44. Cf. pp. 192, 239, 276, 277.
45. P. 262.
46. P. 548ff.

Selected Bibliography

ALLEN, WALTER (1954) *The English Novel: A Short Critical History* (London: Phoenix House).

ANON. (1949) *The Adventures of Lindamira, A Lady of Quality*, ed. Benjamin Boyce (Minneapolis: University of Minnesota Press).

ANON. (1713) *Love Intrigues: Or, The History of the Amours of Bosvil and Galesia, As Related to Lucasia, in St. Germans* [sic] *Garden. A Novel* (London).

APULEIUS (1946) *The Golden Ass of Apuleius*. Trs. William Adlington, 1566. 1639 ed. reprinted verbatim and literatim (London: Lehmann).

—— (1947) *The Golden Ass: Being the Metamorphosis of Lucius Apuleius*. Trs. W. Adlington. Rev. S. Gaselee (London: Heinemann).

ASHLEY, ROBERT, EDWIN M. MOSELY, eds (1966) *Elizabethan Fiction* (New York: Holt, Rinehart and Winston).

AUBIN, PENELOPE (1721) *The Strange Adventures of the Count de Vinevil and his Family. Being an Account of what happen'd to them whilst they resided at Constantinople* (London).

—— (1721) *The Life of Madam de Beaumont, a French Lady; Who Lived in a Cave in Wales above fourteen Years undiscovered, being forced to fly France for her Religion; and of the cruel Usage she had there* (London).

—— (1728) *The Life and Adventures of the Young Count Albertus, The Son of Count Lewis Augustus, by the Lady Lucy: Who being become a Widower, turn'd Monk, and went a Missionary for China, but was shipwrecked on the Coast of Barbary. Where he met with many strange Adventures, and returned to Spain with some persons of Quality who by his Means made their Escape from Africa After which he went again a Missionary to China where he arriv'd and ended his Life a Martyr for the Christian Faith* (London).

BAILEY, CYRIL, ed. (1924) *The Legacy of Rome* (Oxford: The Clarendon Press).

BAKER, EARNEST A. (1924–39) *The History of the English Novel*, 10 vols (London: Witherby).

BAKER, SHERIDAN (1960) 'Henry Fielding's Comic Romances', *Papers of the Michigan Academy of Science, Arts, and Letters*, XLV, 411–19.

—— (1964) 'The Idea of Romance in the Eighteenth-Century Novel', *Papers of the Michigan Academy of Science, Arts and Letters*, XLIX, 507–22.

BALDENSPERGER, FERNAND (1937) '"Romantique", ses Analogues et ses Équivalents: Tableau Synoptique de 1650 à 1850', *Harvard Studies and Notes In Phililogy and Literature*, XIX, 13–105.

BARKER, JANE (1715) *Exilius: or, The Banished Roman. A New Romance* (London).

BASLER, RAY P. (1948) *Sex, Symbolism and Psychology in Literature* (New Brunswick: Rutgers University Press).

BECKER, GEORGE K., ed. (1963) *Documents of Modern Literary Realism* (Princeton: Princeton University Press).

BEER, GILLIAN (1970) *The Romance* (London: Methuen).

BENSON, LARRY D. (1968) 'Sir Thomas Malory's *Le Morte Darthur'*, *Critical Approaches to Six Major English Works: Beowulf through Paradise Lost* (Philadelphia: University of Pennsylvania Press).

BISSELL, FREDERICK O. (1933) *Fielding's Theory of the Novel* (Ithaca: Cornell University Press).

BOCCACCIO, GIOVANNI (1930) *The Decameron*, 2 vols (London: Dent).

BOOTH, WAYNE (1961) *The Rhetoric of Fiction* (London: University of Chicago Press).

—— (1982) 'The Self-Conscious Narrator in Comic Fiction before *Tristram Shandy'*, *PMLA*, LXVII 163–85.

BOYLE, ROGER (1676) *Parthenissa* (London).

BRINKLEY, ROBERTA FLORENCE (1967) *Arthurian Legend in the Seventeenth Century* (London: Frank Cass).

BURY, J. B. (1889) *A History of the Later Roman Empire*, 2 vols (London: Macmillan).

BUTT, JOHN (1954) *Fielding* (London: Longmans Green).

CHADWICK, H. M. (1912) *The Heroic Age* (Cambridge: Cambridge University Press).

CHADWICK, H. M. and N. K. CHADWICK (1932) *The Growth of Literature*, 4 vols. (Cambridge: Cambridge University Press).

CHARITON (1939) *Chaereas and Callirhoe*. Trs. Waren E. Blake (Ann Arbor: University of Michigan Press).

CHASE, RICHARD (1958) *The American Novel and Its Tradition* (London: G. Bell and Sons).

CHURCH, RICHARD (1961) *The Growth of the English Novel* (London: Methuen).

CICERO (1964) *The Speeches With An English Translation: In Catalinam I–IV; Pro Murena; Pro Sulla; Pro Flacco*. Trs. Louis E. Lord (London: Heinemann).

CLIFFORD, JAMES L., ed. (1959) *Eighteenth Century English Literature: Modern Essays in Criticism* (New York: Oxford University Press).

CONGREVE, WILLIAM (1966) *Incognita and The Way of the World*, ed. A. N. Jeffares (London: Edward Arnold).

COOK, ELIZABETH (1969) *The Ordinary and the Fabulous: An Introduction to Myths, Legends and Fairy Tales for Teachers and Storytellers* (Cambridge: Cambridge University Press).

COOKE, ARTHUR L. (1947) 'Henry Fielding and the Writers of Heroic Romance', *PMLA*, LXIX, 984–94.

COWIE, ALEXANDER (1951) *The Rise of the American Novel* (New York: American Book Co.).

CROSS, WILBUR L. (1918) *The History of Henry Fielding*, 3 vols (New Haven: Yale University Press).

CRUMP, G., ed. (1968) *Twentieth Century Interpretations of Samson Agonistes* (Englewood Cliffs: Prentice-Hall).

CURRENT GARCIA, EUGENE, WALTON R. PATRICK, eds (1962) *Realism and Romanticism in Fiction: An Approach to the Novel* (Chicago: Scott, Foresman).

DALZIEL, MARGARET (1957) *Popular Fiction One Hundred Years Ago* (London: Cohen and West).

DANBY, JOHN F. (1952) *Poets on Fortune's Hill: Studies in Sidney, Shakespeare, Beaumont and Fletcher* (Port Washington: Kennikat Press).

DAVIES, CHARLES, ed. (1953) *Prefaces to Four Seventeenth-Century Romances*. Augustan Reprint Society, No. 42 (Los Angeles: University of California Press).

DAVIS, WALTER R. (1969) *Idea and Act in Elizabethan Fiction* (Princeton: Princeton University Press).

DAVISON, MARY C. (1971) 'The Metamoprhoses of Odysseus: A Study of Romance Iconography from the *Odyssey* to *The Tempest*' (Stanford).

DILL, SAMUEL (1911) *Roman Society From Nero to Marcus Aurelius* (London: Macmillan).

DOBRÉE, BONAMY (1959) *English Literature in the Early Eighteenth Century* (Oxford: The Clarendon Press).

DUDDEN, FREDERICK HOMES (1952) *Henry Fielding: His Life, Works, and Times*, 2 vols (Oxford: The Clarendon Press).

DUNLOP, JOHN (1816) *The History of Fiction: being a Critical Account of the Most Celebrated Prose Works of Fiction from the Earliest Greek Romances to the Present Age* (London: Ballantyne).

DURHAM, DONALD B. (1938) 'Parody in Achilles Tatius', *Classical Philology*, XXXIII (January), 1–19.

DUSSINGER, JOHN A. (1966) 'Conscience and the Pattern of Christian Perfection in *Clarissa* (1964)', *PMLA*, LXXXI, 236–45.

EHRENPREIS, IRVIN (1964) *Tom Jones* (London: Edward Arnold).

ELLIOT, ROBERT C. (1970) *The Shape of Utopia: Studies in a Literary Genre* (Chicago: University of Chicago Press).

ELTON, OLIVER (1899) *The Augustan Age* (London: Blackwood).

——— (1928) *A Survey of English Literature 1730–1780* (London: Edward Arnold).

EVERETT, DOROTHY (1955) *Essays on Middle English Literature*, ed. Patricia Kean (Oxford: The Clarendon Press).

FANGER, DONALD (1965) *Dostoevsky and Romantic Realism: A Study of Dostoevsky in relation to Balzac, Dickens, and Gogol* (London: Oxford University Press).

FIELDING, HENRY (1966) *The History of Tom Jones*, ed. R. P. C. Mutter (Harmondsworth: Penguin).

——— (1967) *Joseph Andrews*, ed. Irvin Ehrenpreis (New York: New American Library).

——— (1965) *Joseph Andrews and Shamela*, ed. Martin Battestin (London: Methuen).

'Fielding the Novelist' (1953) Anon. rev., *Times Literary Supplement* (23 January 1953), 56.

Fielding: A Collection of Critical Essays (1962) ed. Ronald Paulson (Englewood Cliffs: Prentice-Hall).

FORSTER, E. M. (1927) *Aspects of the Novel* (London: Edward Arnold).

FOSTER, JAMES R. (1949) *History of the Pre-Romantic Novel in England* (New York: Modern Languages Association).

FRIEDLANDER, LUDWIG (1965) *Roman Life and Manners under the Early Empire*, 4 vols. Trs. J. H. Freese, L. A. Magnus (London: Routledge & Kegan Paul).

GAYLEY, CHARLES MILLS (1937) *The Classic Myths in English Literature and in Art* (Massachusetts: Blaisdell).

GENTLES, FREDERICK (1970) 'Escape to the Other Side of Reality.' *Hangups from Way Back: Historical Myths and Canons* (San Francisco: Canfield Press).

GEROULD, GORDON HALL (1966) *The Patterns of English and American Fiction* (New York: Russell and Russell).

GOLDBERG, HOMER (1969) *The Art of Joseph Andrews* (Chicago: University of Chicago Press).

GOLDEN, MORRIS (1963) *Richardson's Characters* (Ann Arbor: University of Michigan Press).

GORDON, G. S., ed. (1912) *English Literature and the Classics* (Oxford: The Clarendon Press).

GRADON, PAMELA (1971) *Form and Style in Early English Literature* (London: Methuen).

GRANT, DAMIEN (1970) *Realism* (London: Methuen).

GRIFFIN, NATHANIEL E. (1923) 'The Definition of Romance', *PMLA*, XXXVIII, 50–70.

GROSSVOGEL, DAVID I. (1968) *Limits of the Novel: Evolutions of a form from Chaucer to Robbe-Grillet* (London: Cornell University Press).

HADAS, MOSES (1950) *A History of Greek Literature* (New York: Columbia University Press).

———, ed. (1953) *Three Greek Romances* (New York: Doubleday and Co.).

HAIGHT, ELIZABETH H. (1943) *Essays on the Greek Romances* (New York: Longmans Green).

——— (1945) *More Essays on the Greek Romances* (New York: Longmans Green).

HAYWOOD, ELIZA (1719) *Love in Excess, or the Fatal Enquiry, A Novel* (London).

——— (1723) *Idalia: or, The Unfortunate Mistress. A Novel* (London).

——— (1724) *Lasselia: or, the Self Abandon'd. A Novel* (London).

——— (1724) *The British Recluse: or, the Secret History of Cleomira, Suppos'd Dead. And the Injured Husband: or, the Mistaken resentment. Two Novels.* Third edition (Dublin).

——— (1725) *Memoirs of a Certain Island Adjacent to the Kingdom of Utopia* (London).

HEER, FRIEDRICH (1962) *The Medieval World: Europe 1100–1350.* Trs. Janet Sondheimer (London: Weidenfield & Nicholson).

HIGHET, GILBERT (1949) *The Classical Tradition: Greek and Roman Influences on Western Literature* (London: Oxford University Press).

HIRSCH, DAVID (1969) 'The Reality of Ian Watt', *Critical Quarterly* II (Summer), 164–79.

HOFFMAN, DANIEL (1965) *Form and Fable in American Fiction* (New York: Oxford University Press).

HOMER (1946) *The Odyssey.* Trs. E. V. Rieu (Harmondsworth: Penguin).

HORACE (1968) *The Odes and Epodes With an English Translation*. Trs. C. E. Bennett (London: Heinemann).

HUIZINGA, JOHAN (1924) *The Waning of the Middle Ages* (London: Edward Arnold).

—— (1970) *Homo Ludens: A Study of the Play Element in Culture* (London: Temple Smith).

HUMPHREYS, A. E. (1954) *The Augustan World* (London: Methuen).

HUNTER, G. K. (1962) *John Lyly: The Humanist as Courtier* (London: Routledge & Kegan Paul).

JAMES, HENRY (1962) *The Art of the Novel: Critical Prefaces*. Introduction by R. P. Blackmur (New York: Scribners).

JOHNSON, MAURICE (1965) *Fielding's Art of Fiction* (Philadelphia: University of Pennsylvania Press).

JOHNSTON, ARTHUR (1964) *Enchanted Ground: The Study of Medieval Romance in the Eighteenth Century* (London: Athlone Press).

JUSSERAND, J. J. (1890) *The English Novel in the Time of Shakespeare*. Trs. E. Lee. (London: Unwin).

KENYON, F. G. (1932) *Books and Readers in Ancient Greece and Rome* (Oxford: The Clarendon Press).

KER, W. P. (1908) *Epic and Romance* (London: Macmillan).

KRUTCH, JOSEPH WOOD (1931) *Five Masters: A Study in the Mutations of the Novel* (London: Jonathan Cape).

LEAVIS, F. R. (1960) *The Great Tradition* (London: Chatto and Windus).

LEAVIS, Q. D. (1965) *Fiction and the Reading Public* (London: Chatto and Windus).

LEWIS, C. B. (1932) *Classical Mythology and Arthurian Romance* (Oxford: Oxford University Press).

LEVIN, HARRY (1958) 'What is Realism', *Contexts of Criticism* (Cambridge, Mass.: Harvard University Press).

LEWIS, C. S. (1936) *The Allegory of Love: A Study in Medieval Tradition* (London: Oxford University Press).

—— (1966) *Studies in Medieval and Renaissance Literature*. Collected by Walter Hooper (Cambridge: Cambridge University Press).

LIDDELL, ROBERT (1947) *A Treatise on the Novel* (London: Jonathan Cape).

Literary Influence of the Middle Ages, The' (1964) *The Cambridge History of English Literature*, Vol. X (Cambridge: Cambridge University Press).

LIVINGSTON, R. W. (1912) *The Greek Genius and Its Meaning to Us* (Oxford: The Clarendon Press).

LOBEIRA, VASCO (1872) *Amadis of Gaul*. Trs. Robert Southey, 3 vols (London: Russell Smith).

LODGE, DAVID (1969) 'The Novelist at the Crossroads', *Critical Quarterly* II (Summer), 105–32.

LOOMIS, ROGER S., ed. (1959) *Arthurian Literature in the Middle Ages* (Oxford: The Clarendon Press).

LUCIAN (1961) *Satirical Sketches*. Trs. Paul Turner (London: Penguin).

LUKÁCS, GEORGE (1963) *The Theory of the Novel*. Trs. Anna Bostick (London: Merlin Press).

McARTHY, B. G. (1944) *Women Writers: Their Contribution to The English*

Novel (Cork: Cork University Press).

McKILLOP, ALAN D. (1956) *The Early Masters of English Fiction* (Lawrence: University of Kansas Press).

MALORY, SIR THOMAS (1967) *The Works of Sir Thomas Malory*, ed. Eugène Vinaver, second ed., 3 vols (Oxford: The Clarendon Press).

MANLEY, MARY DE LA RIVIÈRE (1709) *Secret Memoirs and Manners of several Persons of Quality, of Both Sexes. From the New Atalantis, an Island in the Mediterranean* (London).

—— (1741) *The Power of Love: in seven Novels*. Duplicate of 1720 ed., with new titlepage (London).

MATTINGLY, HAROLD (1987) *Roman Imperial Civilisation* (London: Edward Arnold).

McBURNEY, WILLIAM H. (1959) 'Mrs Mary Davys: Forerunner of Fielding', *PMLA*, LXXIV, 348–55.

—— (1957) 'Mrs Penelope Aubin and the Early English Novel', *HLQ*, xx, 245–67.

Middle English Verse Romances (1964) ed. W. H. French and C. B. Hale, 2 vols (New York: Russell and Russell).

Middle English Verse Romances (1966) ed. Donald B. Sands (London: Holt, Rinehart and Winston).

MILLER, PERRY (1967) 'The Romance and the Novel', *Nature's Nation* (Cambridge, Mass.: Belknap Press).

MISH, CHARLES, ed. (1963) *Short Fiction of the Seventeenth Century* (New York: New York University Press).

MOORE, ROBERT ETHERIDGE (1951) 'Dr. Johnson on Fielding and Richardson', *PMLA*, LXI, 162–81.

MORGAN, CHARLOTTE E. (1911) *The Rise of the Novel of Manners: A Study of English Prose Fiction Between 1600 and 1740* (New York: Columbia University Press).

MUIR, EDWIN (1928) *The Structure of the Novel* (London: Hogarth Press).

MURRAY, GILBERT (1934) *The Rise of the Greek Epic* (London: Oxford University Press).

NASHE, THOMAS (1966) *The Works of Thomas Nashe*, ed. R. B. McKerrow, 2 vols (Oxford: Blackwell).

NEILL, S. D. (1951) *A Short History of the English Novel* (London: Jarrolds).

OVID (1939) *Ovid: With An English Translation: Tristia: Ex Ponto*. Trs. Arthur L. Wheeler (London: Heinemann).

PARKER, A. A. (1967) *Literature and the Delinquent* (Edinburgh: Edinburgh University Press).

PEPYS, SAMUEL (1848–9) *Diary and Correspondence of Samuel Pepys*. Deciphered by Rev. J. Smith, third ed., 5 vols (London).

PETRONIUS, GAIUS (1960) *The Satyricon and Poems*. Trs. Jack Lindsay (London: Elek Books).

—— (1965) *The Satyricon and The Fragments*. Trs. John Sullivan. (Harmondsworth: Penguin).

—— (1961) *Works: With an English translation by Michael Heseltine*. (London: Heinemann).

PERRY, BEN EDWIN (1967) *The Ancient Romances: A Literary-Historical Account of their Origins* (Berkeley: University of California Press).

PHILLIMORE, J. S. (1912) 'The Greek Romances', *English Literature and the Classics*, ed. G. S. Gordon (Oxford: The Clarendon Press).

PINNER, H. L. (1948) *The World of Books in Classical Antiquity* (Leiden: Sijthoff).

PITOU, SPIRE, JR (1938) *La Calprenède's Faramond: A Study of the Sources, Structure, and Reputation of the Novel* (London: Oxford University Press).

PLINY (1961) *Natural History with an English Translation in Ten Volumes.* Vol. IX. Trs. H. Rackham (London: Heinemann).

PRITCHETT, V. S. (1946) *The Living Novel* (London: Chatto and Windus).

RAGLAN, LORD (1936) *The Hero* (London: Methuen).

RALEIGH, SIR WALTER (1916) *Romance: Two Lectures* (Princeton: Princeton University Press).

——— (1894) *The English Novel: being a Short Sketch of its History from the Earliest Times to 'Waverley'* (London).

RANK, OTTO (1932) *The Myth of the Birth of the Hero and other Writings* (New York: Vintage Books).

RANKIN, H. D. (1971) *Petronius the Artist: Essays on the Satyricon and its Author* (The Hague: Nijhoff).

R., C. [CLARA REEVE] (1785) *The Progress of Romance through Times, Countries and Manners; with Remarks on the good and bad effects of it, on them, respectively; in the course of Evening Conversations.* (Colchester).

RICHARDSON, SAMUEL (1962) *Pamela*, 2 vols (London: Dent).

——— (1962) *Clarissa or, The History of a Young Lady*, 4 vols (London: Dent).

——— (1964) *Selected Letters*, ed. John Carroll (Oxford: The Clarendon Press).

RICHETTI, JOHN J. (1969) *Popular Fiction before Richardson: Narrative Patterns 1700–1739* (Oxford: The Clarendon Press).

RODAX, YVONNE (1968) *The Real and the Ideal in the Novella of Italy, France and England* (Chapel Hill: The University of North Carolina Press).

ROGERS, PAT (1972) *Grub Street: Studies in A Subculture* (London: Methuen).

ROLFE, FRANKLIN P. (1934) 'On the Bibliography of Seventeenth-Century Prose Fiction', *PMLA*, LXIX, 1071–86.

ROSTOVTZEFF, M. (1927) *A History of the Ancient World*, 2 vols (Oxford: The Clarendon Press).

ROWE, ELIZABETH (1755) *Friendship in Death: in Twenty Letters From the Dead to the Living. To Which are added, Letters Moral and Entertaining in Prose and Verse* (Edinburgh). *Friendship in Death* first published 1728; *Letters Moral and Entertaining* 1728–1732.

SAINTSBURY, GEORGE (1917–19) *A History of the French Novel*, 2 vols. (New York: Russell and Russell).

——— (1913) *The English Novel* (London: Dent).

——— (1897) *The Flourishing of Romance and the Rise of Allegory* (London: Blackwood).

SALE, WILLIAM M. JNR. (1964) 'From *Pamela* to *Clarissa*', *The Age of Johnson*, ed. F. W. Hilles (New Haven: Yale University Press).

SCARRON, PAUL (1902) *The Comical Romance, and Other Tales*. Trs. Tom Brown *et al.*, ed. J. D. Jusserand (London: Lawrence and Bullen).

SCHLAUCH, MARAGARET (1963) *Antecedents of the English Novel 1400–1600* (London: Oxford University Press).

SCHOLES, ROBERT (1967) *The Fabulators* (New York: Oxford University Press).

SCHOLES, ROBERT, ROBERT KELLOG (1966) *The Nature of Narrative* (New York: Oxford University Press).

SCHRODER, MAURICE (1967) 'The Novel as a Genre', *The Theory of the Novel*, ed. Philip Stevick (New York: Free Press).

SCOTT, SIR WALTER (1928) *The Lives of the Novelists* (London: Dent).

SCUDÉRY, MADELEINE DE (1683) 'On the Way to Invent a Fable', *Conversations Upon Subjects*. Trs. F. Spence, 2 vols (London).

—— (1674) *Ibrahim: or The Illustrious Bassa*. Trs. Henry Cogan (London).

—— (1655–61) *Clelia, An Excellent New Romance* (London).

SEVERS, J. BURK, ed. (1967) *A Manual of the Writings in Middle English* (New Haven: Connecticut Academy of Arts and Sciences).

SHEPARD, LESLIE (1973) *The History of Street Literature* (Newton Abbot: David and Charles).

Shorter Novels: Elizabethan (1929) Introduction by George Santisbury (London: Dent).

SIDNEY, SIR PHILIP (1867) *The Countess of Pembroke's Arcadia* (London: Sampson Low, and Marston).

SOUTHERN, R. W. (1953) *The Making of the Middle Ages* (London: Hutchinson)

SPEARMAN, DIANA (1966) *The Novel and society* (London: Routledge & Kegan Paul).

SPENCER, T. J. B. ed. (1968) *Elizabethan Love Stories* (London: Penguin).

STEEVES, HARRISON R. (1966) *Before Jane Austen: The Shaping of the English Novel in the Eighteenth Century* (London: George Allen and Unwin).

STEPHEN, LESLIE (1963) *English Literature and Society in the Eighteenth Century* (London: Methuen).

—— (1876) *History of English Thought in the Eighteenth Century*, 2 vols (London: Smith and Elder).

STEVENS, JOHN (1973) *Medieval Romance* (London: Hutchinson).

STEVENSON, LIONEL (1960) *The English Novel* (London: Constable).

STUCKEY, JOHANNA H. (1972) 'Petronius the "Ancient": His Reputation and Influence in Seventeenth-Century England', *Rivista di Studi Classici*, XX, ii, 3–11.

SULLIVAN, JOHN (1968) *The Satyricon of Petronius: A Literary Study* (London: Faber and Faber).

TAYLOR, A. B. (1930) *An Introduction to Medieval Romance* (London: Heath Cranton).

TAYLOR, HENRY O. (1903) *The Classical Heritage of the Middle Ages* (New York: Columbia University Press).

THOMPSON, J. A. K. (1948) *The Classical Background of English Literature* (London: George Allen and Unwin).

—— (1956) *Classical Influences on English Prose* (London: George Allen and Unwin).

THOMPSON, STITH (1961) 'Literature for the Unlettered', *Comparative*

Literature, eds N. P. Stallknecht and H. Frenz (Carbondale: Southern Illinois University Press).

TIEJE, ARTHUR JERROLD (1913) 'A Peculiar Phase of the Theory of Realism in Pre-Richardsonian Fiction', *PMLA*, XXVIII, 213–52.

TILLYARD, E. M. W. (1954) *The English Epic and its Background* (London: Chatto and Windus).

—— (1958) *The Epic Strain in the English Novel* (London: Chatto and Windus).

TODD, F. A. (1940) *Some Ancient Novels* (Oxford: Oxford University Press).

TRENKNER, SOPHIE (1958) *The Greek Novella in the Classical Period.* (Cambridge: Cambridge University Press).

TROTTER, CATHERINE (1718) *Olinda's Adventures: or, the Amours of a Young Lady* (London).

TUVE, ROSEMOND (1966) *Allegorical Imagery: Some Medieval Books and Their Posterity* (Princeton: Princeton University Press).

UPHAM, ALFRED HORATIO (1911) *The French Influence in English Literature from Elizabeth to the Restoration* (New York: Columbia University Press).

Valentine and Orson (1937) Trs. Henry Watson, ed. Arthur Dickson (London: Oxford University Press).

VAN GHENT, DOROTHY (1953) *The English Novel: Form and Function* (New York: Holt).

VINAVER, EUGÈNE (1971) *The Rise of Romance* (Oxford: The Clarendon Press).

WINNY, JAMES (1957) *The Descent of Euphues* (Cambridge: Cambridge University Press).

WALSH, P. G. (1970) *The Roman Novel* (Cambridge: Cambridge University Press).

WATT, IAN (1963) *The Rise of the Novel: Studies in Defoe, Richardson and Fielding* (Harmondsworth: Penguin).

WOLFF, SAMUEL LEE (1912) *The Greek Romances in Elizabethan Prose Fiction* (New York: Columbia University Press).

WOODHOUSE, A. S. P. (1968) 'Tragic Effect in *Samson Agonistes*', *Twentieth Century Interpretations of Samson Agonistes* (Englewood Cliffs: Prentice-Hall).

YARROW, P. J. (1967) 'The Seventeenth Century', *A Literary History of France*, Vol. II (London: Benn).

Index